Contestations of Memory in Southeast Asia

Contestations of Memory in Southeast Asia

Edited by

Roxana Waterson and Kwok Kian-Woon

NUS PRESS
SINGAPORE

Published by:

NUS Press
National University of Singapore
AS3-01-02, 3 Arts Link
Singapore 117569

Fax: (65) 6774-0652
E-mail: nusbooks@nus.edu.sg
Website: http://www.nus.edu.sg/nuspress

ISBN 978-9971-69-506-4 (Paper)

Earlier versions of Chapters 1, and 4–9, appeared in the *Asian Journal of Social Science*, Vol. 29, No. 3 (2001). They are reproduced here with the kind permission of the publisher, Brill Academic Publishers. These chapters have been extensively revised and updated.

National Library Board, Singapore Cataloguing-in-Publication Data

Contestations of memory in Southeast Asia / edited by Roxana Waterson and Kwok Kian-Woon. – Singapore: NUS Press, 2012.
p. cm.
Includes bibliographical references and index.
ISBN: 978-9971-69-506-4 (pbk.)

1. Collective memory – Southeast Asia. 2. Nationalism and collective memory – Southeast Asia. 3. Southeast Asia – History. I. Waterson, Roxana. II. Kwok, Kian Woon.

DS525
959 — dc22 OCN742519248

Cover: War memorial statue at Kham Thien Street, Hanoi, commemorating the families of three houses in the street destroyed by an American bomb in 1972. Photo: Sharon Seah.

Typeset by: Scientifik Graphics
Printed by: Mainland Press Pte Ltd

CONTENTS

Introduction 1
Roxana Waterson and Kwok Kian-Woon

Part I: Southeast Asia within the Field of Memory Studies

Chapter 1 The Work of Memory and the Unfinished Past: Deepening and Widening the Study of Memory in Southeast Asia 17
Roxana Waterson and Kwok Kian-Woon

Part II: Nationalisms and the Construction of Destinies

Chapter 2 Remembering Kings: Archives, Resistance and Memory in Colonial and Post-colonial Burma 53
Maitrii Aung-Thwin

Chapter 3 Shifting Visions of the Past: Ethnic Minorities and the 'Struggle for National Independence' in Laos 83
Vatthana Pholsena

Chapter 4 Truth and Memory: Narrating Viet Nam 106
Sharon Seah Li-Lian

Chapter 5 Textual Construction of a Nation: The Use of Merger and Separation 125
Dayang Istiaisyah bte Hussin

Chapter 6 Remembering, Misremembering and Forgetting: The Struggle over *Serangan Oemoem 1 Maret 1949* in Yogyakarta, Indonesia 156
Heddy Shri Ahimsa Putra

Part III: Traumatic Memories: Interpenetrations of Collective and Personal Experience

Chapter 7 War and Violence, History and Memory: The Philippine Experience of the Second World War 185
Ricardo T. José

Chapter 8 The Past in the Present: Memories of the 1964 'Racial Riots' in Singapore 201
Adeline Low Hwee Cheng

Chapter 9 Memories at the Margins: Chinese-Educated Intellectuals in Singapore 230
Kwok Kian-Woon and Kelvin Chia

Chapter 10 Living with the Spectre of the Past: Traumatic Experiences among Wives of Former Political Prisoners of the '1965 Event' in Indonesia 270
Budiawan

Contributors 292

Index 296

Introduction

Roxana Waterson and Kwok Kian-Woon

This volume brings together case studies in social memory from a wide range of historical contexts in different Southeast Asian countries. They all, in diverse ways, draw inspiration from the newly expanding literature on social memory, to which the authors seek to make a fresh and substantial contribution. Since the early 1990s, the burgeoning cross-disciplinary concern with social memory has heightened awareness that remembering, as a dimension of social relationships, is nothing if not a political matter. In different ways, the papers in this volume seek to ask: "What are the stakes involved in memory?" This question is inextricably tied to another — "What are the stakes involved in people's efforts to arrive at a more accurate or complete account of the past, different from official or other selective but dominant accounts?" How does the multiplicity of individual memories existing in any social context become shared, entering into the flow of collective memory? How do they work against the grain of hegemonic narratives that seek to suppress that diversity in the interests of presenting a more unitary, simplified view of the past, a view that all citizens are invited to adhere to?

In our opening chapter, we as editors attempt to sketch a framework for memory studies by taking some account of the psychological literature. It is our opinion that not enough effort has been made on either side to build the necessary bridges between psychological and sociological approaches to the study of memory, or to examine systematically how concepts currently being developed by psychologists can be applied to the understanding of memory as a social phenomenon. We seek at least to begin the business of linking the insights of the psychological literature to the concerns that drive memory studies in sociology and history. Dimensions of individual recall, such as selectivity, distortion and elaboration, need to be patiently traced and analyzed in social contexts too. But the important question for students of social, as opposed to purely individual, memory is transmission. Since processes of memory transmission are so elusive, we are obliged to seek clues through close-grained analysis of particular case studies. Those we have collected here contribute, we believe, a wealth of insights into these processes. We set out to propose an agenda for such studies in Southeast Asia, taking account of themes that might link crucial events in this region to those that have happened elsewhere. The focus is on the often tumultuous events of the twentieth century, and it will soon become clear that most of the memory issues dealt with here are traumatic. We ask what effect this trauma has on social memory processes, and whether indeed events perhaps have to be traumatic to feature so largely in collective recall. Troubling moral questions and a persisting sense of injustice surround the most contentious of these events, causing continued political tensions within and between countries throughout the region. The obvious uniqueness or historical specificity of each event should not prevent us from drawing comparisons between them. Indeed there may be a moral necessity to do so, in search of the possibly more universal aspects of the human potential for good or evil, resistance or corruption, violence or reconciliation.

The studies gathered here suggest that memory as a social phenomenon is marked by a multitude of tensions and oppositions: between the individual and the social, the popular and the official, between forgetting and remembering, or between dominant and suppressed narratives, the remembering of one story rather than another. Closer examination may prove some of these oppositions too crude: endless shades of ambiguity mark the continuum between remembering and forgetting, for instance.[1] One must consider what are the motivations or desires driving remembrance or forgetfulness; it is not always easy to determine whether the supposedly forgotten object is really removed from consciousness, or why at a particular moment it may dramatically return to public awareness. The chapters in Part II of the book revolve around stories of nations, destinies and identities; those of Part III concern the traumatic memories of specific events or of smaller groups within nations. Often, these two themes of trauma and identity are intertwined, so that it was not easy to structure the chapters into clearly defined sections. Through them all, we seek to pursue the more general questions raised in the opening chapter: How do we human beings work at the business of memory, and how does memory work on us?

Why is there such a compulsion to return to the past, especially to difficult, traumatic issues? Why is the work of memory often so slow, with long delays before these issues become matters of widespread public debate and renewed concern? How does the work of memory reflect and embody particular interests or moral impulses in the present, leading potentially to major shifts in the world of discourse and ideas?

Questions of identity are clearly an area in which memory has a special part to play. Just as the individual's sense of identity depends on being able to remember who you were yesterday, collectivities too almost inevitably derive identity from shared memories. However, since memory is always highly selective, as well as potentially unreliable (Schacter, 1995), the processes by which collective memories are built and maintained deserve careful investigation. These processes can be seen particularly clearly where the groupings concerned are relatively new. Several of the papers in this volume address the question of how the ruling parties of newer nation-states have gone about constructing a narrative of the past in the interests of creating a national identity, and persuading their citizens of its plausibility. Theorists of the modern nation-state (Anderson, 1983; Gellner, 1983; Benjamin, 1988, to mention only a few) have helped us to see that nations and their identities are artefacts, produced through a great deal of symbolic labour, whose outcomes are by no means a foregone conclusion. These papers probe into the actual processes involved in the work of identity construction, reminding us that the stories could have been told differently, and revealing sometimes unresolved problems about the past.

Maitrii Aung Thwin's paper explores how a historical event, the Saya San Rebellion of 1930–31, had been constructed by colonial administrators and the legal process to justify the state's counter-insurgency policy. Administrators had resorted to a counter-insurgency guidebook that had been written 15 years prior to the Saya San rebellion to interpret and frame the rationale for their suppression of dissenters. Bertram Carey, author of the guidebook, had cast the Burmese peasants as being easily incited by a teacher (*saya*) who claimed supernatural powers and monarchical aspirations. Due to their inclination toward nostalgia for the monarchy, the peasants were seen as being "superstitious", "traditional" and consequently unable to engage in modern political discourse. Thus the colonialists were able to make use of Carey's model to frame the rebellion in political terms as the outcome of the protagonist's kingly ambitions and his followers' ignorance. In contrast, U Saw, who later served as a legislative representative for Saya San, provided a counter-narrative that took into consideration the peasants' economic marginalization, which was partly the result of colonial tax policies. In the trials that ensued, however, the prosecutors appropriated Carey's model to legitimate the tribunal's decision to execute Saya San, as well as to provide 'historical precedence' for future dealings with rebels. Maitrii's study highlights the contestation of memory in archival records: in the hands of the colonialists, these records are not just preservative but also prescriptive for future policies.

Vatthana Pholsena's paper brings a welcome insight into recent Laotian history and memory processes. She examines the tensions between remembering and forgetting in official state historiography, as well as between the national narrative and local ethnic identities. The paper discusses the case of a local hero, Ong Keo, of the Nge ethnic minority, who fought against the French in the early years of the twentieth century, and who has been elevated to the status of a national hero for his resistance to colonialism. Pholsena interviewed the villagers of his birthplace, Ban Paktai, including a surviving companion of Ong Keo. The villagers trace an unbroken line of descent between Ong Keo and themselves as revolutionary heroes, and in so doing, seek to link their own identities to the larger collective destiny. Yet there are a number of others besides Ong Keo who fought and suffered in Laos' long struggle for independence, whom the villagers feel have never received the recognition they deserve from the state. Over the years, the role of ethnic minorities as key actors in Laotian revolutionary struggles, once celebrated in official communist accounts, has become increasingly marginalized. As a result, the villagers' own accounts now appear to go 'against the flow' of a nationalist narrative that is constructed as much from a sort of 'willed amnesia' as it is from memories of the past.

Sharon Seah's paper examines the tensions concealed within Vietnam's official view of itself. Here, the harrowing experiences of a war that was at once a war against an external invader as well as a civil war, and the ruptures involved in the imposition and subsequent removal of a border between North and South, have left their own deep scars. One might begin from the simple observation that the war is known to Vietnamese as the 'American War', and not the 'Vietnam War', which in itself involves a salutary shift of perspective. But at the same time as the official, patriotic narrative tries to suture over the split between North and South in inscribing an account of the resistance to

American imperialism, it also silences the memory of those who died on the 'wrong side' of this confrontation: soldiers of the southern ARVN forces are excluded from commemoration in the ubiquitous national monuments to the fallen, and the southern regime is demonized in museum displays. Seah highlights the difficulties of finding any reconciliation with this "other within" the state, especially when the financial remittances and investments of the "other" outside of Vietnam (overseas Vietnamese or *Viet Khieu*) are so important for the economic well-being of the country. The painful dismembering of the state might have been physically overcome, yet the scars remaining suggest that, in another sense, it is not fully over yet. It is characteristic of the dominant, official narrative that, in its claims to 'truth', it cannot do justice to the plenitude of individual and group memories, some of which are consequently suppressed. As Seah proposes, the telling of one story occludes another — the "already-said", that which is taken for granted, at the same time conceals the "never-said", that which becomes unspeakable. But herein lies another danger: the citizens, bombarded too frequently with a single story about the past, may become cynical and detach themselves from the national narrative of the power holders. Too much propaganda results in apathy toward the past. In the meantime, just as in the Philippines, with the passage of time and the inevitable shifts in economic developments, even judgments about former enemies may have to be modified in the interests of establishing working relations in the present.

Whereas the case of Vietnam hinges around the difficulties of mending a breach imposed internally, the birth of Singapore and Malaysia as independent nation-states offers a contrasting example of the splitting of a former — if fleeting — unity. If Singapore's brief 'merger' with Malaysia in 1963 had endured until now, instead of ending abruptly two years later, how many official speeches would its citizens have heard by now endorsing the idea that Singapore's 'natural' destiny lay within Malaysia? As it transpired, a different story had to be told. Dayang Istiaisyah's paper offers an analysis of newspaper texts of the period, providing empirical evidence of the work that had to be put into presenting events in a particular way, and exposing the constructive processes involved. It goes without saying that if one were to perform the same operation on Malaysian accounts of the same events, we would find them presented in a somewhat different light.

Wartime memories provide the theme for Heddy Shri Ahimsa Putra's paper about Indonesia; in this case the memories concern an incident in the 1945–49 war for Independence. Since the watershed events of 1997 and 1998, which brought an abrupt end to Suharto's 'New Order', it has suddenly become possible to re-examine many issues of recent history that had been either suppressed or presented in a particular light by the Suharto regime. Whatever the perceived shortcomings of former President Abdurrahman Wahid, he must be given credit for the initiatives he took during his presidency (1999–2001) to facilitate this reassessment of the past. The incident examined here is known as the General Attack of 1 March 1949, when forces of the Republic of Indonesia, led by then Lieutenant-Colonel Suharto, succeeded in driving the Dutch out of Yogyakarta (which at that time functioned as the capital of the Republic). The Attack marked a watershed in the Independence struggle and is remembered as much for its political as its military importance. During the 1980s, Suharto's own account of this event became the focus of extensive public commemorations. There were annual celebrations incorporating the reading of a speech prepared by Suharto himself; a huge monument was built in Yogya; and several popular films were made, which were widely screened for schoolchildren. But a suppressed controversy existed about who was really the initiator of the Attack: was it, as he claimed, Suharto himself, or was it Sultan Hamengkubuwono IX of Yogya? It now appears that Suharto exaggerated his role in the affair. Heddy Shri Ahimsa Putra draws our attention to the very important question of the various media, besides written texts, by which this somewhat manipulated version of a social memory has been impressed upon the public mind. Historians examining the controversy have paid great attention to written accounts, but none at all to the portrayal of events through monuments or films, although these were clearly designed to exercise powerful emotional effects upon the visitor or the viewer. Can the social memory be revised, without a new programme of socialization as extensive as the old one?

While all the papers in Part I concern issues of national identity and the role of particular narratives about the past in transmitting a nationalist ideology, in Part II the focus is on the interpenetration of popular and official memories in the construction of identities. In all cases, a collective trauma has played a part in shaping a group's identity. In Chapter 1, we draw some parallels between memory issues connected to World War II in Europe and in Asia. In recent years, the discourse on Japanese wartime aggression has moved beyond the borders of East Asia (Kratoska, 1998, 2002, 2005; Fujitani, White and Yoneyama, 2000). Ricardo José's paper in this volume fits within this context of the reassessment of the events of the Second World War in Southeast Asia.[2] José examines the many threads of popular memory surrounding the war in the Philippines. He shows how memories have evolved through several different phases over the past few decades, as relationships with the other main protagonists — in this instance, America and Japan — have undergone shifts. These changes enable — or perhaps compel — a review of previous interpretations of the past. In the immediate aftermath of violent and destructive events, the energies of survivors might have been channelled out of necessity into dealing with the most pressing questions of survival. But as the passing of time creates a distance between the carriers of memories and the events themselves, a more searching reflection becomes possible, especially surrounding difficult questions of unacknowledged guilt and responsibility. Ironically, governments are often the least equipped, and the least willing, to undertake the memory work involved, not least because of desires to maintain present economically beneficial relations.

In the immediate postwar period, many writings patriotically described the wartime pains and suffering endured by Filipinos as a test of national character, with the Americans generally cast in the role of liberating heroes. Attacks on those who had collaborated were also common, especially around election times. As the Marcos period dragged on and the relationship with America soured, American altruism was called into question and a closer consideration was given to the possibility that the Americans had acted, at least partly, out of imperialist self-interest. Feelings of disillusionment were aggravated by the failure of Filipino veterans' groups to win funds from the United States. At the same time, financial assistance from Japan had become such an important part of the Philippines' economic recovery that the Philippine government had its own reasons for wanting normalization of relations. The work of memory involves much more than written texts and is also evidenced in monuments and rituals of commemoration, whether organized at the national, international or local level. José examines a range of these events to expose some of their tensions and ambiguities, and also describes various associations of all political colours, which have some interest in keeping the memory of wartime events alive. These organizations show popular memory at work, operating in the gaps left by official efforts at commemoration, and often going against the grain of the government's own desire to play down tensions in the interests of international relations. Some aspects of popular memory about the war have a legendary quality about them, such as the legend of General Yamashita's buried hoard of gold. But the shifts in emphasis found within historical narratives of the war also contain an element of mythologizing in a deeper sense, in terms of their function as generators of meaning within the bigger story told by the nation about its own identity.

In a case like Singapore, an obvious difficulty facing the architects of nationhood was the question of *which* story to tell about the past, since the citizens themselves were bringing too many diverse kinds of histories and traditions with them to allow for the simple selection of any one of them to create a coherent story. An interim solution was simply to drop history out of the school syllabus altogether, which was in fact the policy adopted in the years between 1972 and the early 1980s. While nationalist mythologies require a conviction of destiny, the historical reality is that territorial borders are often the arbitrary outcomes of historical and political accident. Nor are they by any means as immutable as the notion of destiny might suggest. Adeline Low's paper isolates one event — the so-called 'Racial Riots' of 1964 in Singapore — in order to compare its deployment within official national histories, such as the National Education programme for schools, with its recall in popular memory. This analysis reveals a number of interesting features. The multiplicity of popular memories — for instance, of the possible causes of the riots — contrasts with the singularity of official accounts. Low's paper reminds us that digging into the rich subsoils of collective memory may never result in a definitive disclosure of the 'truth' of 'what really happened', but rather oblige us to acknowledge more ambiguities about it. Different ethnic groups and different individuals have different stories to tell, or they may understand the significance of the event differently because they position it differently in relation to other events of importance to them. Events thus derive their meaning partly from how they are seen in relation to other events. Moreover, where official accounts use the riots to raise the spectre of chaos — of what might happen should citizens fail to accept policies of ethnic management designed for their own good — a strong thread weaving through popular recollections of the riots is the fact that they were actually highly localized, while many neighbours of differing ethnic backgrounds cooperated to protect each other and keep rioters out of their settlements.

The last two papers in the book both deal with periods and experiences that have been very difficult, even taboo, for those who lived through them to talk about. Much recent investigation into the question of traumatic memory does suggest that healing is helped by being able to tell one's story to an appropriate and receptive audience. But what if one has no such audience? In Indonesia since the fall of Suharto, it has at last become possible to readdress many issues in historical memory, none more pressing than the formerly forbidden question of what really happened in the attempted coup and counter-coup of 1965, and its bloody aftermath in which half a million or more suspected 'communists' were massacred.[3] A number of NGOs have formed with the aim of giving support to former political prisoners and gathering their testimonies. Rehabilitation and backlash continue, for instance in the controversy over a new school history textbook that removed references implying the responsibility of the Indonesian Communist Party (PKI) for the alleged attempt of the night of 30 September 1965, in which six generals were murdered.[4] Budiawan's paper makes an unusual contribution to the process of reassessment of memories of the 1960s by discussing what happened, not to political prisoners themselves, but to their wives. The latter found themselves stuck in a state that might be described as symbolic or political "widowhood" (Ramphele, 1997), since there was no way of knowing when, or if, their husbands would ever be returned to them. In the South African cases discussed by Ramphele, women whose dead or imprisoned husbands had the status of heroes within the ANC and the anti-apartheid movement became a valuable resource to these organizations, who made as much political capital out of them as they could. This was not straightforward, however, since widowhood places a woman in a position of ambiguity and liminality in which she becomes the embodiment of loss and pollution, her body and her sexuality summoning ideas of ritual danger. But by making her into a public figure, and thus converting her private pain into public loss, she can be made to embody "a desired social memory about the fallen [or imprisoned] hero", a memory that "has to be cultivated and kept alive" (1997: 102; 110). As Ramphele points out, ironically in a patriarchal society, ideas of nobility and heroism are not easily associated with a woman's body, which tends to be conceived of as incomplete and inadequate to such representations. The woman herself finds her own agency constrained, since she is being made to stand in for a fallen man. While some women might have mixed feelings about their enforced transformation into public figures, others whose own personality or whose husbands' personalities did not lend themselves so well to this process were neglected. Still, certain women, notably Winnie Mandela, as the wife of the most celebrated of South Africa's political prisoners, did through her own force of personality achieve a unique status, becoming a symbol of resistance in her own right.[5] Ramphele suggests that, whatever the ambiguities of this process, it had some positive aspect, since public acknowledgment of personal pain serves the purpose of transforming it into "social suffering", enabling sufferers to "stake their historical claims and thereby restore their dignity" (1997: 114). In the Indonesian cases discussed by Budiawan, however, conditions were almost the inverse of those in South Africa. Far from being incorporated into a larger 'political family' which would help to give public voice to their loss, the political formation to which their husbands had belonged (if indeed they really had belonged to any organization, which was by no means always the case) had been totally demolished and banned, and family members found themselves ostracized by the wider society as a result of the official policy of *bersih lingkungan* (literally, 'clean environment'). This decreed that family members were also polluted by association with the victim and were not to be given employment or helped in any way. In the meantime, these women had to survive and raise their children somehow. Not surprisingly, under such circumstances, some of them entered into other relationships, but in doing so they were often subjected to hostile gossip and further isolation within their own communities. Burdened by feelings of shame or anger at society's (and sometimes their own husbands') hypocrisy, they have no audience waiting to hear their stories or acknowledge their pain. Thus they have tended to bear the burden of memory in silence. Budiawan concludes that a far more radical transformation of patriarchal structures in the Indonesian urban middle classes would be necessary before these women have a chance to heal their own trauma.

In Singapore, ethnic groups tend to be officially subsumed under the concept of 'races', the three main ones being 'Chinese', 'Malay' and 'Indian'. The Chinese, by their strength in numbers, are considered the majority race. Yet, as Kwok Kian-Woon argues in his paper, the historical bifurcation between the Chinese-educated and the English-educated belies the common reference to the Chinese as a race or a community in Singapore. Throughout the post-Independence decades, the Chinese-educated have had to face the problem of marginalization, in effect becoming a minority within a so-called majority race. The experience of marginalization, Kwok suggests, also entails contestation over the memory of past events on the part of Chinese-educated intellectuals. Memory is a burden that has to be carried by individuals, but it is also the channel through which they make sense of their place in history and society.

In conclusion, we propose that the problem of memory cannot be uncoupled from the problem of truth. Truth, however, is an elusive concept, even more so today in a 'postmodernist' context that tends to treat the concept as absolutistic and hence also totalitarian. Relativism, indeed, has its virtues. The recognition of the plurality of recollections and interpretations of any past event renders any single, dominant version suspect. The work of deconstructing socially constructed truths, however, is motivated by a quest for truth and subverts itself if the very concept of truth is abandoned. A realistic acceptance of the never-ending nature of the search does nothing to diminish its importance. Historian John Lukacs (1994: 357) states the case bluntly. Making an eloquent call for the democratization of history by extending it from "the recorded past toward the remembered past", he tells us that: "The purpose of the historian should be the reduction of untruth." This, we believe, is the driving force behind the study of social memory. And in this connection, perhaps we should also bear in mind the words of the French sociologist Edgar Morin (1962: 5), who had this to say about what he called "the enduring problem of truth": "When all is said and done, the great merit of the search for truth is not so much to find the truth but to raise the problem of what constitutes the truth."[6]

Notes

1. See Connerton (2009) for an illuminating inquiry into the different forms of forgetting.
2. Works on Singapore include Chou (1995), Kratoska (1995), *Journal of Southeast Asian Studies* 27/1 (1996), Lim and Wong (2000), Frei (2004), Modder (2004) and Lee (2005).
3. See Zurburchen (2005) for an insightful review of this process and some of its results so far.

4. *The Straits Times*, 29 June 2005. In the official discourse of the Suharto era, that event was categorically blamed on the PKI, being cryptically labelled 'G30S/PKI' — shorthand for *Gerakan 30 September* or '30th September Movement', the PKI tag conveniently affirming the guilt of the Communist Party. The accusation facilitated Suharto's seizure of power and provided the chief justification for the massacres that followed. Other deails of this event were blatantly falsified; whether it really was an attempted coup, and who may have been behind it, remains open to debate (Zurburchen, 2005). All the same, public backlash caused the new history textbook to be immediately withdrawn. An interesting detail concerns the date: since the murders took place after midnight, technically they occurred on 1 October, and not 30 September, but the choice of the latter date enabled Suharto to present his New Order as commencing on the first of the month, doubtless a psychologically more gratifying choice.
5. Ramphele refers to her own unusual experience in being socially transformed into "a political widow who could never be" (1997: 112), as a result of her intense personal relationship with Steve Biko, to whom she was not, however, married.
6. Morin collaborated with anthropologist Jean Rouch in the well-known experimental film *Chronicle of a Summer* (1960). He was discussing the question of the truthfulness of documentary or ethnographic film, but his comments have an equal bearing on the problematic of memory.

References

Anderson, Benedict (1983). *Imagined Communities: Reflections on the Origin and Spread of Nationalism*. London: Verso.

Benjamin, Geoffrey (1988). "The Unseen Presence: The Nation-State and Its Mystifications". Singapore: National University of Singapore, Department of Sociology Working Papers no. 91.

Chou, Cindy (1995). *Beyond the Empires: Memories Retold*. Singapore: National Heritage Board.

Connerton, P. (2009). *How Modernity Forgets*. Cambridge: Cambridge University Press.

Frei, Henry (2004). *The Guns of February: Ordinary Japanese Soldiers' View of the Malayan Campaign and the Fall of Singapore*. Singapore: Singapore University Press.

Fujitani, T., Geoffrey White and Lisa Yoneyama (eds) (2000). *Perilous Memories: The Asia-Pacific War(s)*. Durham, N.C.: Duke University Press.

Gellner, Ernest (1983). *Nations and Nationalism*. Oxford: Blackwell.

Journal of Southeast Asian Studies (1996). "Special Issue: The Japanese Occupation in Southeast Asia", vol. 27/1, March.

Kratoska, Paul (1998). *The Japanese Occupation of Malaya: A Social and Economic History*. London: C. Hurst.

——— (2005). *Asian Labour in the Wartime Japanese Empire: Unknown Histories*. Armonk, N.Y.: Sharpe.

Kratoska, Paul (ed.) (1995). *Malaya and Singapore during the Japanese Occupation. Journal of Southeast Asian Studies*, Special Publication no. 3.

——— (2002). *Southeast Asian Minorities in the Wartime Japanese Empire*. London: RoutledgeCurzon.

Lee Geok Boi (2005). *The Syonan Years: Singapore under Japanese Rule*. Singapore: National Archives of Singapore/Epigram.

Lim Pui Huen, P. and Diana Wong (eds) (2000). *War and Memory in Malaysia and Singapore*. Singapore: ISEAS.

Lukacs, John (1994 [1968]). *Historical Consciousness: The Remembered Past*. New Brunswick: Transaction Publishers.

Modder, Ralph (2004). *The Singapore Chinese Massacre, 18 February–4 March 1942*. Singapore: Horizon Books.

Morin, Edgar (1962). "Preface", in Luc de Heusch (ed.), *The Cinema and Social Science: A Survey of Ethnographic and Sociological Films*. UNESCO Reports and Papers in the Social Sciences, no. 16.

Ramphele, Mamphela (1997). "Political Widowhood in South Africa: The Embodiment of Ambiguity", in A. Kleinman, V. Das and M. Lock (eds), *Social Suffering*. Berkeley: University of California Press, pp. 99–117.

Schacter, Daniel (ed.) (1995). *Memory Distortion: How Minds, Brains and Societies Reconstruct the Past*. Cambridge, Mass.: Harvard University Press.

The Straits Times, 29 June 2005. "Uproar over 'gaps' in Jakarta history textbooks".

Zurburchen, Mary (2005). *Beginning to Remember: The Past in the Indonesian Present*. Singapore/Seattle: Singapore University Press/University of Washington Press.

PART I

Southeast Asia within the Field of Memory Studies

CHAPTER 1

The Work of Memory and the Unfinished Past: Deepening and Widening the Study of Memory in Southeast Asia

Roxana Waterson and Kwok Kian-Woon

The past two decades have seen a remarkable development in the study of human memory. There has been a great burst of writing, crossing the boundaries between several disciplines and offering a wealth of new insights into this complex and multi-faceted phenomenon. Recent advances in neurology have been so spectacular as to transform our knowledge about the brain and its biochemistry, providing for the first time a detailed and coherent picture of how memories are actually created and retrieved in the brain (Rose, 1992). Schacter (1996: 6) sees the possibility of a new synthesis arising with the increased co-operation between, as he terms it, the "separate tribes" of cognitive psychologists, clinicians and neuroscientists. Tellingly, he makes no mention of historians, sociologists or anthropologists — "tribes" whose spheres of interest have been even more sharply separated from those who investigate memory in a laboratory context. But there has been a significant surge of interest in memory within concrete social contexts. While new works in psychology probe the role of memory in the formation of personal identity and life stories (Ross, 1991; Neisser & Fivush, 1994), scholarship in the disciplines of history, anthropology and sociology has also turned to the study of memory as a social phenomenon. For memory is as intrinsic to the construction of collective identities as it is integral to the individual's sense of self.

This outpouring of literature on all aspects of memory presents us with something of a puzzle. If memory is an indelible feature of social life, why should there be such a heightened awareness of its importance only in recent times? Perhaps memory was a fact of life too obvious to attract attention, so that it was simply taken for granted — in much the same way as the body, for instance, which had also excited little sociological attention prior to the 1990s. Then — not least because of feminist contributions to social theory — the fact of embodiment was suddenly reappraised as a facet of the human condition so fundamental as to demand proper analysis, prompting a similar outburst of academic activity. Since recasting the obvious in a new light has always been one of the most useful goals of the social sciences, breakthroughs of this kind are always valuable. But once we begin to reflect on the many social aspects of memory, its earlier comparative neglect still strikes us as surprising. Moreover, while Bloch (1996) suggests that there has been a real effort on both sides to bridge the gap between the natural and social sciences, a fuller integration between the insights of neurologists and psychologists and those of social scientists and historians on the workings of memory has yet to be achieved today. In this chapter, we offer our own particular take on the broader issues at stake in the study of social memory, with the aim of providing a theoretical framework for the more detailed case studies presented in the subsequent chapters.

Memory and Mind: Bridging Psychological and Sociological Perspectives

Until recently, psychological research on memory was predominantly focused on short-term memory — the kind that enables us to remember a phone number while searching for a pencil, and which typically lasts less than a minute — and was carried out in laboratory contexts far removed from real-life settings (Neisser, 1978; Bloch, 1996). However, some researchers in the mid-1960s were beginning to consider the possibility that short-term or 'working memory' of this kind forms a separate, though closely related, memory system to 'long-term' memory. Building on this distinction, Endel Tulving (1972, 1983) went further and distinguished, in long-term memory, between what he termed "semantic" and "episodic" memory. The term "semantic" memory was first used to refer to the stored knowledge necessary for the deployment of language, but was extended by Tulving to include knowledge in general, all that we have learned about the world and how to do things. "Episodic" memory by contrast refers to recall of personally experienced events. One way to express this difference is to distinguish what happens when we retrieve such memories. We would say that we 'know' the contents of semantic memory, whereas we 'remember' specific personal experiences. This idea that there might be multiple (if closely integrated) memory systems, rather than a single unitary one, was radical when first proposed, but has by now achieved wide acceptance. In fact, memory researchers are continuing to stretch and refine these distinctions to build more elaborate, though still speculative, models of how the functions might be integrated.

Not only must we think of multiple systems performing distinct functions, but the memory process can also be seen to fall into different stages over time: *encoding* (when a memory is originally laid down), *storage* and *retrieval.* Questions about the accuracy and durability of memory arise at each stage. While a variety of factors, including the degree of emotional intensity involved, will affect how vividly a memory is encoded in the first place, during the storage phase memories are especially vulnerable to the two processes of decay and interference (distortions produced by the introduction of new materials). Over time, memory for the smaller details of daily life tends to merge into a generalized picture of the more routine aspects of our activities; still, psychologists who have kept diaries and later tested themselves for recall seem largely to be surprised by the degree of accuracy achieved (Linton, 1986). The possibility of contamination by suggestion or the insertion of new material is sufficiently well recognized to affect the evaluation of eyewitness evidence in courts of law (Loftus, 1979). Context and emotion, as well as the search techniques employed, influence the success of recall or retrieval. What this three-fold schema fails, however, to address is a fourth aspect of memory processes, the one that is of primary interest to anthropologists and historians: *transmission.* In order for memories to become social, rather than purely personal and private, they must first be articulated and shared with others. It is these processes of transmission — or its failure — that are the primary concern in a study of *social* memory. This also requires the basic recognition that all of us are the carriers of memories that are not part of our direct personal experience, but which have been transmitted to us by others. These "vicarious memories", as Climo (1995) calls them, as much as purely personal ones, have the potential to contribute to our sense of personal identity or to provide motivations for future action.

What light might research by cognitive psychologists have to shed upon processes of social remembering? Cohen (1996) and Baddeley, Conway and Aggleton (2002) describe a number of characteristics of memory functions that are worth reflecting on in the social context. For instance, although the selectivity of memory at the encoding stage is stressed, what is selected is itself subject to *elaboration*, that is to say, it is linked to context and associations, framed within existing stores and schemas of knowledge, and linked to cues and reminders (Cohen, 1996: 312). As to the storage stage, memory is *dynamic*, being readily subject to revision, updating and modification, since fixed memory structures are always at risk of obsolescence. Mental models used for planning activities, for instance, are infinitely adaptable. Just what are the limits to this dynamism, and whether certain social groups would appear, by contrast, to have become extremely fixated on certain key memories or narratives, is one topic we should consider in studying memory as a social phenomenon. Memory is *integrative*: Cohen (1996: 313) states that "the most important function of memory in the real world is to link past, present and future". *Prospective* memory is that function which enables us to draw upon past experience in order to plan for the future. It has to be constructive, able to conceive of things not present, imagine hypothetical situations, and predict outcomes that have not happened yet. Again, the integrative uses of memory for the future at the wider communal, social and transnational levels are key questions in social memory research. Retrieval is "the most vulnerable aspect of everyday memory", with significant differences in performance revealed in tests on recognition as opposed to recall, and much information stored being implicit (held out of consciousness, or able to be inferred), rather than explicitly represented. Furthermore, there must be *metalevels* of memory for memory processes to work well in everyday life: "The operations of working memory need to be driven by some form of central executive or supervisory attentional system linking memory to goals and actions" (Cohen, 1996: 316).

Whereas the terms "episodic" and "autobiographical" memory were originally used more or less interchangeably, in a more recent volume (Baddeley, Conway and Aggleton, 2002), several of the authors distinguish between them. Tulving (2002) now proposes a hierarchical relationship between *perceptual* memory (which stores information about the properties of objects, and makes it available to other systems), *semantic* memory (which enables us to know the present) and *episodic* memory (which enables us to remember the past). One of the important questions is how different kinds of memories get encoded in the first place. The model implies that information has to pass through the lower levels of the system before it can be stored in episodic memory. Testing the model still depends crucially on study of brain-injured or other amnesic patients, who may display different degrees of impairment of each of these three functions, sometimes losing one while retaining the others intact. Individuals who have lost their autobiographical memory of the past are still able to draw upon old semantic knowledge, or to acquire new knowledge, enabling them, for instance, to play a game of bridge, though they will not remember that they have learned it. Conway (2002) pushes further in distinguishing between episodic and autobiographical memory, proposing that episodic memory should be reconceived as a system that retains highly detailed perceptual knowledge of recent experience over short intervals of minutes or hours. Thus, we can think back over what we did this morning, but in a week's time we may have lost most of that information and will retain only a broader outline of things to be incorporated into long-term memory. Only a small proportion of our immediate impressions will end up being laid down in autobiographical memory, whose time spans of recall are much longer, and may even last a lifetime. Over time, many of our memories of repeated daily activities will blur into a generalized picture of 'my school days', 'work', 'when I lived in such and such a place', and so forth. Conway calls these "lifetime periods". They generally contain feelings and evaluations ('this was a good/bad time for me'), and "may be chunked into higher order units to form life story schema[ta] which in turn form part of the self concept" (Conway, 2002: 57). Conway thus seeks to propose that "episodic memories provide a link from working memory to long-term memory and in so doing suggest ways in which momentary experience might be retained and later incorporated into consciously formed memories" (Conway, 2002: 67).

To summarize considerations thus far, it is important to realize that our understandings of how memory works for the individual are still to a surprising degree speculative. Models of the processes involved are becoming more complex and layered, and are likely to continue to change. As working models become more nuanced, they may in turn help to shed light on social memory. A consideration of transmission in human relationships extends and complicates the picture of memory's functions beyond their immediate uses to the individual, and beyond what is normally considered by psychologists. But many of the characteristic features of individual memory — its layered quality, its shaping by context and emotion, and its dynamism and vulnerability over time — must also be taken into consideration when thinking about memory as social. In one sense this is no surprise, for what could 'social memory' be composed of if not the sum of many individuals' powers and acts of remembrance?

Cognitive psychologists have tended to be interested in how much memory capacity we have, how it is organized, and how accurate it is. The tests they devise to investigate these issues tend to be designed in such a way as to provoke failures, since it is hoped that the nature of the mistakes made will be revealing of the processes going on in the subject's mind. One result of this, Cohen (1996: 316) writes, is that "arguably, the methodology has produced a somewhat distorted view of memory efficiency. In daily life, memory successes are the norm and memory failures are the exception." We all exhibit remarkable feats of remembering over an entire lifetime, or of recalling large quantities of information within shorter periods. Besides, as she puts it, "errors are the price of having a constructive memory that can fill gaps with best guesses." When we turn to social memory and its functioning within collective contexts, we find that the whole question of accuracy and truth becomes much more complex. There can be distortions, omissions and fabrications as much in popular oral memory as in 'official' constructions of the past; the crucial question is what *meanings* lie behind them. And when we turn our attention to contexts of transmission, in which memory often has a strongly performative quality, then 'truth' may not be at issue so much as our attempt to understand *why* certain memories, embodied in certain kinds of representation, have salience for people in the present, and *how* they are transmitted from one person to another to become part of the fabric of social life.

The Dialectics of Memory and History

Hence it is perhaps inevitable that a complex lineage of "social memory studies" has been developed by social scientists and historians (Olick and Robbins, 1998). Halbwachs (1992 [1925]) holds a special place in this lineage as the first to have theorized extensively on the collective bases of memory, especially the 'social frameworks' within which the past is reconstructed. In a significant departure from the perspective of his mentor Durkheim, Halbwachs insisted on the existence of multiple and overlapping smaller groupings within the grand collectivity of 'society'. It is from within such groupings, which themselves are bound to represent sometimes conflicting interests, that individuals reconstruct their memories of the past. Memory provides a crucial site for the exploration of the links between the individual and the social, which are arguably still underexplained and undertheorized in the social sciences. That exemplary sociologist, Norbert Elias, pointed out in his *What is Sociology?* (1978), how easily the "brittle façade of reifying concepts" about "society" and social structures can distort our understanding of our own life in society, and he insisted on the necessity to reimagine social life in terms of the "figurations" or "webs of interdependence", with their many different kinds of power balance, that link individuals together (Elias, 1978: 15). If we envisage 'society' as the sum of the interweaving of individual social interactions, then we must study the interface between individuals and larger social structures in order to gain a suitably processual understanding of it, one that can also account for change. Elias himself pursued this project brilliantly in his two-volume work on *The Civilizing Process* (1994 [1939]); his sensitivity to historical questions has served as an inspiration to us to consider more closely the interpenetrations of the individual and the social in memory processes, and the transmission of memories by networks of individuals over time.

Our reference in this book to the *work* of memory also acknowledges a debt to the French oral historian Frédéric Raphaël (1980), whose penetrating analysis of the dynamic and contradictory character of collective memories, based on his own research among Jewish and non-Jewish communities of Alsace and southern Algeria, shares with Elias this quality of casting light on the interface between the individual and the social. As Raphaël contends, memory cannot survive except in the praxis of living individuals. In this process, it is constantly being reconstituted and recreated (Raphaël, 1980: 130). It is useful to keep this concept of praxis constantly in view.

Rather than adopting fixed conceptual categories in thinking about memory, some have argued that a long historical perspective is required to understand memory as a continually emergent phenomemon, expressed differently in specific times, locations and for different purposes

(Carruthers, 1990; Coleman, 1992; Le Goff, 1992; Matsuda, 1996). One of the most prominent works on the historicization of memory is Nora's (1996) monumental analysis of French society and its "sites of memory" (*lieux de mémoire*). In the tradition of Halbwachs, Nora asserted that whereas in pre-modern times people lived in continuity with the past, with the advent of modernization, the nation-state took centre stage in connecting the past with present identities. In the third phase, post-modernity is marked by the declining significance of the nation-state. As Kansteiner has put it, "the media culture of the late twentieth century spews out identities as representations of the past which have little relation to any shared traditions, life worlds or political institutions other than the frantic fact of media consumption itself" (Kansteiner, 2002: 183). According to this argument, we are now obsessed with memory precisely because the conditions for remembering have become so tenuous. But when Nora (1996: 1) goes so far as to declare that "[m]emory is constantly on our lips because it no longer exists", he is looking back to a putative peasant past when memory, rather than crystallizing around specific "sites" (*lieux*), whether material or symbolic, simply saturated local settings (*milieux*) as "a real part of everyday experience". This idealization of a presumed unself-conscious wholeness and naturalness of past experience seems to parallel the suppositions of Hobsbawm and Ranger (1987) concerning life and "tradition" prior to the age of nationalisms, which they memorably characterized as marked by the "invention of tradition". We should be critical of these dualities, deeply rooted as they are in Western sociological thought, even as we try to decipher the new forms of memory creation — and their potential ephemerality — in the new media forms that inhabit cyberspace. If remembering is as integral to human functioning and sociality as we are proposing, it may take unexpected forms but it is unlikely to disappear.

We wish to emphasize that the so-called divide between history and memory as opposites has been the subject of debate, but our own position is that the two are deeply implicated in each other. As Portelli (1991) has demonstrated, written historical accounts are rarely constructed without recourse to oral testimony, and where this reaches the historian at second hand, for instance through a newspaper report, one must already take account of the witnesses' own positions: a police report, for instance, may present the same event very differently from how it is described by other participants, and in countries with a free press, one must also take into consideration the political positions of different newspapers which may have given a different slant to their reporting. Moreover, although historians have often claimed for their craft a greater objectivity and accuracy, in opposition to memory, which is seen as unreliable and partial, it is clear that much historical writing has itself been driven by mythical metanarratives concerning issues such as national 'destiny'.[1] There are no grounds for supposing that textual history is intrinsically more objective than social memory, and as LaCapra (1998) has pointed out, a history that insists on sticking to the 'facts' may be inadequate to deal with the moral issues raised by the most difficult events, such as the Holocaust. Merely stating the 'facts' about that event leaves one at a loss, since many of them are so bizarre as to defy understanding. A different kind of engagement is thus demanded of the historian, a moral engagement which cannot afford to affect a 'neutral' position or to ignore testimony (that is, memory).

Fentress and Wickham (1992: 47) make the fundamental point that for a memory to be transmitted, it must first be articulated or recalled through social practices. This process of transmission involves the schematization and conceptualization of what is recalled (Tanabe, 2000). It is this conceptualization of meanings that provides the basis for the contestation of interpretations of the past between various social groups (Irwin-Zarecka, 1994; Thelen, 1989). Interest groups can lend their voices to the shaping of national memory only if their concerns fit within the framework of current interests (Zerubavel, 1995). Conceptualization of past events always entails, voluntarily or involuntarily, some form of "organized forgetting", a salient feature of the politics of identity (Tanabe and Keyes, 2002: 24). Because all memories become collectively relevant only when they are represented in a social setting, analyzing the means of representation can provide valuable clues about how collective memories evolve (Kansteiner, 2002: 190). The centrality of the social context is demonstrated in the "presentist" mode of inquiry, which focuses on the ways in which images of the past change over time and how groups use the past for present purposes. In this perspective, the past is viewed as "a particularly useful resource for expressing interests" (Olick and Robbins, 1998: 128).

The use of images of the past for present interests, often against the grain of the dominant account, is exemplified in feminist historiography and oral historical approaches. Counter-memory, in Foucault's terminology (Foucault, 1977), provides alternative perspectives from below. The approach tends to favour groups that have traditionally been marginalized in official versions of history. However, as Olick and Robbins (1998: 128) have rightly pointed out, one should not assume that the dominant account of the past is monolithic, or that the account from below is necessarily authentic. Identity is not a substance, but something that can be reshaped depending on differing circumstances. Tanabe and Keyes (2002: 23–4) have explored the concept of *appropriation* in their attempt to understand how individuals construct their identities in the context of power relations. Subjects act pragmatically by selecting those elements of the past that are relevant for constituting one's present identity. The anthropological literature contains many instances that point to the appropriation of aspects of cultural practices (such as rituals) and narratives about the past that are relevant for the constitution of the self. An important point to note is that modernity changes the place of traditions and "makes them objects that can be talked about and strategically manipulated". This unmooring of traditions, or "de-contextualization", makes it possible for people to "appropriate from them meanings to confront actively the contradictions of modernity" (Tanabe and Keyes, 2002: 25). These three processes — conceptualization, decontextualization and appropriation — call into question the objectivity of historical knowledge. Indeed, Burke (1989) maintains that both histories and memories are subject to interpretation and distortion, which, in turn, are socially conditioned. The relation between history and memory, far from being a settled issue, remains a theoretical challenge in the literature (Kansteiner, 2002: 184).

Cultural Trauma and Contestation

The merging of the personal with the social can be examined in stark relief in cases of what has been called "cultural trauma" (Alexander, 2004). Alexander argues that not all social disruptions necessarily become traumatic. For traumas to emerge at the collective level and become "cultural" as he defines it, they must be publicly *represented* in such a way that a wider audience can identify with the original sufferers and become "able to symbolically participate in the experience of the originating trauma" (2004: 14), and acknowledge it as a threat to the collectivity's own sense of identity. Alexander makes a number of significant points about how this process is likely to unfold in complex societies such as nation-states. Noting that national cultures are typically "problematic with respect to unity" and coherence, he observes that:

> a claim of traumatic cultural damage ... must be established by deliberate efforts on the part of cultural carriers — cultural specialists such as priests, politicians, intellectuals, journalists, moral entrepreneurs, and leaders of social movements. In most cases the process of establishing is a contested process, with different political groups divided as to whether a trauma occurred (historical contestation), how its meaning should be regarded (contestation over interpretation), and what kinds of feelings — pride, neutrality, rage, guilt — it should arouse (affective contestation). Furthermore, once society has to be held in some way responsible, its status as trauma has to be continuously and actively sustained and reproduced in order to continue in that status.

Delineation of these features can help us to draw distinctions, at least in theory, between the trajectories of cultural as opposed to psychological traumas, but what of cases where public working through is delayed by official repression or, for other reasons, has not yet been fully possible? Perhaps inevitably, most of the problematic memory issues of recent history concern traumatic events, such that the question of the interplay between personal and social trauma, and how these might best be addressed, remains a particularly pressing one. In this context, Arthur Kleinman, as a physician and medical anthropologist, is one researcher who has tried to bridge what he refers to as "the fundamental divide between anthropology, sociology, social history, and political science, on the one side, and psychology, psychiatry, neurosciences, and biomedicine on the other" (A. & J. Kleinman, 1994: 708) — the same gap to which we have pointed at the start of this chapter. Arthur and Joan Kleinman have sought to identify the sociosomatic processes by which memories of a traumatic historical event, in this case the Chinese Cultural Revolution, pass to and fro between collectivities and individuals. These memories find embodied expression in the continuing health problems of those who were victimized during that period. As they note, it is ironic that, in spite of all the recent writing in sociology and anthropology on the subject of embodiment, it remains largely an *assumed* phenomenon, and very little progress has been made in detailing the actual social and physiological processes involved. They write (1994: 708): "Because few social theorists have bothered to explore the methods of remembering that underwrite the incorporation of the social body into the physical body, the theoretical cartography that maps the processes that mediate (and transform) the nexus between the collective and the individual is undeveloped to an alarming degree. The map is almost empty." There can be no "experience" without memory, but this also implies a social context; experience, they insist, "is not limited to the isolated person but is shared across persons and even classes of persons" (1994: 712). The question posed by the Kleinmans is: "How do political processes of terror (and resistance) cross over from public space to traumatize (or reanimate) inner space and then cross back as collective experience?" (1998: 711).

The Kleinmans' work in China in the early 1980s documented patients' narratives of illness, which included accounts of what they had suffered during the Cultural Revolution. Their most paradigmatic symptoms — dizziness, exhaustion and pain, often given the locally salient and acceptable diagnosis of "neurasthenia" — mirrored the social experience of many during that chaotic period, and were "as close as many could come to expressing political opposition and cultural criticism at a time when overt expression of hidden transcripts carried dangerous political outcomes, such as public reprimand, disgrace, demotion, forced self-criticism, exile, imprisonment." Inner and outer anguish and resentment merged in the body as "lived metaphor", becoming "a moral commentary, first about a delegitimated local world, ultimately about the delegitimation of Chinese society" (1994: 715–6). The Kleinmans propose that what is needed is a model of "the interpersonal flow of experience, in which cognitive and affective processes aggregate, disaggregate and reaggregate around different axes of experience, from the deeply subjective through the dialogical to the communal" (1994: 718). We would agree with them that the interactive processes that produce societal memory remain insufficiently described.

Social Amnesia, Competing Narratives and the "Return of the Repressed"

Since only a tiny proportion of all possible memories can be preserved, whatever is remembered in the present is highly selective, and to be remembered at all, this selection must have some relevance to current concerns. Consequently, questions of memory are always political. Therefore we seek to ask, "What are the stakes involved in memory?" What exactly happens at the social level when incidences of forgetting, amnesia or oblivion occur? Do popular memories serve individuals or smaller groupings in part as a defence against being swallowed up by larger structures, with their (too often sanitized and manipulated) 'official versions' of the past? What are the forces that bring the 'unfinished business' of memory to the surface, sometimes half a century or more after the event? And if remembering is something we have to work at, how on the other hand do memories work on us, shaping our own sense of connection to the past, and our mapping of possible futures? Raphael Samuel (1994: x) expressed this quality of memory well when he proposed that "memory, so far from being merely a passive receptacle or storage system, an image bank of the past, is rather an active, shaping force; that it is dynamic — what it contrives symptomatically to forget is as important as what it remembers — and that it is dialectically related to historical thought, rather than being some kind of negative other to it."

The creation of any particular narrative of the past may almost inevitably result in the occlusion of some other story. As power balances change, one dominant version of the past is likely to displace or suppress others. Since 1989, this process has been very conspicuously at work in the post-Communist regimes of the Baltic States, Eastern Europe and other regions of the former Soviet Union, where the movement to recover all that was suppressed in the process of constructing an official Communist version of the past was accompanied by the simultaneous erasure of that now discredited version itself, symbolized most immediately and dramatically by the removal of hundreds of monuments to Communist heroes. This "war of monuments" involves its own kind of violence to the urban fabric (Tchervonnaya, 1997). After Gorbachev came to power, the first of the Soviet Socialist Republics to make a unilateral reassertion of sovereignty was Estonia, in 1987, and over the next few years, the unravelling of the Soviet Union gathered an unstoppable momentum. This example provides an especially vivid illustration of the processes of popular memory imaginatively brought to bear against a totalitarian regime, the moment that *glasnost* provided the long-awaited opening. It is noteworthy that three organizations which became very active in the late 1980s were all concerned with aspects of social memory: the Estonian Heritage Society (which worked to restore significant historic buildings), the Estonian Life Histories Association (which collected hundreds of personal narratives describing the deportations to Siberia and other privations previously dangerous to mention; see Kirss, Kõresaar and Lauristin, 2004), and the famous five-yearly Song Festival (which had its origins in the first surge of Estonian nationalism in the mid-nineteenth century). The singing of folk songs by massed choirs, which had been throughout the Soviet era a covert expression of nationalist resistance, had by 1988 become a mass protest movement, creating a social momentum that was dubbed "Singing Nationalism" (Aarelaid-Tart, 2006) or the "Singing Revolution". Before the close of the century, another momentous regime change would also occur in Southeast Asia — Indonesia's watershed election, precipitated by the Asian Monetary Crisis of 1998, brought the downfall of Suharto after 32 years in power. In this case, too, the drive to re-examine history manifested itself almost immediately and still continues today, involving sometimes sharp contestation between different interest groups (Zurburchen, 2005; and see Chapters 6 and 10, this volume). Particularly potent here was the breaking of the taboo on examination of the events of 1965 with their appalling massacres of alleged communists that claimed at least half a million lives. This in itself produced immediate backlash from groups unwilling to let go of the demonization of communism that had been such a key element of the national narrative, constructed under the previous regime, to which for their own reasons they had found it useful to subscribe.

These examples raise important questions about the pressures of enforced silence under certain oppressive regimes, and the degree to which those pressures precisely generate resistances in social memory, accentuating the need to hold on to "forbidden" memories that are denied public expression.[3] Yet, beyond such extreme cases, no doubt there are many ways, more or less subtle, in which people can be robbed of their past, not just as individuals but also as groups. What limits are there to the psychic violence involved in this process? Fred Astaire sang of his memories, "They can't take that away from me"; but are the individual's memories really as inviolate as we like to think they are? How much are they open to manipulation by hegemonic processes? The cruelty of Russia's suppression of Estonia, with all of the arbitrary arrests, executions and deportations to Siberia that it involved, clearly never extinguished the desire to recover a treasured autonomy, and indeed made all the more urgent the work of individuals in resolutely holding on to dangerous memories until such time as they could safely be brought back into the public domain. Perhaps softer forms of authoritarian control pose a different threat to memory, lulling citizens into a state of heedlessness or self-censorship rather than enforced silence.

In several of the countries represented in this volume, there are periods of the recent past about which discussion has been officially discouraged. In Singapore, for instance, the 1950s is a problematic decade, memories of which still form an unspoken "burden" for some people (see Chapter 9, this volume), and whose alternative threads of narrative and "paths not taken" have only very recently received renewed attention from historians (Barr and Trocki, 2008). Then again, by contrast with what Harvey Kaye (1996: 18) has called the "politics of amnesia", there is also the politics that remembers too well, what might be termed a "hypermnesia" that dwells obsessively and destructively on past events as a justification for present acts of violence (the Battle of Blackbird Field or of the Boyne). Both these extremes of enforced forgetting, and obsessive remembering, can warp identities, and be causes of deep harm.[4] Either way, one is obliged to recognize the existential importance of memory for groups as much as for individuals. If without memory, there is no identity, the obverse may also be true — that without identity it is difficult to remember. We must have some structure within which to remember things, but the structure may itself be made of memory, so that memory and identity themselves become fused.

Understanding memory's continuing salience in the affairs of the present requires us to address a number of questions. One of the most problematic and interesting is the question of why it often takes so long for 'unfinished business' from the past to surface and make its demands on current consciousness. It seems that history cannot be well understood until after the event; at the time, caught in the midst of events, people may not even be able to grasp their significance, and some degree of distance and perspective is necessary before an accurate understanding of them can even be attempted. In the European context, this sense of delay has been especially vividly demonstrated in the memory of the Holocaust, which, as Primo Levi wrote, remains "exemplary" and unique in its horror, and, "if nothing more happens in the coming years", will be remembered as "the central event, the scourge of the twentieth century". Levi tells us that the truth about the concentration camps has come to light "down a long road and through a narrow door", an image which well conveys the urgency and difficulty of the work of memory (Levi, 1988: 19). The "truth", in other words, is not simply "there", in the past — "what really happened" — but travels along with us, continuing to arrive long after the event. 1995, as the fiftieth anniversary of the Second World War, saw the re-emergence of a number of troubling issues that had never been satisfactorily dealt with and, in some instances, deliberately suppressed. If the former West Germany had struggled to come to terms with the Holocaust, the end of the Cold War raised new questions about the integration of former Nazis into the post-war communist government of East Germany, where the agony of self-questioning had by no means been so rigorously pursued (Buruma, 1994). At the same time, fresh queries arose regarding the complicity of other players: Vichy France; the Vatican; Swiss banks; the fascist regime of Portugal; a French chemicals company that may have profited from the manufacture of Zyklon-B gas for Nazi uses; the Dutch finance ministry, which in the late 1960s clandestinely auctioned among its employees a hoard of valuables plundered from Dutch Jews in the 1940s; Swedish firms that sacked Jews to please the Nazis; and the governments of Britain and America, which received intelligence about Nazi massacres from as early as 1941 but apparently saw the mass murder of civilians as merely a distracting sideshow of the war — all of these came under fresh exposure and scrutiny in the closing years of the twentieth century. Such efforts to find a more complete truth about the recent past may even stir unease about more distant events: in September 1995, the French army, "after a hundred years of lying, hedging and misinformation", for the first time officially admitted that Captain Alfred Dreyfus had been framed. Newspaper reports suggested that it was condemnation by President Jacques Chirac of the Vichy regime's anti-Semitic collaboration with the Nazis during the Second World War that may have somehow made it possible for the army after all that time to admit to an infamous injustice.[5]

Since that anniversary, research and reflection on the events of World War II and the Holocaust have continued unabated. The sixtieth anniversary of the war's end, in 2005, again saw widespread rituals of commemoration. At Auschwitz, many heads of state attended the moving event held on 27 January, a bleak day of falling snow, to commemorate the camp's liberation. Although carefully choreographed, a sense of heightened drama was conveyed by the irruption of several unprogrammed contributions, including one impassioned outburst from a survivor from Israel, now in her late seventies, who recalled how at the age of 16 she had stood in the camp, stripped naked as a newly arrived inmate, 60 years before. The presidents of Poland, Russia and Israel played prominent roles, each drawing their own moral from the event for present purposes. Polish President Aleksander Kwasniewski expressed the dilemma of trying to speak about the unspeakable when he said, "We're in a place where no words can tell the truth about what happened ... but they have to", while German President Horst Koehler declared, "We have to come back here again and again" to keep alive the memory of this, "the worst crime in history", for later generations. Israeli President Moshe Katsav, calling the Holocaust "a failure of humanity", reminded the former Allied countries how little they had done to prevent it, and urged them never to abandon Israel. President Vladimir Putin pointed out that 27 million Russians sacrificed their lives as part of the Allied resistance against Fascism, and declared that yesterday's Fascists have their equivalent in today's terrorists, who must never be allowed to prevail. As compelling as the ceremony was, attention to detail did fail in one respect: at its conclusion, the heads of state were whisked away in their limousines, closely followed by the press, while the survivors, many of whom were in their 90s and who had stood for hours in subzero temperatures in the snow, were left to wait till the end before their buses came to pick them up.

If we pause to reflect on the Holocaust in a book about Southeast Asia, this is because of that "exemplary" status to which Primo Levi alerts us. Of all memory issues, this is the most difficult and intractable, also the largest and most inescapable, so transgressive of moral norms that LaCapra (1998: 183) dubs it a "limit-event". The enormity of what happened simply resists explanation, and will continue to do so. At the same time, the need to prevent forgetting, as well as to counter crude denials, remains understandably urgent. In the field of Holocaust studies, some of the greatest intellects of our time have applied themselves to asking the most searching questions about the nature of memory itself. Moreover, many of them speak with the special authority that attaches to survivors. This in itself must give pause to any ordinary person, not directly touched by those events, for how can we even find a viable position from which to speak about them? Yet we cannot avoid mentioning them here for several reasons: firstly, because of the powerful resonances of certain ideas about memory, mourning and trauma put forward by Holocaust historians such as Friedländer (1992, 1993), Santner (1992) and LaCapra (1992, 1998), in their probing of the "limits of representation"; and secondly, because those events did reverberate with others that directly affected millions of Southeast Asians, who experienced Japanese Occupation during World War II. And in this part of the world, too, we observe that the major memory issues are traumatic, with just the same delay in confronting unsettled moral problems. In the case of Japan, there has indeed been a chronic evasiveness of the issues on the part of successive governments and rightist organizations, which contrasts sorely with the investigative efforts of those within Japanese society who have worked hard to research and document them, digging out evidence with which to challenge official revisionism and forgetfulness. Thirdly, while acknowledging and respecting the Holocaust's "uniqueness", as LaCapra proposes, it is still possible, and arguably necessary, to think about it comparatively, in relation to other genocides — in so far as that effort might help us to a better understanding of significant similarities or differences. Cambodia, as a main candidate for this kind of comparative study, once again draws our attention to Southeast Asia (Hinton, 2005). The Cambodian case raises perplexing questions of its own, notably the fact that the victims here were not obviously identifiable as an "out-group", except in so far as difference could be manufactured by means of an ideology of class warfare — a point which begs still further comparisons, most obviously with China's Cultural Revolution and prior to that, with Russia's Stalinist purges.

A most significant contribution of the above-mentioned authors has been their engagement with concepts derived from psychoanalysis, and their rigorous consideration of how these might be brought to bear upon questions of collective memory. It is notable that many writers have not been able to resist an apparently metaphorical application, in social contexts, of some of Freud's more compelling notions, such as "a return of the repressed". But too often they have not really bothered to examine what might be involved in such sliding between individual psychic processes and collective memory problems. Friedländer, Santner and LaCapra stand out as three theorists who have attempted a more systematic inquiry. They all pay careful attention to the affective investments that an individual or group may have in a particular narrative; that, as LaCapra is at pains to consider, must include the investment of the investigating scholar as a "secondary witness", who must find an appropriate balance between empathy and critical (or self-preservative) distance (Santner, 1992: 144; LaCapra, 1998: 69, 182). Importantly, LaCapra offers a possible way out of the difficulty of bridging individual and collective processes when he reminds us, quite correctly, that in reality psychic processes never take place in a social vacuum. A person in psychoanalysis, for instance, must of necessity be in relationship with at least one other person, if only the analyst. Perhaps psychology, of all Western modes of thought, is the one most prone to a reification of the individual as autonomous subject. Mourning, a process central to all these writers' discussions of trauma, is also not an entirely private matter; it is more usually a social, even a ritual, practice. "To be effective, mourning would seem to require a supportive, or even solidaristic, social context", LaCapra observes (1998: 184), wondering at the same time whether Western societies have forgotten how to provide sufficient support to people at such times. Above all, he warns us of the need for a particular quality of attention in talking of traumatic events; of the need when assessing contradictory narratives of the past to affirm only that which deserves affirmation; and of the necessity for the inquirer to be self-critical and reflexive in working out an appropriate subject-position from which to speak. He asserts the need for an "ethicopolitical" approach that understands politics "not simply as power but in terms of normatively guided life in common"; while cautioning against self-indulgence, he insists that "it is also the case that one's implication in a set of problems can exist and be explored by virtue of the fact that one is indissolubly a scholar, an ethical agent, and a citizen or political being" (1998: 210).

Santner (1992: 144) extends Freud's idea of fetishism to historical narratives, proposing that groups as well as individuals may at times allow themselves to privilege a compulsively repeated narrative that blocks the work of mourning. He defines narrative fetishism as:

> the construction and deployment of a narrative consciously or unconsciously designed to expunge the traces of the trauma or loss that called that narrative into being in the first place. The use of narrative as fetish may be contrasted with that rather different mode of symbolic behaviour that Freud called *Trauerarbeit* or the "work of mourning". Both narrative fetishism and mourning are responses to loss, to a past that refuses to go away due to its traumatic impact. The work of mourning is a process of elaborating and integrating the reality of loss or traumatic shock by remembering and repeating it in symbolically and dialogically mediated doses.... Narrative fetishism, by contrast, is the way an inability to mourn emplots traumatic events; it is a strategy of undoing, in fantasy, the need for mourning by simulating a condition of intactness, typically by situating the site and origin of loss elsewhere. Narrative fetishism releases one from the burden of having to reconstitute one's self-identity under "posttraumatic" conditions; in narrative fetishism, the "post" is indefinitely postponed.

Freud himself observed that trauma is typically belatedly (*nachträglich*) registered, after a period of latency. This observation resonates with the delay we have already noted in the working through of problems in social memory, and the gathering of testimony about them. In parallel with Santner, LaCapra (1998: 185) seeks to develop an application of Freud's concepts of "acting out" and "working through" to the analysis of social trauma. He recognizes that the two are best not seen as polar opposites, since some degree of acting-out may be unavoidable, while for its part, working-through is a recurrent process that may never be entirely completed. But working-through does allow one to recover some reinvestment in life and the future, with a loosening of the narcissistic identification with the lost "other", who is nevertheless still remembered and honoured. Acting-out, on the other hand (which in Freud's work is associated, by contrast with the work of mourning, to the fixated state of melancholia) has a compulsive and evasive quality. One way of remembering may here be used as a substitute or 'screen' for another, creating a blockage that arrests any movement beyond closed, stymied positions, any shift in articulation that might allow of some forward progression.

In the politics of memory, questions of responsibility are constantly being revisited; the work of these historians helps us to gain some insight into why this process takes so much time. The link between the personal and the collective can be seen, for instance, in how the different narratives constructed by the German historians who participated in the 'Historians' Debate' of the 1980s, whether revisionist or radical, articulate through their own political and emotional commitments the impulses of the wider society, either in acting-out or working-through the difficulties of remembering the past. Once published, their works in turn enter public discourse, influencing the further directions of popular debate. The effect of such individual efforts may be incremental. In many social contexts, close scrutiny will show that the work of memory is going on all the time, without necessarily attracting much attention. But longer-term shifts in the social, political and economic climates in various countries, or the eruption of new events that threaten to repeat the past, can lead with apparent suddenness to dramatic watersheds in public awareness. In the early 1990s, the war in Bosnia, with its nightmare of 'ethnic cleansing', was one such event that directly challenged Europeans to consider whether the lessons of the Holocaust had been properly learned. The Serbian mass rape of women prisoners in that conflict also provoked an International Commission of Inquiry which demanded a new international recognition of rape as a war crime, instead of just an age-old 'accident' of war. In February 2001, the Yugoslav War Crimes Tribunal in the Hague confirmed this recognition when it made a landmark ruling in the case of three Bosnian Serbs who ran 'rape camps' where they tortured women and girls in Foca, southeast Bosnia, during the war of 1992–95. This was the first case in which mass rape and sexual enslavement have been officially categorized as crimes against humanity, and the three were sentenced to a combined total of 60 years in prison.[6] This ability to rethink categories in a fundamental way has been made possible partly by the success of feminist movements in bringing women's concerns into the mainstream of public awareness. Significantly, the redefinition of rape as a war crime has given new impetus to an older issue, the movement for the compensation of former 'Comfort Women' or military sex slaves of the Japanese army in East and Southeast Asia during World War II.

It is sometimes argued that it is anachronistic, and therefore pointless or unfair, to judge the past by present moral standards. This exact argument has been offered by the Japanese government in defence of the army's wartime treatment of women. Yet, in the search for justice, restitution or reconciliation, people will continue to do precisely this. The argument can easily be posed disingenuously, containing as it does the hidden assumption that there was uniform agreement about the moral standards of the past.[7] The continuous interrogation of the past in the light of present-day concerns and opinions reveals that memory is not just a political, but in some much more profound sense, a moral issue. One of the most intriguing phenomena of the past several years has been the spate of apologies for historical injustices, even those for which the apologizers can claim only a very indirect responsibility as descendants of the perpetrators. Perhaps it is precisely this impulse to make a *moral* engagement with the past that, more than anything else, keeps it alive for us. More than just a matter of sanctimonious sentiment, it demands rather the recognition that even harms inflicted generations ago may still be working themselves out in the present. It is this feeling of a need to face up to the past that drives the reconciliation movement in Australia, for example, a movement whose present, startling momentum throughout a wide cross-section of Australian society is itself the result of decades of effort on the part of activists both Aboriginal and white. Kevin Rudd's public apology in the Australian parliament, as one of his first acts in office, in January 2008, brought a profound sense of relief in view of the tension generated by his predecessor John Howard's obstinate refusal over the years to make such a gesture. It was taken by many Australians as a moment of moral renewal for the nation as a whole.[8]

The work of memory may appear to be slow, then, while its cumulative effects may be far-reaching. If the Holocaust continues to figure prominently in wider European and American scholarly and public discourses, Japanese military aggression during the Second World War has emerged as a focus of international debate in Asia. It was in the changed context of the 1990s that surviving Comfort Women, benefiting from the progress of women's movements in their own countries, began to speak up for the first time about their experiences, and campaign for compensation. Many of the survivors had by now outlived their parents, and their children, if they had any, were themselves grown up. The powerful factor of shame which had forced them to keep their memories secret was thus no longer such an inhibiting factor (Howard, 1995; Piper, 2000). Howard notes that during the 1960s and 1970s, investigative research (a significant amount of it by Japanese writers and film-makers), had already done something to bring to light the story of the Comfort Women. The first former Korean Comfort Woman to break the silence was actually Pae Ponggi, who appeared in a Japanese documentary film in 1979. Several others published their testimonies in the 1980s. Yet it was not until 1990 that this slowly gathering momentum finally achieved the big breakthrough into public awareness, when another survivor, Kim Haksun, became the first to tell her story publicly (Kim, 1995). The next year, Kim and two others filed a lawsuit in Tokyo to demand compensation from the Japanese government, which initially denied that there had been military involvement in the organization of Comfort Women. Soon after, former Comfort Women of China, Taiwan, the Philippines and elsewhere, also joined the movement for compensation (Ruff-O'Herne, 1994; Hicks, 1995). Further lawsuits followed in 1992, 1993 and 2000, while in 1997 a suit was brought by survivors of the Rape of Nanjing, some with the support of Japanese human rights groups and the Japan Federation of Bar Associations. None have succeeded in obtaining compensation, and to date, the issues of military sexual slavery, as well as of acknowledgment of responsibility for what happened at Nanjing, remain unsettled.

Successive Japanese governments have evinced a deep-seated resistance to offering any written apology for the country's actions during World War II. Attempts to analyze the reasons for this resistance have themselves become the object of numerous newspaper reports, scholarly articles and books.[9] Junichiro Koizumi's time in office was marked by mounting strains between China, South Korea and Japan over his persistent visits to the notorious Yasukuni Shrine where Japan's war dead, including 14 Class A war criminals, are deified (the latter, incidentally, having been enshrined there only in a recuperative movement in 1978). In 2005 a lawsuit was brought by around 1,000 individuals — including politicians, ordinary Japanese citizens and relatives of South Korean war dead — seeking damages for Koizumi's visits to the shrine and requesting that they be ruled unconstitutional. The Tokyo District Court dismissed this suit, and Koizumi's visits continued to make headlines. There were also regular irruptions over the publishing of revisionist school history textbooks. On the other side of the balance, the American decision to bomb Hiroshima has also come under microscopic re-examination and critique, its complexities generating fierce and polarizing debates in US society.[10] Another issue complicating any moral judgements about wartime events is the disturbing complicity of the United States in covering up some shameful deeds and granting immunity to prosecution for participants who might otherwise have stood trial for war crimes (Ward, 1992; Harris, 1994). Behind all these events are deeper questions about the rapidly shifting balance of power in East Asia. Will Japan become sufficiently 'normalized' in the eyes of the international community to be allowed to rearm itself? Can a nation that refuses to accept responsibility for past wrongdoing be trusted not to go to war again? Or will China, as its economy booms and its military buildup continues, become powerful enough to present a real threat to Japan?

The motivations behind Koizumi's dedication (or obduracy) are potentially rather complex, providing opportunity for reflection on the interface between public and private memory, while Yasukuni itself, as a "site of memory" in Pierre Nora's terms (1996), is especially contentious (Murakami, 1980; Hardacre, 1989). Whereas before the war, the state enjoyed effective hegemony in articulating what the shrine should mean, this is no longer the case; it has become a site of ideological struggle within Japan, as much as between Japan and its neighbours. As for Koizumi himself, he has a cousin who died as a kamikaze pilot and is enshrined at Yasukuni. His father, Junya Koizumi, was a senior defence agency official who was instrumental in having an airfield built in his prefecture of Kagoshima, from which 201 kamikaze pilots departed. It is said that Junya Koizumi remained deeply affected by their deaths, and in subsequent years felt remorseful over their sacrifices; did he transmit this feeling of grief to his son?[11] Or did the younger Koizumi continue his visits, in spite of the international rancour they caused, because of his pre-election pledge to the conservative Nippon Izokukai or Bereaved Society of Japan, which represents the families of war dead, and which has campaigned since 1956 for the reinstatement of government support for Yasukuni? Koizumi's public actions, which he disingenuously claimed as private, surely provide a classic example of the repetition-compulsion of "acting out", in the terms of LaCapra's analysis. His motivations remain ambiguous; perhaps only Koizumi himself could tell us where exactly for him lies the line between personal and public remembrance, or between individual, partisan and national pride. But if anyone hoped for a relaxation of Japan's relations with its neighbours once he stepped down as Prime Minister, they were quickly disabused. His successor, Shinzo Abe, promptly continued the pattern of "acting out" rather than "working through" by claiming, in March 2007, that the Comfort Women had been willing volunteers, and that no coercion had been involved in their recruitment. This statement, which caused understandable further outrage, flies in the face of the documentary evidence marshalled by Japan's own historians (notably Yoshimi, 2000).

It has often been said that the Japanese did not undergo the national soul-searching that was manifested in post-war Germany. Indeed, both academic scholarship and public discourse on the Holocaust have deepened the understanding of the mass participation of ordinary Germans in the voluntary mass murder of Jews. In particular, there are two prominent works based on the same set of materials on the Reserve Battalion 101: Christopher Browning's *Ordinary Men* (1992) and Daniel Goldhagen's *Hitler's Willing Executioners* (1996). The contrast in the two lines of analysis have yielded precious insights into what Browning, following Primo Levi's "grey zone" has called "that murky world of mixed motives, conflicting emotions and priorities, reluctant choices, and self-serving opportunism and accommodation wedded to self-deception and denial — a world that is all too human and too universal" (Browning, 1998: 67). We submit that analyses along these lines, that is, of the motivations of ordinary Japanese as *ordinary men* placed under a specific set of social conditions, would add immeasurably not only to the self-understanding of contemporary Japanese of that dark period but also to the international debate on their distorted memories of the war, which Koreans, Chinese, Taiwanese and Southeast Asians continue to remember as victims.[12] But such analyses, too, must come from the Japanese themselves. As Kuo Pao Kun, the late Singapore dramatist, asked in a forum of the conference "'We Asians': Between Past and Present" (Kwok *et al.*, 2000: 73–4): "What is there in the Japanese psyche, what is there in Japanese culture that stops a people capable of deep profound thinking, coming out strongly as a people, not just a few individuals but as a people, to reflect openly and deeply about the war? Because what you have in you is an insight into the war that none of us have in such depth." He was addressing Japanese scholars who were also his friends, and commenting on the fact that the Japanese had been "at the same time a very cruel aggressor and a victim of the cruellest experience of war which we've had in the last century". As one of the characters in his allegorical play about the War, *The Spirits Play*, asks: "How come we have suddenly become so dark and cold, so murderous and cruel?" (Kuo, 2003). Ironically, he also commented on the fact that when this play was performed in Singapore, some Singaporeans criticized it for being pro-Japanese; but when the play was proposed for production in Japan, neither the Ministry of Culture nor the Tokyo municipal government would support it.

Such forms of self-questioning in the process of remembering, however, are rare. In China's case it is ironic that its students seem to have a greater knowledge, and feel more intense emotion, about the events of World War II, than about troubling episodes in their country's own more recent past such as the Cultural Revolution — which also involved millions of 'ordinary' Chinese, especially youths, who were led to commit morally reprehensible acts under the spell of ideological fervour (Esherick, Pickowicz and Walder, 2006). The Communist regime in China has long pursued a "Technique of Forgetting History" (Fang, 1991: 268), suppressing memories of each succeeding purge and crackdown. Its history textbooks are far from perfect, and it is still dangerous to discuss the events that took place in Tiananmen Square in 1989, or even to mention the Cultural Revolution.[13] Indeed, the dynamics of social memory on the part of the victims of foreign aggression may be contrasted with that seen in cases of state or state-sponsored violence against dissenters *within* a nation-state context. A few prominent Asian examples may be mentioned here: the Taiwan Uprising of 28 February 1947, often simply referred to as "228" (Lai *et al.*, 1991); the Kwangju Massacre of May 1980 in South Korea (Han, 2005); and the October 1976 Massacre in Bangkok (Thongchai, 2002). Thongchai's poignant conclusion to his reflections on the Thai case (2002: 279) also speaks volumes for other cases of state violence against citizen populations: "I doubt ... if this state crime will ever be officially condemned, or that the history of Thai radicalism ever be fully acknowledged. The October 1976 massacre is likely to remain in the shadows of Thai history for years to come." This pessimistic conclusion is certainly understandable, and yet historic shifts of power can sometimes take us by surprise, opening up new spaces for the reconsideration of the past, as we currently see in Indonesia (Budiawan, this volume).

Conclusion: Destinies, Identities and Traumatic Memories

In this chapter we have attempted to sketch out some of the major frameworks currently shaping the development of social memory studies. We have proposed some connections between the theorizing of memory processes in relation to contestations of memory in Europe, and what we see as some of the leading memory issues in the region of East and Southeast Asia. In this attempt, we have sought to go beyond oppositions that might be too simplistically and rigidly conceived between memory and history, the individual and the social, the popular and the official, and to begin to trace the interpenetration of politics and lived bodily experience, of communal and personal memories, and of dominant and suppressed narratives. We have noted how many of the most heavily contested and politically salient memory issues of our time involve collective and cultural trauma. Their unfinished quality is something we should come to expect, even to regard as a healthy sign of the process of "working through"; "normality" may require that such efforts never be entirely laid to rest in some cases (Olick, 2003).

In the chapters that follow, we shall also see how transnational, national and subnational politics may be closely interwoven. Minorities and smaller groups of various kinds have often experienced suppression in the name of a dominant regime's chosen narrative about the 'nation' and its identity, while that narrative in turn has been shaped by the need for geopolitical positioning in the context of wider international politics. Historical events and their impact upon individuals and groups can involve many different degrees of trauma, but it is the events that are difficult or traumatic in some way that become problematic from the perspective of social memory. The case studies gathered in this book do not all concern events as violent as those just referred to above, but they are nevertheless traumatic in their various ways. That is just the reason why they have been contentious, and why they serve to map some of the great diversity of issues in which memories can become a site of contestation between interest groups within nations. Though their focus is on Southeast Asian nations, we can see that in different ways their particular struggles over memory and identity have been caught up in bigger historical movements that have reverberated through a larger Asian region. These include colonialism, and the different experiences of resistance to, or struggle for independence from, European domination; World War II and Japan's former dream of dominance over what it once called the 'Greater East Asian Co-Prosperity Sphere'; and further, the pursuit of socialism's alternative grand narrative of modernity in some Southeast Asian countries, and the demonization of communism that formed the sharp reaction to it in others. The latter trope is one that has strongly shaped the official narratives of nation and identity in countries like Singapore, Malaysia and Indonesia, leaving its marks on individual lives in the process.

While acknowledging the uniqueness, that is, the historical specificity, of each such event, we have argued for the necessity of comparative analysis in the search for possible insights into more universal aspects of the human potential to become either perpetrators, victims or bystanders. Only through such a study can we hope to learn how to avert such human disasters in future. In a number of ways, the study of social memory provides vital insights into the dynamics of social processes, as people at all levels in society find ways to use their powers of remembrance to shape the future.

Notes

1. On the question of narrative structures in historical writing, see especially White (1973, 1978), Ricoeur (1983) and Carr (1986).
2. Holocaust survivors also suffer from a wide range of continuing health problems and higher rates of morbidity than control groups, decades after

their initial traumatic experiences. Dysphoria-related problems may even accentuate in old age, when the normal inclination to look back over the past — in this case, a past with which reconciliation is hardly possible — will cause renewed pain (Krystal, 1995).

3. A further example is the recent exhumation of mass graves of victims of the Franco era in Spain, accompanied by the narrating and recording of long-silenced testimonies (Ferrándiz, 2006). Here too, different groups have taken up differing positions about the desirability of exhumation, what forms of further memorial activity should ensue, and the degree to which these are politicized.
4. The Battle of Blackbird Field (1389) in Kosovo has been bitterly remembered by Serbs as the occasion of their humiliating defeat by Muslim Ottoman forces, ending the Serbian empire and instituting 500 years of Turkish rule. It has fuelled ideas of vengeance over the centuries, and served a justificatory purpose in the ideologizing of 'Greater Serbia', which drove the murderous 'ethnic cleansings' in the former Yugoslavia during the 1990s. The Battle of the Boyne (1690), in which the Protestant English King William III (William of Orange) defeated the Catholic James II, ensured Protestant dominance in Ireland and is still celebrated in an inflammatory manner by Northern Ireland's Protestants in their annual Orange marches.
5. *Guardian Weekly*, 24 September 1995.
6. *Guardian Weekly*, 1–7 March 2001.
7. Actually, Japanese military regulations stipulated that rape was a crime punishable by a seven-year prison sentence, but this regulation was not implemented.
8. Another remarkable example is the recent reopening of two famous murder cases in America's deep south. In June 2005, Edgar Killen, now aged 84 and confined to a wheelchair, was finally prosecuted and found guilty of felony manslaughter for the 1964 Ku Klux Klan murders of three civil rights activists, Michael Schwerner, James Chaney and Andrew Goodman, in Neshoba County, Philadelphia. The same month saw the reopening of an equally notorious case, the murder of Emmett Till, a 14-year-old black youth, in Money, Mississippi in 1955. Rosa Parks has said that when she refused to give up her seat on a bus in Montgomery, Alabama, three months later (the incident generally credited with triggering the Civil Rights Movement in America), it was Emmett Till who was on her mind.
9. For an in-depth discussion, see Buruma (1994).
10. The fiftieth anniversary of the end of World War II, and the controversy surrounding the Enola Gay exhibition in Washington, provoked an extensive new literature on the Hiroshima question. See Takaki (1995) and Lifton and Mitchell (1995) for two good examples.

11. *The Straits Times*, 28 May 2005.
12. H. and T. Cook (1992) go some way to providing such insights in their remarkable collection of oral testimonies from ordinary Japanese caught up in the historical events of the Sino-Japanese War and World War II.
13. *Lifeweek*, a popular magazine, was publicly reprimanded in October 2006 for running an article commemorating the thirtieth anniversary of the end of the Cultural Revolution, featuring a cover photo of Mao's wife Jiang Qing standing trial. The editors were forced to do a self-criticism. In January 2007, the authorities banned eight books touching on historical subjects of the past few decades, including a novel about the SARS epidemic, and threatened their publishers with "severe punishment" (*The Straits Times*, 1 December 2006 and 20 January 2007).

References

Aarelaid-Tart, Aili (2006). *Cultural Trauma and Life Stories*. Helsinki: Kikimora Publications.

Alexander, Jeffrey (2004). *Cultural Trauma and Collective Identity*. Berkeley: University of California Press.

Baddeley, A., M. Conway and J. Aggleton (eds) (2002). *Episodic Memory: New Directions in Research*. Oxford: The Royal Society/Oxford University Press.

Barr, Michael and Carl Trocki (eds) (2008). *Paths Not Taken: Political Pluralism in Post-War Singapore*. Singapore: NUS Press.

Bertaux, Daniel and Paul Thompson (eds) (1993). *Between Generations: Family Models, Myths and Memories*. International Yearbook of Oral History and Life Stories, vol. II. Oxford: Oxford University Press.

Bloch, Maurice (1996). "Internal and External Memory: Different Ways of Being in History", in Paul Antze and Michael Lambek (eds), *Tense Past: Cultural Essays in Trauma and Memory*. New York: Routledge, pp. 215–33.

——— (1998). *How We Think They Think: Anthropological Approaches to Cognition, Memory, and Literacy*. Boulder: Westview.

Browning, Christopher (1992). *Ordinary Men: Reserve Police Battalion 101 and the Final Solution in Poland*. New York: Harper Collins.

——— (1998). "Ordinary Men or Ordinary Germans", in Robert Shandley (ed.), *Unwilling Germans? The Goldhagen Debate*. Minneapolis: University of Minnesota Press, pp. 55–73.

Burke, Peter (1989). "History as Social Memory", in T. Butler (ed.), *Memory: History, Culture and the Mind*. New York: Blackwell, pp. 97–113.

Buruma, Ian (1994). *Wages of Guilt: Memories of War in Germany and Japan*. London: Vintage.

Carr, David (1986). "Narrative and the Real World: An Argument for Continuity". *History and Theory* 25/2: 117–31.

Carruthers, Mary (1990). *The Book of Memory: A Study of Memory in Medieval Culture*. Cambridge: Cambridge University Press.

Chang, Iris (1997). *The Rape of Nanking: The Forgotten Holocaust of World War II*. New York: BasicBooks.

Climo, Jacob (1995). "Prisoners of Silence: A Vicarious Holocaust Memory", in M. Teski and J. Climo (eds), *The Labyrinth of Memory: Ethnographic Journeys*. Westport: Begin and Garvey, pp. 175–84.

Cohen, Gillian (1996). *Memory in the Real World* (2nd edition). Hove: Psychology Press.

Coleman, Janet (1992). *Ancient and Medieval Memories: Studies in the Reconstruction of the Past*. Cambridge: Cambridge University Press.

Connerton, Paul (1989). *How Societies Remember*. Cambridge: Cambridge University Press.

Conway, Martin (2002). "Sensory-perceptual episodic Memory and Its Context: Autobiographical Memory", in A. Baddeley, M. Conway and J. Aggleton (eds), *Episodic Memory: New Directions in Research*. Oxford: The Royal Society/Oxford University Press, pp. 53–70.

Elias, Norbert (1978). *What is Sociology?* London: Hutchinson.

______ (1994 [1939]). *The Civilizing Process*. Oxford: Blackwell.

Esherick, Joseph, Paul Pickowicz and Andrew Walder (2006). *The Chinese Cultural Revolution as History*. Stanford: Stanford University Press.

Fang Lizhi (1991). "The End of Forgetting History", in his *Bringing Down the Great Wall: Writings on Science, Culture, and Democracy in China*. New York: Knopf, pp. 267–75.

Fara, Patricia and Karalyn Patterson (1998). *Memory*. Cambridge: Cambridge University Press.

Fentress, James and Chris Wickham (1992). *Social Memory*. Oxford: Blackwell.

Foucault, Michel (1977). *Language, counter-memory, practice: Selected essays and interviews*. Edited/introduced by Donald F. Bouchard. Oxford: Blackwell.

Friedländer, Saul (ed.) (1992). *Probing the Limits of Representation: Nazism and the "Final Solution"*. Cambridge, Mass.: Harvard University Press.

______ (1993). *Memory, History and the Extermination of the Jews of Europe*. Bloomington: Indiana University Press.

Goldhagen, Daniel (1996). *Hitler's Willing Executioners: Ordinary Germans and the Holocaust*. New York: Knopf.

Halbwachs, Maurice (1992 [1925]). *On Collective Memory*. Edited, translated and with an introduction by Lewis Coser. Chicago: Chicago University Press.

Han, In-sup (2005). "Kwangju and Beyond: Coping with Past State Atrocities". *South Korea Human Rights Quarterly*, vol. 27, no. 3, Aug. 2005: 998–1045.

Hardacre, Helen (1989). *Shintō and the State, 1868–1988*. Princeton: Princeton University Press.

Harris, Sheldon (1994). *Factories of Death: Japanese Biological Warfare, 1932–45, and the American Cover-Up*. London: Routledge.

Hicks, George (1995). *The Comfort Women: Sex Slaves of the Japanese Imperial Forces*. St Leonard's, NSW: Allen and Unwin.

Hinton, Alexander Laban (2005). *Why Did They Kill?: Cambodia in the Shadow of Genocide*. Berkeley: University of California Press.

Howard, Keith (ed.) (1995). *True Stories of the Korean Comfort Women*. London: Cassell.

Irwin-Zarecka, Iwona (2007). *Frames of remembrance: The dynamics of collective memory*. New Brunswick, N.J.: Transaction Publishers.

Journal of Southeast Asian Studies (1996). "Special Issue: The Japanese Occupation in Southeast Asia", vol. 27/1, March.

Kansteiner, Wulf (2002). "Finding Meaning in Memory: A Methodological Critique of Collective Memory Studies". *History and Theory* 41: 179–97.

Kaye, Harvey (1996). "Why do Ruling Classes Fear History?", in Kaye Harvey, *"Why Do Ruling Classes Fear History?" and Other Questions*. New York: Saint Martin's Griffin, pp. 7–28.

Kim Haksun (1995). "Bitter Memories I am Loath to Recall", in K. Howard (ed.), *True Stories of the Korean Comfort Women*. London: Cassell, pp. 32–40.

Kirss, Tina, Ena Kõresaar and Marju Lauristin (2004). *She Who Remembers Survives: Interpreting Estonian Women's Post-Soviet Life Stories*. Tartu (Estonia): Tartu University Press.

Kleinman, Arthur and Joan Kleinman (1994). "How Bodies Remember: Social Memory and Bodily Experience of Criticism, Resistance, and Delegitimation Following China's Cultural Revolution". *New Literary History* 25: 707–23.

Krystal, Henry (1995). "Trauma and Aging: A Thirty-Year Follow-Up", in Cathy Carruth (ed.), *Trauma: Explorations in Memory*. Baltimore: Johns Hopkins University Press, pp. 76–99.

Kuo Pao Kun (2003). *Two Plays by Kuo Pao Kun: Descendants of the Eunuch Admiral and The Spirits Play*. Edited by C.J. W.-L Wee and Lee Chee Keng. Singapore: SNP Editions.

Kwok Kian-Woon *et al.* (eds) (2000). *"We Asians": Between Past and Future*. Singapore: Japan Foundation Asia Centre/National Archives of Singapore/ Singapore Heritage Society.

LaCapra, Dominique (1992). "Representing the Holocaust: Reflections on the Historians' Debate", in S. Friedländer (ed.), *Probing the Limits of Representation: Nazism and the "Final Solution"*. Cambridge, Mass.: Harvard University Press, pp. 108–27.

——— (1998). *History and Memory After Auschwitz*. Ithaca and London: Cornell University Press.

Lai *et al.* (1991). *A Tragic Beginning: The Taiwan Uprising of February 28, 1947*. Stanford: Stanford University Press.

Le Goff, Jacques (1992). *History and Memory*. New York: Columbia University Press.

Levi, Primo (1988). *The Drowned and the Saved*. New York: Vintage International.

Lifton, Robert and Greg Mitchell (1995). *Hiroshima in America: A Half Century of Denial*. New York: Avon Books.

Linton, Marigold (1986). "Ways of Searching and the Contents of Memory", in D. Rubin (ed.), *Autobiographical Memory*. Cambridge: Cambridge University Press, pp. 50–67.

Loftus, Elizabeth (1979). *Eyewitness Testimony*. Cambridge, Mass.: Harvard University Press.

Matsuda, Matt (1996). *The Memory of the Modern*. New York: Oxford University Press.

Murayami, Shigeyoshi (1980). *Japanese Religion in the Modern Century*. Tokyo: University of Tokyo Press.

Neisser, Ulric (1978). "Memory, What are the Important Questions?", in M. Gruneberg, P. Morris and R. Sykes (eds), *Practical Aspects of Memory*. London: Academic Press.

Neisser, Ulric and Robyn Fivush (eds) (1994). *The Remembering Self: Construction and Accuracy in the Self-Narrative*. Cambridge: Cambridge University Press.

Nora, Pierre (1996). *Realms of Memory: Rethinking the French Past* (3 vols.). New York: Columbia University Press.

Ohnuki-Tierney, Emiko (2004). "Betrayal by Idealism and Aesthetics: Special Attack Force (Kamikaze) Pilots and their Intellectual Trajectories (Part I)". *Anthropology Today* 20/2: 15–21.

Olick, Jeffrey (2003). "What Does It Mean to Normalize the Past?: Official Memory in German Politics since 1989", in J. Olick (ed.), *States of Memory: Continuities, Conflicts, and Transformations in National Retrospection*. Durham, N.C.: Duke University Press, pp. 259–88.

Olick, Jeffrey and Joyce Robbins (eds) (1998). "Social Memory Studies: From 'Collective Memory' to the Historical Sociology of Mnemonic Practices". *Annual Review of Sociology* 24: 105–40.

Pennebaker, James (1997). "Writing About Emotional Experiences as a Therapeutic Process". *Psychological Science* 8/3: 162–6.

Piper, Nicola (2000). "Victim Identity and War — The Unsettled Issue of the 'Military Comfort Women' in Japan". *NIASnytt* (*Nordic Newsletter of Asian Studies*), 1: 4–9.

Raphaël, Frédéric (1980). "Le Travail de la Mémoire et les Limites de l'Histoire Orale" (The Work of Memory and the Limits of Oral History). *Annales E.S.C.*, 35: 127–45.

Ricoeur, Paul (1983). "Can Fictional Narratives be True?". *Analecta Husserliana*, vol. XIV: 3–19.

Rose, Stephen (1992). *The Making of Memory*. London: Bantam.

Ross, Bruce (1991). *Remembering the Personal Past: Descriptions of Autobiographical Memory*. New York: Oxford University Press.

Ruff-O'Herne, Jan (1994). *Fifty Years of Silence: Comfort Woman of Indonesia*. Singapore: Toppan.

Samuel, Raphael (1994). *Theatres of Memory* (2 vols). London: Verso.

Santner, Eric (1992). "History Beyond the Pleasure Principle: Some Thoughts on the Representation of Trauma", in S. Friedländer (ed.), *Probing the Limits of Representation: Nazism and the "Final Solution"*. Cambridge, Mass.: Harvard University Press, pp. 143–54.

Schacter, Daniel (1996). *Searching for Memory: The Brain, the Mind and the Past*. New York: Basic Books.

Schacter, Daniel (ed.) (1995). *Memory Distortion: How Minds, Brains and Societies Reconstruct the Past*. Cambridge, Mass.: Harvard University Press.

Takaki, Ronald (1995). *Hiroshima: Why America Dropped the Atomic Bomb*. Boston: Little, Brown & Co.

Tanabe, Shigeharu (2000). "The Person in Transformation: Body, Mind and Cultural Appropriation", in S. Tanabe & C. Keyes (eds), *Cultural Crisis and Social Memory: Modernity and Identity in Thailand and Laos*. Hawai'i: University of Hawai'i Press, pp. 43–67.

Tanabe, Shigeharu and Charles F. Keyes (2002). *Cultural Crisis and Social Memory: Modernity and Identity in Thailand and Laos*. Hawai'i: University of Hawai'i Press.

Tchervonnaya, Svetlana (1997). "The War of Monuments in the Post-Soviet Space". Paper presented at the Symposium on "History and Memory". University of Turku, Finland, 9–11 September 1997.

Thelen, David (1989). "Memory and American History". *The Journal of American History* 75: 1117–29.

Thongchai Winichakul (2002). "Remembering/Silencing the Traumatic Past: The Ambivalent Memories of the October 1976 Massacre in Bangkok", in S. Tanabe and C. Keyes (eds), *Cultural Crisis and Social Memory: Modernity and Identity in Thailand and Laos*. Hawai'i: University of Hawai'i Press, pp. 243–83.

Tonkin, Elizabeth (1992). *Narrating Our Pasts: The Social Construction of Oral History*. Cambridge: Cambridge University Press.

Tulving, Endel (1972). "Episodic and Semantic Memory", in E. Tulving and W. Donaldson (eds), *The Organization of Memory*. New York: Academic Press, pp. 381–403.

——— (1983). *Elements of Episodic Memory*. Oxford: Clarendon Press.

——— (2002). "Episodic Memory and Common Sense: How Far Apart?", in A. Baddeley, M. Conway and J. Aggleton, *Episodic Memory: New Directions in Research*. Oxford: The Royal Society/Oxford University Press, pp. 269–87.

Ward, Ian (1992). *The Killer They Called A God*. Singapore: Media Masters.

Yoshimi, Yoshiaki (2000). *Comfort Women: Sexual Slavery in the Japanese Military during World War II*. New York: Columbia University Press.

Zerubavel, Eviatar (1996). "Social Memories: Steps to a Sociology of the Past". *Qualitative Sociology* 19/3: 283–300.

Zurburchen, Mary (2005). *Beginning to Remember: The Past in the Indonesian Present*. Singapore/Seattle: NUS Press/University of Washington Press.

Newspaper Articles

Guardian Weekly, 24 September 1995. "Apology for Dreyfus".

______ 1–7 March 2001. "Mass rape ruled a war crime as Bosnian Serbs jailed".

______ 26 April–2 May 2001. "School textbook rewrites Japan's role in Second World War".

______ 17–23 June 2005. "Murder that powered a revolution".

The Straits Times, 13 February 1997. " 'Rape of Nanjing' trial begins in Tokyo".

______ 4 April 2001. "Revisions to Japan history book not good enough; Beijing regrets Tokyo's decision to approve book".

______ 4 May 2005. "Yasukuni no simple shrine to war dead".

______ 28 May 2005. "Much more to Yasukuni shrine than war criminals".

______ 13 June 2005. "Time to stop shrine visits, party veteran tells Koizumi".

______ 23 June 2005. "Yasukuni visits 'do not hurt relations': Koizumi denies his trips to shrine are reason for anger in Seoul and Beijing".

______ 23 June 2005. "Mastermind of 1964 KKK killing convicted".

______ 29 June 2005. "Uproar over 'gaps' in Jakarta history text books".

______ 1 December 2006. "Weekly ticked off for piece on Cultural Revolution".

______ 20 January 2007. "Beijing bans eight books to curb dissent".

Part II

Nationalisms and the Construction of Destinies

CHAPTER 2

Remembering Kings: Archives, Resistance and Memory in Colonial and Post-colonial Burma

Maitrii Aung-Thwin

Memory, Nation, and Kings

The study of memory in Southeast Asia studies continues to be a topic of much attention, especially in the field's critical reassessment of national histories (Zurburchen, 2005; Hong and Huang, 2008; Pelly, 2002; Ileto, 1998). Scholarship on the region has benefited from post-colonial critiques that have begun to resituate national narratives by exploring the particular contexts and roles of social memory in a variety of memorial and commemoration projects (Winter, 2008; Winichakhul, 1994). Broadly speaking, many of these studies reveal that nationalist agendas contributed significantly to the production of collective memory as efforts to define the national community required a reconfiguration of multiple pasts into a single, dominant narrative (Amin, 1995; Reid, 2010). Even today, Southeast Asian nations still make defining their identity through history and memory a significant priority since the particular processes and challenges associated with national integration (and resistance to these trends) are often readily apparent (Ahmad and Tan, 2003). Contemporary examples of autonomy movements in southern Thailand/northern Malaysia, southern Philippines, northeast/southeast Burma, and in numerous Indonesian locales suggest that the question of belonging to the nation has yet to be resolved by various communities throughout the region (Montesano and Jory, 2008; Gravers, 2007; Reid, 2006). The study of memory-making projects has become an important angle through which the critique of contemporary nation-building and resistance to these efforts has been engaged (Winter, 2007).

With these issues in mind, Myanmar (Burma) provides an attractive field for the study of memory and the critique of the national project as domestic, regional, and international commentators connect the debate over the country's political future to the management and interpretation of its pasts (Skidmore, 2004; Fink, 2001; Collignan and Taylor, 2001; Lang, 2002). Recent scholarship has considered how individuals, institutions, and events in recent Burmese history have been represented, appropriated, and remembered in order to assess issues surrounding the current and future direction of the country (Michael Aung-Thwin, 1998; Silverstein, 1972; Maung Maung, 1999; Taylor, 2001; Maung Aung Myoe, 2001; Litner, 1990). Specifically, studies have attended to interpretations surrounding the political legacy and memory of Aung San (the 'father' of post-colonial Burma), the tumultuous 14-year period of 'democratic' rule following independence (1948–1962), and the more divisive memories of the 1988 uprising and 1990 constituent elections respectively (Houtman, 1999; Skidmore, 2005). While this body of scholarship recognizes attempts by Burmese (and various other communities) to define, articulate, and imagine the national community — an internal process that has been ongoing since at least World War II — it has not begun to comment on how memory has become an analytical category in the assessment of Burmese culture, politics, and history. This paper explores and compares the colonial linkages to this contemporary discourse that makes Burmese memory of past kings a defining characteristic of and method towards the construction of Burmese identity and political potential.

One recurring theme that has emerged within current assessments of the country's political future is the role of traditional Burmese kingship in relation to the state's patronage of Buddhist institutions (Skidmore, 2005). Despite the dissolving of the monarchy by the British at the close of the third Anglo-Burmese War (1886), Burmese kingship continued to be a relevant issue in colonial and post-colonial discourses on leadership and moral authority (Michael Aung-Thwin, 1985; Miksic, 2002). Scholars suggest that the dismantling of the monarchy fundamentally altered crucial institutional, economic, and socio-religious networks that structured the pre-colonial state — a fate that neighbouring Thailand managed to avoid. Furthermore, the banishment of the last king Thibaw and his court to India also represented a significant change in the order of the (Buddhist) universe as there was no longer a monarch to protect and preserve the sanctity and purity of the Buddhist religion (Sarkysianz, 1965; Adas, 1979). Without the king, common Burmese were thought to have experienced a psychological and deeply traumatic cultural crisis, which engendered an enduring hope that one day, a king of Burma might return (Sarkysianz, 1965; Adas, 1979; Michael Aung-Thwin, 1985). Rebellions and resistance movements in the 1890s were regarded as being directly linked to this nostalgia, with former court members, provincial elites, or peasant cultivators adopting royal personalities in order to rally followers in the name of the king (Tarling, 1992; Scott, 1976). While colonial administrators pointed to these expressions of protest and apparent longing for the monarchy as evidence of Burmese cultural lethargy and an inability to comprehend, let alone engage, the potential of colonial modernity, many area studies scholars would see these memories of kings in a different light. Highlighting the persistence and importance of the monarchy in the Burmese conceptual worldview enabled scholars to bridge the pre-colonial/colonial divide while demonstrating a sensitivity to indigenous categories and symbols, which were a methodological concern to scholars in Southeast Asian studies (Heine-Geldern, 1942; Mabbett, 1969; Michael Aung-Thwin, 1985; Tarling, 1992).

In recent years, a variation of those views offered by early colonial commentators has resurfaced in issues over state cultural resource management and commemoration (Matthews, 1993). Specifically, sharp criticism has been raised over the management and patronage of archaeological and historical spaces (such as the preservation of Bagan, the 'classical state' of Myanmar), drawing attention to disputable heritage policies and the state's perceived inability to manage its past (Montlake, 2004). Specialist, media, and activist observers alike have questioned the refurbishment of pagodas in styles that are deemed inconsistent with the period in which they were constructed, providing a critique of the political direction of the country through debates about the country's public past (Priestly, 2005; Tourtellot, 2002; Harding, 2005). Though some foreign and local Burmese archaeologists involved with these renovation projects offer informed explanations (Hudson, 2000), the important issue for this analysis is to recognize how the debate over Bagan's commemoration has been appropriated by competing discourses over the country's political future. For instance, objections raised over the building of access roads constructed within the ancient city and complaints over the building of a new observation tower (ironically to protect the temples from over-exposure to tourists) provided a similar line of critique that discredits the Burma government's restoration and preservation policies while simultaneously questioning its political legitimacy (Skidmore, 2005).

In a similar vein, the reconstruction of palaces, museums, and the preservation of historical sites in and amongst the various ancient capitals/centres of the country (Mandalay, Shwebo, Pegu, and Pagan) have also drawn attention to the ways in which the Burma authorities attempt to build a national community through their control of and identification with the country's material past (Houtmann, 1994; Marshall, 2002; Philip and Mercer, 2002). Involvement of government officials in public festivals, the building of new religious edifices, and other commemorative projects have drawn the attention of external observers, who question these allusions to roles established by former kings. The erection of larger-than-life statues of kings in the new capital Naypyidaw seems to many observers to indicate that the state is attempting to establish a tenuous continuity with the memory and legitimacy of the Burmese monarchy. On the other hand, the Burma government sees itself as adhering to principles of authority and legitimacy that have been defined and shaped over the past 1,000 years or so by various Burmese polities, so the erection of three 'unifiers' in the context of the country's history since 1948 might be seen from this more nuanced perspective (Michael Aung-Thwin, 1998, 2001; Taylor, 2009). While these debates have both contributed to and constrained understandings of contemporary Burma, exploring these varying positions is not the aim of this paper as much as recognizing how memory of the monarchy (in terms of moral authority and legitimacy) has been employed as a category through which some contemporary debates have been contextualized — a dialogue over the future of post-colonial Burma that began during the high colonial era (1885–1942).

Kings and Rebellion

The manner in which Burmese are said to remember and make reference to past kings has been an integral part of the colonial and nationalist record, especially in regard to matters of rebellion and resistance. In numerous documents (Burma Rebellion General File L/PJ/2020–2022)

Burmese political potential was often cast in terms of their enduring nostalgia for the past: reports described peasants and monks as clinging hopelessly to the idea that their monarchy would eventually be restored while histories labelled Burmese as unable to conceptualize ideas of progress, change, and development (Maung Maung, 1989). Casting the population in this manner served to legitimize and reify colonial rule by representing the rural cultivators as incapable of participating in the modernist projects of the state, thus further entrenching their reasons for rule while limiting representation in the legislature to British-educated elites (Cady, 1958).

This alleged yearning for past kings and institutions of old was as much a colonial category that framed perceptions of the ideological propensities of the colonized as it was a discourse that came to be associated with the ethnographic representation of rural Burmese. This nostalgia for the returning monarchy became an enduring paradigm in the colonial archive, whose structures of knowledge production contributed to the maintenance of this image and cast rural Burmese nationalist leaders as incapable of embracing the language of modern political discourse and accepted norms of governance (Cohn, 1987; Dirks, 2001; Maitrii Aung-Thwin, 2003; Sadan, 2007). Just as contemporary discourses use memory as a means of contestation and criticism, so too did British scholar-officials make Burmese memory a criterion upon which modernity and political potential was assessed. The colonial archive reified this ethnology, prescribing the way in which Burmese notions of authority would be defined while registering the legitimacy and power of the colonial state (Maitrii Aung-Thwin, 2003, 2008). As numerous studies have suggested, the archive becomes a site of memory production and commemoration that reified and enabled the policies of the colonial administration (Axel, 2002). However, a closer look at the archive reveals that it was not a site immune to moments of contestation, especially in regard to its memory-making potential.

This study seeks to examine one such moment in the archive that was constructed around the events that posthumously came to be known as the Saya San Rebellion (1930–32). The 'archive' under review will be those documents compiled under the designation 'Burma Rebellion General File', a collection of roughly 2,500 documents within the India Office Records that represent an attempt to define rebellion in colonial Burma in ethnographic terms (Maitrii Aung-Thwin, 2003). The file will be assessed not only for its role and function in the memory-making process but for the ways in which memory became an ethnographic category through which Burmese political potential was discussed. Specific attention will be given to a counter-insurgency guidebook that made resistance a particular ethnographic trait of rural Burmese communities.

Second, the essay will explore the ways in which this pamphlet and its assertions about Burmese memory were memorialized by special rebellion tribunals, which became the primary sites for producing and preserving the understanding of the rebellion (Nora, 1989; Klein, 2000). Much of the Burma Rebellion General File contained legal documents that reconstructed the context in which the idea of the rebellion came to be known within the evidential record. Not only were these sources instrumental in the formation of the narrative associated with Saya San, they also offered important insight into how memory about Burma's past was used to condemn and criminalize political stakeholders in the present. Through the special tribunal trials of the rebellion, views that condemned Burmese political potential to stagnation informed assessments of the revolt and confined future interpretations to a rigid framework that merely repeated the arguments of government prosecutors.

Third, this study will investigate attempts to contest this memory-making process through the efforts of one Burma Legislative Council member who offered a different reading of the rebellion as the official record was being constructed. This document, a mirror-image of official documents he set out to challenge, sought to affect the way in which events of the Rebellion were being understood by textualizing memory in the same manner employed by the colonial administration. While it reveals that archives can be contested from within, the said document only served to further entrench the official government position that saw the rebellion through a particular lens. Finally, contemporary uses of Saya San as a figure of resistance on the one hand, and of national unity on the other, will be examined.

Archiving a Rebellion

Within the unassumingly named Public and Judicial Department section of the India Office Records lies a repository of knowledge and memory under the category 'Burma Rebellion General File'. As part of a much larger archive of documents related to British Burma, and more generally to colonial India, this specific file attends to the official records associated with the Saya San Rebellion of 1930–32. Despite its original classification as the 'Burma Rebellion', post-colonial scholars named the series of uprisings that erupted in the outlying districts of Rangoon in December 1930 after its alleged leader Saya San, signalling the importance attributed to the ex-monk/medicine man who was charged with organizing the resistance movement that would eventually spread from Lower Burma into the northern regions of the province (Cady, 1958). The official narrative (which would continue to influence the historiography and understanding of the rebellion 70 years later) identified Saya San as the peasant leader who had reportedly revived the ancient symbols of Burmese kingship in order to inspire the peasantry to move against the colonial state. Operating through a network of village associations founded by him and his lieutenants, Saya San convinced his followers that he would restore the Burmese monarchy and revitalize the Buddhist religion, which had been in decline since the annexation of the country in 1886 (Michael Aung-Thwin, 1985). Peasant cultivators, already frustrated by the drop in paddy prices, the privatization of communal forestry lands, and the increasing demand of state taxes, were quick to respond to Saya San's ideological campaign, which presented a mixture of anti-tax rhetoric, familiar Buddhist prophesies, and invulnerability rituals. Despite Saya San's capture, trial, and execution in November 1931, the rebellion continued until it finally dissolved into seemingly random incidents of banditry and crime. By the end of the insurrection, 1,300 rebels had been killed and up to 9,000 had surrendered (Government of Burma, 1934).

The archive preserving this event consists of a wide range of documents, including legislative proceedings, official correspondence, reports, memos, newspaper clippings, and judicial records related to the rebellion and its recording. The files continue to serve as the primary evidential foundation for what we know of the resistance movement that saw thousands of peasants mobilize in what was arguably British Burma's most violent and widespread series of peasant revolts. In addition to tracing the history of this rebellion(s), scholars consulted these documents in order to explore the dynamics of Burmese nationalism, political mobilization, peasant worldviews, and related aspects of the colonial encounter (Scott, 1976; Adas, 1979; Tarling, 1992; Herbert, 1982; Brown, 2005; Ghosh, 2000). Until recently, many treated the colonial archive and its files as a neutral site of knowledge, regarding its contents as unproblematic so long as corrective measures were employed in interpreting the documents' data. Many scholars felt that by reading against the grain and beyond the gaze of scholar-administrators, important insights into Burmese culture, history, and society could be accomplished using sources such as the Rebellion Files (Guha, 1994).

Recent scholarship, however, has begun to reconsider how these and other sources within the archive 'became' part of the historical record in the first place (Maitrii Aung-Thwin, 2003). Specifically, we are now attuned to how processes related to the colonial documentation project were connected to the ways in which colonial prerogatives and policies conditioned understandings of the cultures they sought to collect, codify, and control (Cohn, 1987, 1996; Asad, 1973; Axel, 2002). Many commentators, following Michel Foucault, have already begun to regard archives such as the Burma Rebellion File as expressions of colonial power and authority (Axel, 2002). Closer assessments of how archives are made and the context in which documents are produced have also contributed to our treating of the archives as sites for and expressions of colonial knowledge and self-reflection. Recognizing that records may have misread, mislabelled, or misconstrued the societies they represented is but one level of critique — we now accept, furthermore, that the very act of representation through documents and the objectification of culture is crucial to our critique of archival sources and the social contexts that produced them (Cohn, 1996).

As numerous studies have shown, the categories for organizing the colonies reveal as much about the particular historical contexts in which the archives were being compiled as they demonstrate the interpretive strategies of officials. Nicholas B. Dirks's exhaustive research into the idea of caste in British India has argued that its earliest manifestations in the sources were often shaped by administrative demands to understand the workings of pre-British land tenure networks, which would ultimately affect revenue collection and policy (Dirks, 2001). Similarly, our knowledge of pre-colonial Balinese water management strategies were informed by Dutch priorities to read and record agricultural village relations in order that they might eventually be taken over by the colonial state (Lansing, 1991). Turning our attention to the archive in this manner has exposed these multiple contexts and drawn attention to the narratives and audiences to which these sources and meanings were directed. We can no longer take for granted that the categories within the colonial archive were disconnected from the institutions and individuals which produced them, from the competition among colonial offices throughout the Empire, or from the debates within which many of their findings were constructed (Cooper and Stoler, 1997).

Records were made not only to preserve the past but to prescribe the future, since policy formation and legal interpretation relied on the archive to establish the legitimizing authority of documentary precedence. Textualization of the colony — from maps to surveys, gazetteers to guidebooks — became as much a part of the colonial project as roads, policing, and taxation. These texts encapsulated entire cultures onto the 'flattened' surface of the archive document, smoothing over the complexities of societies they purported to represent while stifling the variances within them (Mrazek, 2002). Memory-making and commemoration control was what archiving was all about: colonial documents were organized and managed to preserve particular meanings and understandings of the past in order to register future interpretations. Memory was essential to the workings and administrative functioning of the colonial state, which relied on principles of legal precedence, while archives produced and preserved its very own documentary mode of remembering. Memory was not only a subject that saturated the documents within the Burma Rebellion General File, it informed and prescribed the archive's very function, identity, and raison d'être. Ironically, this site of memory, to quote Pierre Nora, reveals not only the institutional mechanisms of colonial memory; it also illustrates how the colonial state managed the memories of the colonized, describing and delineating how Burmese longed to remember while asserting what they could not possibly forget. Thus, categories such as kingship, superstition, and tattooing — three themes that were essential ingredients in characterizing the Burma Rebellion — reveal much about how ethnologies of memory were produced, preserved, and prescribed within the confines of the archive.

Genealogies within the Archives

In addition to reassessing the Burma Rebellion Files as a site of memory production, we may gain further insight by viewing the archive as one moment in the epistemological story of 'Burmese Rebellion', treating the final reports and documents found there as part of a much longer genealogy of memory whose stories could be traced back to previous institutions and contexts. For instance, the definitive report on the rebellion, "The Origins and Causes of the Burma Rebellion 1930–1932" (Burma Rebellion General File, 1 March 1934) reveals a rich ancestry of previous incarnations that could be traced back to special tribunal hearings in 1931, locally oriented situation reports, and even further in time to a guidebook published in 1914 on how 'future' rebellions would occur in Burma, a document examined below (BRGF, 1934). Similarly, but in the opposite direction, the idea of 'Burmese' rebellions might be retraced forward, beyond the archival 'moment' into its various subsequent manifestations in the hands of scholars who relied on the archive as the source for their interpretations. In this manner, archives refer to the past and to the future, preserving particular memories while providing the foundation for future versions as well. As this article will illustrate, memories of the once reigning monarchy, and hopes for its resurrection, formed an over-arching vision that was not only prescribed on behalf of rebelling peasants in the 1930s but also objectified through the legal system by colonial administrators in their attempts to create counter-insurgency policies. In the turbulent years of 1930–32, memory became a criminal component of a 'Rebellion Ethnology' — a set of essential characteristics and paradigms that bound Burmese to particular definitions of resistance defined by culture, tradition, and political potential. Documents that articulated this ethnology were recorded and maintained in order to account for actions and policies in the past, as well as for the adoption of actions and policies in the future. As a result, not only did these documents deal with 'Burmese' memory, they functioned within the colonial state as memory-making practices of knowledge production. Whether these sources were court judgments, legislative proceedings, or official correspondence, they functioned as registered memories for the future, prescribing and enabling policies deemed necessary to deal with putatively similar contexts.

Much of the material connected to the official narrative of the rebellion has its origin in an obscure counter-insurgency guidebook issued nearly 15 years previous to the events of 1930. Bertram Carey, a political officer who had taken part in the pacification of the Chin tribes in the late 1880s, wrote a pamphlet entitled "Hints to the Guidance of Civil Officers in the Event of Outbreak of Disturbances", describing how resistance movements in the future would be characterized by and founded upon peasants' memories of the exiled monarchy.

According to Carey, rural dissidents should automatically be regarded as incapable of pursuing standard avenues of political dialogue with the colonial authorities due to their 'natural' propensity to conceptualize political discourse through kingship and their continuing nostalgia for the past (Eliade, 1991). This guidebook provided the rationalization for defining and understanding the series of anti-colonial movements that spread through the country (BRGF, 3 October 1914). Officials attempting to make sense of the outbreak saw in Bertram Carey's guidebook a document that could connect the memory of past rebellions to the events in the 1930s — and secure the extension of Emergency powers to the Government of Burma. Not only would Carey's guidebook remind administrators in the 1930s of past rebellions and the form they would likely take in the future, it also projected a particular memory of past kings into the minds of twentieth-century local Burmese communities (BRGF, 1931). Burmese political thought was confined to behaviour forever compensating for an empty throne (Heine-Geldern, 1942). While documents in the Burma Rebellion General File (including Carey's guidebook) preserved the past in particular ways, the archive also conditioned the manner in which the Burmese would be perceived to remember their own past as well.

Some of the earliest telegrams and situation reports reveal that in the early days of the rebellion, British officials were caught by surprise and failed to grasp the scope and breadth of the uprising (BRGF, 1931). The violence that erupted in Tharrawaddy was initially considered a local disturbance, though subsequent cases in neighbouring districts forced officials to reconsider these assessments. The Rangoon administration's request for supplemental military support and permission to enact tough counter-insurgency legislation from New Delhi, the political centre of the Indian administration, had to be backed up by a well-constructed explanation. Although two narratives were actually employed to explain the outbreak of violence in Rangoon (one posited that Bengali revolutionaries were behind the rebellion), the story involving local monks and disgruntled medicine men would soon evolve into the familiar narrative involving Saya San that we know today. Most interesting was how memory played a role in this construction as British officials combined ethnographic images of Burmese memory with their own memories of pacification and conquest to forge an early reading of the rebellion that would last well beyond the British period in Burma. Under pressure from New Delhi and London, officials in

Rangoon looked desperately to find an explanation for the revolt, and in doing so reprinted the 1914 guidebook by B.S. Carey.

Most scholars have not examined the relationship between Carey's guidebook and the Saya San Rebellion, although Patricia Herbert was the first to raise doubts about interpreting the rebellion primarily through Carey's *minlaung* (incipient king) model (Herbert, 1982). Herbert reassessed the traditional reading of the rebellion in the light of overwhelming evidence that it had in fact been conceptualized and organized along more contemporary strategies for mobilization, specifically through the deployment of village associations (*wunthanus*) and their corresponding networks. Carey's formula posited that from time to time, a Burmese *Saya* (teacher/elder) will envision himself as fulfilling the prophecy of the 'return of the king' and would seek to enlist ignorant peasants to his calling. The actions of this 'pretender' (the British translation for the term *minlaung*) would follow a prescribed pattern: he would lead isolated attacks on outposts, luring followers with promises of protective tattooing and amulets, and would undoubtedly set up his headquarters at traditionally sacred spaces or historically meaningful centres. Buddhist monks were also thought to be a threat because during the pacification of Upper Burma in the late nineteenth century, monks took up arms in battle. Officials were advised to listen carefully and to take seriously rumours of "soothsayers", "charm-givers" or other men claiming "supernatural powers" for if these figures were left alone, they would "get such a hold on the imagination of the people that they will first shelter and then follow him" (BRGF, 3 October 1914).

The guidebook was as much an ethnographic statement about Burmese memory as a prediction of the ways in which Burmese would rebel in the future. It argued that for the most part "what will happen in the future will be very much the same as what happened in the past", regulating the way in which Burmese remembered monarchy as constricting their abilities to engage the technologies and progress of the modern (British) world (BRGF, 3 October 1914). The formula cast Burmese as "imaginative", prone to "credulity", and by nature "restless subject(s)", whose "history is a record of sudden and successful rebellions resulting in the seizure of the throne" (BRGF, 3 October 1914). For instance, Carey recounted how when a past *minlaung* promised that his amulets would protect his followers from bullets, it was his fantastic claims and extraordinary character that attracted followers — even though wounded limbs from gunfire should have rendered these claims implausible. As such, officials were advised to expect history to repeat itself for the superstitious nature of the Burmese went hand in hand with their willingness and innate hope that monarchy and state-protected Buddhism would once again be restored in Upper Burma. The memory of past kings and the hope for a restored throne consumed the conceptual and political world of the peasant, enabling British officials to predict how the Burmese would remember and how they would act upon those memories.

Even a cursory review of the sources would reveal how Carey's *minlaung* model was adopted and projected onto the events of the 1930s in order to cast the movement in a traditional mould. The result of this memory production, both textually and ethnographically, can be found amongst the earliest telegrams and reports at the onset of the rebellion. Though the original descriptions of Saya San's alleged mountain headquarters called it a bamboo stockade with a flag, this site would later be refashioned as Saya San's "palace", considered by officials (and later by scholars) to be evidence of his attempt to resurrect the Burmese monarchy along traditional lines (Adas, 1979; Herbert, 1982; Sarkysianz, 1969; Aung-Thwin, 2003). The basis for reading the events surrounding the battle of Alantaung (the name of the hill upon which the stockade was located) through the prism of kingship is actually very thin, though several provocative assessments have suggested that this event fits a formula for Southeast Asian conceptions of revolt and resistance, not unlike Carey's model for Burmese rebellion. By inscribing in the memories of peasants a nostalgia for the monarchy, officials created an ethnographic understanding of rebellion that cast Burmese peasants as forever rooted to the past and unable to move beyond the symbols, rituals, and authority of past kings. Establishing the encampment as the "palace" of Saya San also rendered rural peasant protest as qualitatively different from the nationalist movements in the cities, despite evidence suggesting that taxes, loss of access to forestry products, and Burma's imminent separation from India were shared issues of concern. For counter-insurgency purposes, British administrators were resurrecting the memory of kings among the Burmese peasantry, relegating peasant political dissent to mere 'superstition' while simultaneously making it difficult for urban-based nationalists within the Burmese Legislative Council to associate themselves with peasant concerns (Cady, 1958). These peasant combatants, silenced by the categories of reports and telegrams, were also muted by the memories that were being attributed to them by officials. To British sensibilities, rendering rebellion in these terms not only relegated the Burmese to certain modes of political expression, it also helped to justify and enable counter-insurgency policy.

These initial projections would find their way into the earliest documents that would provide the textual basis for the special tribunal hearings and official reports that emerged that year (BRGF, 1931). In short, British officials hoped to establish that Burmese memories for the return of the king could explain the rebellion, while administrators simultaneously wanted to document the basis for that assessment by republishing Carey's guidebook. Carey's model of future rebellions depended on people remembering his predictions, as much as it depended on the Burmese rebelling. In some ways, the guidebook provided documentary evidence that administrators knew such disturbances were possible, as suggested in the final Blue Book report. Drawing upon Carey's guidebook provided Rangoon officials with a template that could be inserted whatever the circumstances, for the document established clear operational strategies for dealing with new outbreaks while rekindling at the same time the memory of rebellions during the pacification. For administrators in Rangoon, remembering rebellions in the past influenced the way they engaged and represented rebellions in the present. The early documents closest to the outbreak of the Saya San Rebellion reveal how easily the models established by Carey were inserted into the events of early 1931. For police and civil administrators, the outbreak in Tharrawaddy and demands from London and New Delhi would require them to remember quickly.

Codifying Memory

Yet referring to the guidebook's contents was only one part of the story. Infusing contemporaneous documents with Carey's assertions and narrative structures required a consolidated effort, as seen in R.C. Morris's "Causes of the Tharrawaddy Rebellion", one of the earliest comprehensive reports on the rebellion. Carey's formula for rebellion was resurrected by Morris in his delineation of how Saya San planned the rebellion, focusing on the alleged leader's recruitment practices and promises to restore the Burmese monarchy. Just as Carey predicted, Saya San's supposed lieutenants recruited followers by promising them protection from bullets with tattoos and amulets. These members were instructed to tattoo on their bodies the figure of the Galon (Garuda), the mythical bird that is the arch-enemy of the Naga (snake). It was also argued during the trial of Saya San that this symbol stood for the very idea of rebellion in Burma, since the Galon supposedly represented the Burmese while the Naga denoted the British. These assertions, coupled with claims that he would build a palace at Alantaung and call himself the Galon King, completed the profile of kingship and its connections to this prescribed past. Saya San's emergence could thus be seen as not only a characteristic of Tharrawaddy district's past; it was a sign that Burmese peasants were hopelessly bound to a tradition inextricably linked with the memory of an exiled monarchy. In the words of the report, "the unsettled state of the district arose from the disposition of its inhabitants who from time immemorial had been noted as a turbulent and lawless race" (BRGF, 26 March 1931).

Not only was Tharrawaddy made responsible for the emergence of another claimant to the throne, the district was also deemed a criminal region, full of bandits, rebels, and pretenders who had "always been a thorn in the sides of kings and Governments" (BRGF, 26 March 1931). Arguing that "this same disposition to disorder and anarchy continued", Morris attempted to establish that rebellion was a common feature of the district, the memory of which continued — as exemplified by the numerous rebellions that broke out following the dismantling of the monarchy. Curiously, the report also reconstructed the history of nationalist activities in the region, detailing the growth of the Young Men's Buddhist Association, its evolution into the General Council of Burmese Associations, and the role of specific nationalist leaders, apparently aware that urban leaders such as U Oktama and U Soe Thein had as much influence in this region as the memory of kings. Contemporary nationalist leaders were also being associated with the 'rebellious' past of this district. Thus the criminalization of the Tharrawaddy district involved both the memory of British pacification and the memory of lawlessness inherent in the people living there.

The thrust of this early report sought to establish the causes of the revolt in Tharrawaddy, drawing attention to the district's history of engagement with the colonial state. In doing so, the report reintroduced a template of how rebellions were conducted in the past, continuing a framework through which the current disturbance would be evaluated.

In effect, Morris hoped to establish that the propensity for revolt in the Tharrawaddy district was culturally inscribed in the people and communities of the area, if not the entire colony. Pointing to disturbances and "dacoities" in the 1880s, the report recounts how monks attracted peasants to their causes through oaths, royal proclamations, and protective tattooing (BRGF, 26 March 1931). Similarly, politically active monks of the 1920s were successfully woven into the memory of resistance movements in the Tharrawaddy District in an attempt to establish a straight line between nationalist organizations, the immediate events surrounding the rebellion, and the individuals being held responsible for them. In doing so, the report cast recent memory of events in early 1931 into the form of an older memory of rebellions dating back to the pacification campaigns of the 1880s. Not only was the rebellion in Tharrawaddy being connected to a different historical context (which froze Burmese peasant memory in the context of kingship), it was also being diverted from current domestic issues (worldwide depression, capitation taxes, privatization of public forests, and the Separation Issue), containing it instead in a framework of timeless nostalgia. As the memory of early 1931 was being recast along traditional lines, it was being authenticated by Morris's report and preserved for future remembering, as subsequent reports (such as the comprehensive "The Origins and Causes of the Burma Rebellion 1930–1932", 1934) would use it as basis for their own narrative making.

Contests within the Archives

Even though the Burma Rebellion Files were very much a product of counter-insurgency policy, there are elements within the archive that expose the presence of counter-'memory-making', documents that contested the way in which the present and the future were being represented. One important example that has received very little scholarly attention can be found in a pamphlet prepared by U Saw, an important Burma Legislative Council representative who would later participate as supporting legal counsel for Saya San. During the opening months of 1931, local government attempted to account for the outbreak of rebellion and at the same time secure administrative powers that would enable them to cope with the rising incidents of disturbances. Several government-level reports, basing their assessments of Carey's *minlaung* model, began to carve out the narrative that we associate with Saya San today. In an effort to intervene in this process and in reaction to the way in which the rebellion was being used to discredit Burmese members of the Burma Legislative Council, U Saw used his publishing connections to print a document entitled "The Burmese Situation (1930–1931)", which he addressed to the then Secretary of State for India, William Wedgewood Benn. The letter was visually provocative, containing several graphic pictures of counter-insurgency operations in Burma, especially one that showed 16 decapitated heads of 'rebels' that had been brought back to a police station to be placed on display. Not only did U Saw's letter initiate an investigation from London to ascertain the nature of counter-insurgency measures initiated by the Rangoon authorities, it also contested the government's image of the rebellion and their overall policies of rule — the implementation of the Village Act, the suppression of village associations, and the collection of the capitation tax. Local administrators were naturally concerned about the letter and moved quickly to suppress its publication and distribution within Burma. On the one hand, the document can be viewed as U Saw's attempt to challenge current counter-insurgency policies; on the other hand, his pamphlet can also be examined for how it attended to and dealt with the nature of Burmese peasant memory.

"The Burma Situation" reconstructs the early events of the rebellion, stressing the economic hardship faced by communities in Tharrawaddy, the suburb of Rangoon that witnessed the original outbreak of violence and the district U Saw represented as a member of the Burma Legislative Council. His account contrasted significantly with the official interpretation, which identified political motivation as the sole cause of the rebellion. Though only four months had passed since the outbreak of violence, memories of kings had already begun to surface in official discourse in accordance with the *minlaung* pattern. While the letter sought to establish a separate interpretation of events in Burma, significant similarities with British ethnographic images of the Burmese persisted. As can be seen in several official reports, U Saw made reference to many 'rebellious characteristics' of the Burmese. He described peasants collectively as having little voice or agency, a silent mass that had little connection to the urban rhythms and communities of Rangoon and which merely reacted to external pressures posed by the colonial economy. Rural cultivators were stereotyped as simple-minded or inherently and uncontrollably agitated. Most importantly, the peasant population was described as being incapable of articulating protest or disagreement in terms other than what was deemed traditional — an underlying theme consistent with British reports. In short, U Saw's description of the rebellion unintentionally fell along the same lines as the government's official narrative, although he lent more weight to the economic circumstances preceding the rebellion as the cause for the uprising.

In order to explain the behaviour of the peasant, U Saw described the normal reaction of cultivators facing the current economic conditions, a rather formulaic approach that mirrored colonial ethnographic accounts and confined the quintessential peasant to particular behaviour. He stated that Burmese peasants would resist the collection of taxes by any means possible if their livelihood were threatened. Caricatures of the Burmese peasant as being "short-tempered" and "often venturesome, unmindful of the consequences" resonated with the way British officials spoke of the "superstitious" and "restless" nature of village communities (BRGF, "The Burmese Situation", 1931). Following Carey's profiling of peasants, U Saw went on to suggest that such men (driven to these levels of poverty) would collect firearms and other weapons, deal with "the little overlord of the village", and destroy tax records or else "undergo the trials of 1923–1924 and 1927–1928 afresh" (BRGF, "The Burmese Situation", 1931). Perhaps in an attempt to produce an alternative 'official' account, as well as respond to the criticism that the rebellion originated in 'his' district, U Saw adopted the form and tone of earlier situation reports. Just as Morris had developed his theory on the Tharrawaddy Rebellion by focusing on the criminalized history of the district, so too did U Saw use Tharrawaddy as his focus by describing economic conditions experienced by village communities in the period leading up to the outbreak of violence. While U Saw's letter redirected the treatment of memory away from past kings and towards the colonial authorities and their policies, it nonetheless contributed to the rebellion's enduring image by using memory as a means of categorizing the behaviour and nature of rural peasants. Rather than making the palace of Mandalay the ultimate reference of the Burmese worldview, U Saw created an image of rural peasants who were engaged with and attuned to the demands and challenges of policies being constructed in colonial Rangoon.

Overall, U Saw sought to emphasize different memories in connection to the rebellion than those prescribed in the *minlaung* model. In his estimation, it was the memory of economic decline in the early and late twenties that prompted peasants to respond more aggressively to the circumstances of the 1930s, especially since the threat of the capitation tax remained constant while indebtedness and unemployment increased. These memories of economic destitution and unrelenting tax pressure were at the heart of the peasant response, he opined, not the nostalgia for a returning king as maintained in official circles. At the same time, U Saw's ethnology of memory seems to have constructed a contradictory image of the peasant: on the one hand, they were seen as active participants within the economic dynamics of the colonial economy, sensitive to challenges in the market and fully aware of how taxation policies affected circumstances on the ground; yet they were still bound to the same essentialist definitions, behaviour, and contexts written for them by external observers situated in the urban setting. Given the growth of countryside village associations that connected rural constituencies with urban nationalists, it would seem that a more complex picture, as Patricia Herbert has argued, needs to be considered (Herbert, 1982).

In the end, U Saw's pamphlet had its desired effect on its London audience — members of Parliament began to question what officials were doing in Burma, why its police forces were decapitating suspected rebels, and whether or not Rangoon-based tax policies were somehow connected to the instability in the colony. With pressure from London and New Delhi, an inquiry was launched to investigate the incident, resulting in a few officers being mildly disciplined. However, the dispute over which memory was at the heart of the rebellion and the process by which the past would be preserved for the future would continue through procedures dictated by the Special Rebellion Tribunals.

History, Memory, and the Law

The 'trials' of suspected rebels were conducted under the newly formed Special Rebellion Tribunals, a result of special emergency power legislation that was designed to create a fast-track judicial system outside the normal purview of the civil courts. The tribunals were deemed necessary in order to process suspects quickly so they would not be encumbered by committal hearings, *habeas corpus*, or standard rules of evidentiary procedure. Suspects were often drawn from different villages and tried by the hundreds, with charges being levied towards them *en masse*, despite notable lapses in the evidence and significant flaws in the prosecution's arguments (Aung-Thwin, 2003). Consolidating the trials of detainees who allegedly took part in uprisings in other districts under the overarching jurisdiction of the Special Tribunal also reinforced the image of the rebellion as coherent, unified, and connected to Saya San's Tharrawaddy Rebellion. Furthermore, the identity, motivations, and memories of those incarcerated were subsumed under the rubric of the 'Rebellion Ethnology' and legal procedure. Thus, the administrative shape of counter-insurgency measures, and the way in which the trials were being managed, was in fact influencing how the rebellion was understood and recorded. As one Burma official commented, installing special tribunals would be able to "stop the activity of leaders of whose guilt they are convinced but of which they cannot produce sufficient evidence to secure conviction in the courts" (BRGF, January 1931).

The trials are important to this ethnology of memory for it was here that the *minlaung* idea became the dominant theme in the case against Saya San and his various lieutenants. According to the government's interpretation, the rebellion was caused by a deep-seated nostalgia for the monarchy. This is in concurrence with Carey's prediction that peasants could only remember the rule of the Konbaung kings (Burma's last dynasty), a sign of the rebellion's 'political' rather than 'economic' character. Saya San, envisioning himself as that returning king, took advantage of this 'memory' and used it to dupe an otherwise passive populace. Government advocates, relying on this ethnology to contextualize and colour its evidence, produced a case that illustrated and reinforced the royal aspirations of Saya San. They focused on reconstructing the events of Saya San's alleged coronation ceremony, the building of his palaces, his issuing of royal proclamations, and his allusions to symbols of traditional kingship. Although this evidential record has been shown to be flawed (which renders the entire narrative and the interpretations that depended on it untenable), the trial records served as the basis for the comprehensive report on the rebellion that became the primary source for future historians studying Saya San. Thus, counter-insurgency law enabled the British to give the *minlaung* memory its 'materiality' and textual character by codifying and documenting it for the archive.

As the series of legal records on the various Special Rebellion Trials reveal, Carey's *minlaung* model and the official reports that followed it effectively marginalized U Saw's explanation for the rebellion. Perhaps a result of the British common-law tradition — where like cases are to be treated alike and judges are encouraged to adhere to decisions made in previous similar cases — the series of rebellions that erupted in various parts of the province in 1930–31 were envisioned as being part of a coherent movement orchestrated by Saya San. Rulings, evidence, and witnesses from one trial were used for another, while the dominant *minlaung* trope continued to characterize the arguments of the prosecution. From this perspective, the memory of kings was directly infused into the record, providing an overarching *modus operandi* that connected often disparate communities with varying concerns and priorities into a single, underground network of insurgency. Even though Saya San may not have been directly involved in a particular local uprising, his 'influence' was either detected by a similarity in pattern (often associated with tattooing) or through a local leader who was made out to be his 'lieutenant'. In this way, suspected rebels were treated as a silent criminal mass, all prone to the same nostalgia for kingship despite testimony suggesting several other motivating factors, tensions, and contexts for resistance. Thus, tribunal judges and government prosecutors were charged with deliberating how Cary's *minlaung* pattern was relevant to and self-evident in the memories of those participating in the rebellion, perhaps driven as much by law's procedural criteria to establish a continuity of precedence as the need to reify the authority of the colonial state (Sarat and Kearns, 1999).

Memory also became an issue of debate in regard to procedure within the trials. The prosecution charged that the memory of past kings stirred the villagers into rebelling. It was also in the slippery terrain of memory that judges decided how the "lines of precedent led to their final conclusion" (Sarat & Kearns, 1999: 6). Lawyers and judges dealt with memory as a contested issue as well as a system of procedural analysis. Just as the tribunal fixed Saya San in a particular relation to the past (a use of memory in making a legal decision), so too was the memory of past kings entrenched and oriented towards the circumstances of the early 1930s. The special tribunals materialized this ethnology of memory in transcripts and written opinions, anchoring the place of rural communities to the past while asserting their limited political potential in the future. As Sarat and Kearns suggest, litigated cases create a record that enable courts to be seen as archives in which that record serves as the materialization of memory. Moreover, the intersections amongst law, memory, and the rebellion narrative are linked in every legal act — the testimony of witnesses, the judges' uses of precedent, the references to Burmese history, and even the monuments that housed the tribunal urged participants to remember. In a sense, counter-insurgency law was forging its own history of the rebellion while simultaneously depending on a particular reading of that history. Carey's *minlaung* memory was appropriated by the legal record to authorize the tribunal's legal decisions over trial defendants and to provide historical precedence for future deliberation over rebellion matters.

Post-colonial Memories

Although Saya San was executed in November 1931, his memory certainly lives on in a variety of post-colonial contexts. U Saw, one of Saya San's lawyers and author of "The Burmese Situation 1930–1931", later adopted the Galon (Garuda) to represent the populist orientation of his own political party (Maung Maung, 1989). Similarly, post-Independence (1948) Burmese historians appropriated the official narrative of Saya San but refashioned him as a reluctant nationalist martyr who led the silent but memory-laden peasantry towards establishing independence and the nation-state (Maung Htin Aung, 1967). In contemporary Burma, Saya San is treated as a nationalist hero, one of many to be honoured during the Peasant Day celebrations (during the Burma Socialist Program Party years) as an instrumental figure in the narrative of the nation. His image has been used on the 90 *kyat* note (Burmese currency) while streets and a memorial hall have been named after him; even his former prison cell has supposedly become a pseudo-shrine. Commemorative statues have even been erected in Tharrawaddy and Magwe to mark his special place in rural and national history. The former Defense Historical Museum in Yangon had a special exhibit for Saya San, separated from the main exhibits recreating the history of the nation from British annexation to the contemporary period. While he is included in this expression of the national memory, he is at the same time distanced from the master narrative that includes key nationalist organizations and political monks who seemingly embraced more modern strategies of political reform rather than the symbols of Burmese kingship. Though studies suggest he was most likely a product of this very urban-based political culture, the memory of him as a simple peasant who embodied traditional Burmese worldviews endures uneasily within the national narrative.

Interestingly enough, critics and opposition dissidents have also adopted Saya San as a figure of their own political agendas, incorporating the rebellion into twenty-first-century discourses of opposition to the state. In all of these cases, the Saya San Rebellion is treated as an important event in social memory that represented a coherent collection of popular, local, and subaltern voices thought to be suppressed by official colonial discourses. Yet, at the source of these collective memories lies the problem of their origin, and the role of colonial counterinsurgency measures that were involved in their production. The contestation is evident not only in the appropriation of those memories, but in how this particular memory constrained and reduced the potential and capability of the Burmese peasantry to a perceived static traditionalism.

The production of and control over memory in the 1930s seems to have some striking parallels to contemporary debates in the twenty-first century. Questions over the future administrative structures of the colony and the willingness of the population to take part in political reform were intimately connected to the way in which the Saya San Rebellion was understood. By presenting the rural population as unable to conceive of a state in terms other than that of a traditional monarchy, British officials in Rangoon made the case for separating from India in order to form an autonomous colonial administration. In the official view, the rebellion demonstrated that the Burmese in the 1930s were just not equipped for the type of political liberalization that was being prepared for the people of India. Just as the memory of monarchy was meant to reflect the inability of the rural peasantry to engage in meaningful political dialogue (an argument that supported the eventual separation of India from the Province of Burma), the frequent references to kingship and the objectification of 'mythical' authority by Burma's military leadership have often been presented as indicative of its inability to adopt the sort of political reforms that are deemed meaningful by external observers (Skidmore, 2005). Whereas rural resistance to the colonial state was defined in terms of nostalgia for the monarchy, contemporary discourses have attributed a similar nostalgia to the Burmese junta as a means of contesting the state's legitimacy and apparent inability to adopt modern forms of governance. The move of the capital (back) to Upper Burma and the erection of three imposing statues of past kings (all unifiers) has been attributed to a wide range of reasons: paranoia about the possibility of a US invasion, an interest in astrology, continued anti-colonial sentiment, and an urge to situate the capital back in the Burmese cultural and historical 'heartland', where nearly every monarch in the past established his exemplary centre (Michael Aung-Thwin, 1994). Assessing the behaviour and actions of the Burma government has relied upon particular definitions of authenticity and how particular memories reflect particular visions of Burma's political future.

Interestingly enough, Aung San Suu Kyi also relies on and is connected to particular memories in constructing her own political identity — the memory of her father's role in post-colonial Burmese history (she even attached his name to her own) and in her role in continuing the 'unfinished' revolution, in reference to the brief experimentation with parliamentary forms of governance between 1948–1962 and her father's premature demise. As such, her political status is inextricably tied to Aung San's even though his memory is appropriated by the state (although less so now), specifically within military narratives of the nation's past. Within the Defense Services Historical Museum, the nation's political struggle against colonialism, separatism, and external interference is represented through exhibits illustrating the efforts by kings, peasants, nationalists, monks, and the military to secure and sustain independence. A massive portrait of Aung San hangs side by side with future leader Ne Win, suggesting continuity between the vision and memories of these two former friends and the legitimacy and policies of the leadership.

The category of memory, like rumours, might be considered and critiqued as an ethnographic characteristic of political discourse in colonial and post-colonial Burma (Skidmore, 2005). Though studies of rumour and memory are currently being explored in contemporary settings, the colonial antecedents to the uses of these categories as markers of 'Burmeseness' and political potential should be considered within the longer epistemological context. Even in the case of Saya San, the idea that 'rumours' of a returning *minlaung* fit seamlessly into the village 'expectations' that a future king would once again restore the Buddhist monarchy found its way into colonial documents and later into scholarship. Bertram Carey, whose guidebook codified the place of kings in Burmese peasant memory, even warned future officials to take these rumours seriously, as they were one of the first indicators of impending violence. Both features prescribe particular behaviour and mentalities to the Burmese, and a study of their uses reveal the varying contexts and discourses to which these traits were often connected.

This study has suggested that memory can be explored from a variety of perspectives: as an object and method of analysis, as an ethnographic category that enabled and was enabled by the ideologies of colonial rule, and as a method towards a cultural history of Burma (Confino, 1997). Specifically, memories of kings served as a colonial template for understanding Burmese rebellions and limited future modes of political expression to movements seeking the resurrection of the monarchy, providing officials with the necessary perspective and documentary trail to connect counter-insurgency policy with modernizing agendas. Though the character and content of the Saya San Rebellion was challenged by Burmese officials and scholars alike, the ways in which colonial and nationalist elites contested memory on the behalf of a silent peasantry remained surprisingly consistent and provides an opportunity for further critique of how social memory is represented (Prakash, 1994). In doing so, we find that memory was part of the narrative production process, embedded in legal procedure and deliberation that accounted for the making of the evidential record upon which our history of the Saya San Rebellion rests. Judges employed memory and precedence as a mode of analysis in the Special Tribunal hearings, which produced the court summaries that would contribute to the eventual historical record emerging from these trials. These records would also fix particular memories as being essential to the character of Burmese, prescribing behaviour and mentalities that would resurface in contemporary debates over Burma's future.

References

Adas, M. (1979). *Prophets of Rebellion: Millenarian Protest Movements against European Colonialism*. Chapel-Hill: The University of North Carolina Press.

Ahmad, A.T. and Tan L.E. (eds) (2003). *New Terrains in Southeast Asian History*. Athens: Ohio University Press.

Amin, S. (1995). *Event, Metaphor, Memory: Charui Chaura 1922–1992*. Berkeley: University of California Press.

Anderson, B. (1991). *Imagined Communities*. London: Verso Press.

Anonymous (1995). "Make the Gallant Morale of March 16th Endure Forever". *Voice of the Peacock*, vol. 2, no. 2.

Asad, T. (ed.) (1973). *Anthropology and the Colonial Encounter*. New York: Humanity Books.

Aung-Thwin, Maitrii (2003). "Genealogy of a Rebellion Narrative: Law, Ethnology, and Culture in Colonial Burma". *Journal of Southeast Asian Studies*, vol. 34, no. 3: 393–419.

Aung-Thwin, Michael A. (1985a). *Pagan: The Origins of Modern Burma*. Honolulu: University of Hawaii Press.

______ (1985b). "The British Pacification of Burma: Order without Meaning". *Journal of Southeast Asian Studies*, vol. 16, no. 2.

______ (1994). "Principles and Patterns of the Precolonial Burmese State," in Uta Gartner and Jens Lorenz (eds), *Tradition and Modernity in Myanmar: Proceedings of an International Conference held in Berlin from May 7th to May 9th, 1993*. Berlin: Humboldt-University zu Berlin, pp. 15–44.

______ (1998). *Myth and History in the Historiography of Early Burma: Paradigms, Primary Sources, and Prejudices*. Athens: Ohio University Press.

______ (2002). "Parochial Universalism, Democracy Jihad and the Orientalist Image of Burma: The New Evangelism". *Pacific Affairs*, vol. 74, no. 4.

Axel, B. (ed.) (2002). *From the Margins: Historical Anthropology and Its Futures*. Durham: Duke University Press.

Brown, I. (2005). *A Colonial Economy in Crisis: Burma's Cultivators and the World Depression of the 1930s*. London: RoutledgeCurzon.

Burma Rebellion General File (BRGF), L/PJ/6/2020–2022, India Office Records:

L/PJ/6/2020, BRGF, "Hints for the Guidance of Civil Officers in the Event of Outbreak of Disturbances in Burma", Confidential, B.S. Carey (Commissioner Sagaing Division), 3 October 1914 [reprinted by Office of the Superintendent, Printing and Stationary, Burma, April 1931].

L/PJ/6/2020, BRGF, Copy of Letter No. C30, G/B to G/I, H/D, 20 December 1930.

L/PJ/6/2020, BRGF, "The Burmese Situation 1930–1931: A Letter to The Right Hon'ble William Wedgewood Benn, M.P., Secretary of State for India", The Burma Guardian Press, 1931.

L/PJ/6/2020, BRGF, Copy of Telegram, Government of India (G/I), Home Department (H/D), to Secretary of State for India (SS/I), repeating telegram from Burma Government (G/B), 24 December 1930–2 January 1931.

L/PJ/6/2020, BRGF, Copy of Telegram, G/I to SS/I, repeating from G/B, 2–4 January 1931.

L/PJ/6/2020, BRGF, Letter No. C30, F.B. Leach, G/B to S/SI, G/I, H/D, 29 December 1930, 5 January 1931, and 12 January 1931.

L/PJ/6/2021, BRGF, W. Johnston, Legal Advisor, Docket, Public and Judicial Department, 11 January 1931.

L/PJ/6/2020, BRGF, F.B. Leach, Confidential Police Letter 429C30, 12 January 1931.

L/PJ/6/2021, BRGF, Secret, Telegram, G/I H/D to S/SI, 18 February 1931, 7:30 pm, 8:30 pm, and 9:00 pm.

L/PJ/6/2021, BRGF, Burma Rebellion Trials Ordinance, No. III of 1931, 12 March 1931.

L/PJ/6/2020, BRGF, "Causes of the Tharrawaddy Rebellion", Criminal Investigation Department, compiled by Ralph Clarence Morris (Deputy Inspector-General of Police for Railways and CI), 26 March 1931.

L/PJ/6/2020, BRGF, "Report on the Recent Rebellion in Burma", Police Letter, No. 429C30, 8 May 1931.

L/PJ/6/2020, BRGF, G/B, Police Department, No. 292C31 and Report of the Special Commissioner (on the Rebellion), W. Booth-Gravely, 30 June 1931.

L/PJ/6/2020, BRGF, Confidential Police Letter No. 423C31, F.B. Leach to Secretary to the Government of India (S/GI), 24 August 1931.

L/PJ/6/2020, BRGF, "The Origins and Causes of the Burma Rebellion 1930–1932", 1 March 1934.

L/PJ/6/2020, BRGF, Extract from Official Report of the Burma Legislative Council Debates, Part B, General Administration, "Release of Under Trial Rebels", 1 March 1935, pp. 356–63.

Cady, J. (1958). *A History of Modern Burma*. Ithaca: Cornell University Press.

Cohn, B. (1987). *An Anthropologist among the Historians and Other Essays*. Delhi: Oxford University Pressds.

——— (1996). *Colonialism and Its Forms of Knowledge: The British in India*. Princeton: Princeton University Press.

Collignan, S. and R.H. Taylor (eds) (2001). *Burma: Political Economy under Military Rule*. London: Hurst and Co.

Confino, A. (1997). "Collective Memory and Cultural History: Problems of Method". *The American Historical Review*, vol. 102, no. 5.

Cooper, F. and A.L. Stoler (eds) (1997). *Tensions of Empire: Colonial Cultures in a Bourgeois World*. Berkeley: University of California Press.

Dirks, N.B. (1996). "Introduction", in B. Cohn. *Colonialism and Its Forms of Knowledge: The British in India*. Princeton: Princeton University Press.

——— (2001). *Castes of Mind: Colonialism and the Making of Modern India*. Princeton: Princeton University Press.

Eliade, M. (1991). *The Myth of the Eternal Return*. Princeton: Princeton University Press.

Fink, C. (2001). *Living in Silence, Burma under Military Rule*. New York: Zed Books.

Ghosh, P. (2000). *Brave Men of the Hills: Resistance and Rebellion in Burma 1825–1932*. London: Hurst and Co.

Gravers, M. (ed.) (2007). *Ethnic Diversity in Burma*. Copenhagen: NIAS Press.

Guha, R. (1994). "The Prose of Counter-insurgency", in N.B. Dirks, G. Eley and S.B. Ortner (eds), *Culture/Power/History: A Reader in Contemporary Social Theory*. Princeton: Princeton University Press.

Harding, A. (2005). "Burma Rebuilding Risks Pagan Jewel". *BBC News World Edition*, <http://news.bbc.co.uk/1/hi/world/asia-pacific/4606759.stm> [accessed 16 March 2010].

Heine-Geldern, R. (1942). "Conceptions of State and Kingship in Southeast Asia", Data Paper no. 18, Department of Far Eastern Studies. Ithaca: Cornell University.

Herbert, P. (1982). *The Hsaya San Rebellion 1930–1932 Re-appraised.* Center of Southeast Asian Studies, Working Paper no. 27. Melbourne: Monash University.

Houtmann, G. (1994). "Why I Believe Academics Should Be Wary of Dealing with Repressive Regimes". *Times Higher Educational Supplement*, vol. 1, no. 1.

______ (1999). *Mental Culture in Burmese Crisis Politics: Aung San Suu Kyi and the National League for Democracy.* Studies of Languages and Cultures of Africa and Asia, Monograph Series no. 33. Tokyo: Tokyo University of Foreign Studies.

______ (2005). "Sacralizing or Demonizing Democracy?", in M. Skidmore (ed.), *Burma at the Turn of the 21st Century.* Honolulu: University of Hawaii Press.

Hudson, B. (2000). "The Merits of Rebuilding Pagan". *Orientations*, vol. 31, no. 5.

Ileto, R.C. (1992). "Religion and Anti-Colonial Movements", in N. Tarling (ed.), *The Cambridge History of Southeast Asia.* Cambridge: Cambridge University Press.

______ (1998). *The Filipinos and Their Revolution: Event, Discourse, and Historiography.* Quezon City: Ateneo de Manila University Press

Khin Maung Nyunt (2004). *Selected Writings of Dr. Khin Maung Nyunt.* Yangon: Myanmar Historical Commission.

Klein, K.L. (2000). "On the Emergence of Memory in Historical Discourse". *Representations*, no. 69, Special Issue: Grounds for Remembering.

Lang, H.J. (2002). *Fear and Sanctuary: Burmese Refugees in Thailand.* Ithaca: Cornell Southeast Asia Program Publications.

Lansing, S.J. (1991). *Priests and Programmers: Technologies of Power in the Engineered Landscape of Bali.* Princeton: Princeton University Press.

Litner, B. (1990). *Aung San Suu Kyi and Burma's Unfinished Renaissance.* Center of Southeast Asian Studies Monographs, no. 64. Clayton Victoria: Monash University.

Marshall, A. (2002). "Centuries of Distrust Divide Burma and Thailand". *Reuters*, 9 June, <http://www.rebound88.net/sp/ngb/sborder2.html> [accessed 17 March 2010].

Matthews, B. (1993). "Buddhism Under a Military Regime: Burma under the Iron Heel". *Asian Survey*, vol. 33, no. 4.

Maung Aung Myoe (2001). *Neither Friend Nor Foe: Burma's Relations with Thailand since 1988*. Singapore: Institute for Defense and Strategic Services.

Maung Htin Aung (1967). *A History of Burma*. New York: Columbia University Press.

Maung Maung (1999). *The 1988 Uprising in Burma*. New Haven: Yale University Southeast Asian Studies.

Maung Maung, U (1989). *Burmese Nationalist Movements*. Edinburgh: Kiscadale Publications.

Miksic, J. (2002). "Early Burmese Urbanization: Research and Conservation". *Asian Perspectives*, vol. 40, no. 1.

Montesano M.J. & P. Jory (eds) (2008). *Thai South and Malay North: Ethnic Interactions on a Plural Peninsula*. Singapore: NUS Press.

Montlake, S. (2004). "Burma Temples in Red Brick". *Christian Science Monitor*, 19 May, <http://www.csmonitor.com/2004/0519/p07s01-wosc.html?s=widep> [accessed 17 March 2010].

Mrazek, R. (2002). *Engineers of Happyland: Technology and Nationalism in a Colony*. Princeton: Princeton University Press.

Nora, P. (1989). "Between Memory and History: Les Lieux de Mémoire". *Representations*, no. 26, Special Issue: Memory and Counter-Memory.

Nwe, T. and J. Philp (2002). "Yangon, Myanmar: The Re-invention of Heritage", in W.S. Logan (ed.), *The Disappearing 'Asian' City: Protecting Asia's Urban Heritage in a Globalizing World*. Hong Kong: Oxford University Press.

Pelly, P. (2002). *Postcolonial Vietnam: New Histories of the National Past*. Durham: Duke University Press.

Pemberton, J. (1994). *On the Subject of Java*. Ithaca: Cornell University Press.

Philp, J. and D. Mercer (2002). "Politicized Pagodas and Veiled Resistance". *Urban Studies*, vol. 39, no. 9.

Prakash, G. (1994). "Subaltern Studies as Postcolonial Criticism". *American Historical Review*, AHR Forum, 9.

Priestly, H. (2005). "Redesigning History". *The Irrawaddy News*, vol. 13, no. 6, 13 June, <http://www.irrawaddymedia.com/article.php?art_id=4762> [accessed 17 March 2010].

Rafael, V. (1988). *Contracting Colonialism: Translation and Christian Conversion in Tagalog Society under Early Spanish Rule*. Quezon City: Ateneo de Manila University Press.

Reid, A. (2010). *Imperial Alchemy: Nationalism and Political Identity in Southeast Asia*. Cambridge: Cambridge University Press.

Reid, A. (ed.) (2007). *Verandah of Violence: The Background to the Aceh Problem*. Seattle: University of Washington Press.

Sarat, A. and T.R. Kearns (eds) (1999). *History, Memory and the Law*. The Amherst Series in Law, Jurisprudence, and Social Thought. Ann Arbor: The University of Michigan Press.

Sarkisyanz, E. (1965). *Buddhist Backgrounds of the Burmese Revolution*. The Hague: Martinus Nijhoff.

Schober, J. (2005). "Buddhist Visions of Moral Authority and Modernity", in Monique Skidmore (ed.), *Burma at the Turn of the 21st Century*. Honolulu: University of Hawaii Press.

Scott, J.C. (1976). *The Moral Economy of the Peasant: Rebellion and Subsistence in Southeast Asia*. New Haven: Yale University Press.

Sears, L. (1996). *Shadows of Empire*. Durham: Duke University Press.

Silverstein, J. (1972). *The Political Legacy of Aung San*. Data Paper no. 86, SEAP, Department of Asian Studies. Ithaca: Cornell University.

Skidmore, M. (2004). *Karaoke Fascism: Burma and the Politics of Fear*. Philadelphia: University of Pennsylvania.

Skidmore, M. (ed.) (2005). *Burma at the Turn of the 21st Century*. Honolulu: University of Hawaii Press.

Smail, J. (1993). "On the Possibility of an Autonomous History of Modern Southeast Asia", in Laurie Sears (ed.), *Autonomous Histories*. Madison: University of Wisconsin Center for Southeast Asian Studies.

Solomon, R. (1969). "Saya San and the Burmese Rebellion". *Modern Asian Studies*, vol. 3, no. 3.

Tanabe, S. and C.F. Keyes (eds) (2002). *Cultural Crisis and Social Memory: Modernity and Identity in Thailand and Laos*. London: RoutledgeCurzon.

Taylor, R.H. (2001). *Burma: Political Economy Under Military Rule*. London: Hurst and Co.

Tosa, K. (2005). "The Chicken and the Scorpion: Rumor, Counternarratives, and the Political Uses of Buddhism", in Monique Skidmore (ed.), *Burma at the Turn of the 21st Century*. Honolulu: University of Hawaii.

Tourtellot, J.B. (2002). "Dictators 'Defacing' Famed Burma Temples". *National Geographic News Travelwatch*, 3 September, <http://news.nationalgeographic.com/news/2004/09/0903_040903_travelwatch.html> [accessed 17 March 2010].

Winichakhul, T. (1994). *Siam Mapped: A History of the Geo-Body of a Nation*. Honolulu: University of Hawaii Press.

Winter, T. (2007). *Post-conflict Heritage, Postcolonial Tourism: Culture, Politics, and Development at Angkor*. New York: Routledge.

Zurbuchen, M.S. (ed.) (2005). *Beginning to Remember: The Past in the Indonesian Present*. Seattle: The University of Washington Press/NUS Press.

CHAPTER 3

Shifting Visions of the Past: Ethnic Minorities and the 'Struggle for National Independence' in Laos

Vatthana Pholsena

Since Ernest Renan's much-quoted essay (1882), the modern nation has been considered by scholars to be constituted of two causal facets, one linked to the past, the other to the present and the future. Horizontal homogeneity is accomplished along an uninterrupted span of time: "we are what you were, we will be what you are" (Renan, 1997 [1882]: 32). However, the national narration involves, in the famous formula, the dual selective process of remembering and forgetting. The past appears seamless because it is constructed as such. The representation of the nation loathes disruptions and discontinuities. One may easily argue that history as written by authoritarian states constitutes the most extreme example of a highly selective, if not distorted, representation of the past. History must be 'correct', that is, it must legitimise the leadership's rule, and in the case of communist states, it must also follow the single party-state's vision. This genre of historiography is still commonly available in Vientiane, the capital of Laos. The state printing press continues to churn out memoirs of Party leaders and histories of Laos as well as of 'heroic' provinces (those that fought the toughest battles against the 'enemy' and subsequently suffered the most, for example, Huaphan and Xieng Khouang in the north, or Saravane/Sekong in the south) — all of which follow the same underlying pattern: the celebration of the party-state's righteous and flawless guidance that led to the liberation of the Lao people from 'colonial tyranny' (the French) and the 'imperialist forces' (the Americans) 30 years ago.

In this essay, my intention will be to transcribe the narratives of some people of ethnic minority origin that have remained concealed in the authoritative national history, and to show that, in the manner of Bhabha, "no political ideologies [can] claim transcendent or metaphysical authority for themselves" (Bhabha, 1995: 299). I will point out the divergent interpretations performed by the state and the villagers of Ban Paktai in Sekong Province (in Southeastern Laos) concerning Ong Keo, an ethnic leader who fought against French colonial rule in the early twentieth century and who was turned into a patriotic figure for the sake of the nationalist history, by investigating the oral memory of some of these villagers. I argue, however, that in the context of transition in contemporary Laos whereby orthodox communist ideology is slowly giving way to "more purely nationalist sources of legitimation" (Evans, 2004: 99), these narratives both reproduce and contest the state's historical discourse as there exist identifications as well as potential disjunctions between the narration told by the rulers and the stories embedded in the lived experience of the ruled.

In the now familiar phrase, Stuart Hall has pointed out the discursive character of the "narrative of the nation"

> ... told and retold in national histories, literatures, the media and popular culture. These provide a set of stories, images, landscapes, scenarios, historical events, national symbols and rituals which stand for, or represent, the shared experiences, sorrows, and triumphs and disasters which give meaning to the nation. As members of such an 'imagined community', we see ourselves in our mind's eye sharing in this narrative. It lends significance and importance to our humdrum existence, connecting our everyday lives with a national destiny that pre-existed us and will outlive us (Hall, 1994: 293).

If it is commonly acknowledged that representations of the past are central to the symbolic constitution of national consciousness, the relation between collective history, on the one hand, and memories based on personal experience, on the other hand, is persistently a vexed one, even when a coercive state is responsible for the production of history. Perhaps it is wise to adopt Rubie S. Watson's cautious statement when she writes: "it is important that we do not credit the socialist state and its agents with too much power or its citizens with too much boldness" (Watson, 1994: 2). The people are not mere passive receivers but neither are they constantly resisting. Homi Bhabha sees the relationships between individuals and the nation's narrative through a dual lens or, in his words, in a "double-time". The people are the "historical 'objects' of a nationalist pedagogy" but they are also "the 'subjects' of a process of signification that must erase any prior or originary presence of the nation-people to demonstrate the prodigious, living principle of the people as that continual process by which the national life is redeemed and signified as a repeating and reproductive process" (Bhabha, 1995: 297).

It is precisely this duality that allows individuals a space for contesting the official representation of the past, which claims to configure the imagining of the national community. Elizabeth Tonkin argues that people are both subjects[1] and agents in the account of memory and the constitution of history. Social conditions and political rhetoric model people's identities; yet their subjectivity is not entirely dominated by the social and by the action of the nation-state. Personal and social identities are clearly intertwined; however, people have a margin for criticism and self-reflection. She states: "[...] oral accounts no less than written ones can be means of comment and reflection, in which different pasts are conceptualised, and, often, contradiction and failure admitted" (Tonkin, 1992: 130–1). In other words, totalising narrations of national history are not themselves homogenous. They serve as a framework, the content and bounds of which may be represented by people. The working of power is neither total nor unilateral.

While acknowledging the existence of space for dissent, we should also, on the other hand, be careful not to reify the other posited, collective field of memory. What happens on the personal level when the narrative of the nation shifts? In the decade following the communist takeover in Laos in 1975, monarchy and Buddhism, the country's most potent national symbols under the former Royal Lao Government (RLG), disappeared from the new rhetoric. Almost 30 years since the Revolution, the 'infamous' past, however, seems to be as relevant as ever in the country. The revival of Buddhism is evident both at the popular and at the state level. The conflation of Buddhism and socialism is, as a matter of fact, openly celebrated and benefits from extensive media coverage.[2] Lao urban society and lowland rural areas are also experiencing a process of re-traditionalisation based mainly upon lowland Lao customs and codes of *savoir vivre* after several years of cultural and social anomie. Meanwhile, the country's economic liberalisation since the late 1980s has given the population, especially the younger generations, access to other means of communication than the official channels, as well as more exposure to outside influences.

In contrast, the blanket theme of the '30-year Struggle for Independence' (the Franco-Viet Minh and Vietnam/American Wars) that gives the standard propagandistic narration a thin thread of continuity and unity appears to have steadily lost its appeal and credibility among the population. From the late 1950s to the mid-1970s, a civil war tore Laos apart along political, ideological and territorial lines. The conflict opposed the Royal Lao Government and the Pathet Lao (the Lao communists). Both sides were heavily dependent on foreign powers: on the one hand, the United States (and the Kingdom of Thailand), and on the other, the Democratic Republic of Vietnam (along with the People's Republic of China). Geographically, the country was also split into two zones. It was as if an imaginary (and fluctuating) line drawn from the north to the south divided the country between the west and the east. Broadly speaking, the government-controlled areas embraced the plains, mostly inhabited by ethnic Lao populations, while the communists dominated the eastern and mountainous territories where non-ethnic Lao peoples were predominant (although some highland ethnic groups also supported the American-backed Royal Lao Government). It is commonly accepted that the highland populations in Laos were caught between the propaganda of the fighting parties, both sides being eager to obtain their loyalty in the aftermath of the Second World War. The decision to rally to either side was contingent and, most often, guided by the imperative of survival.[3]

I. Ong Keo: From Kha[4] Leader to Patriotic Leader

There was a series of highland peoples' rebellions against the French administration in colonial Laos, beginning in 1895, reaching a peak between 1910 and 1916, and finally dying out in the 1930s. As early as 1901, some Mon-Khmer highland groups, led by their chief, Ong Keo, embarked upon armed resistance to French rule on the Bolovens Plateau in southern Laos. I will first briefly present his actions from the perspectives of scholars and of Lao official historiography, then comment on the legacy of Ong Keo's actions in Ban Paktai, based on the villagers' reactions. My brief account of Ong Keo's history is principally drawn from the works of Moppert (1978, 1981), Gunn (1985) and Murdoch (1974).

Ong Keo's real name was My; hence he was condescendingly nicknamed Bac My by the French, which may be roughly translated as 'that bloke My'.[5] He was an Alak[6] from a relatively modest background — his father was the chief of a village. He rapidly distinguished himself by his charisma and intelligence — his command of Lao, and also of Pali, no doubt helped him to build up a certain prestige among his fellow men. He began his actions around 1900 amidst the highland people's sentiments of resentment and anger caused by the French authorities' harsh and insensitive rule. He performed religious *Phi* (spirit) ceremonies on Phu (Mount) Tayun, located a few kilometres east of his native village, during which he urged his followers to throw out the invaders. The rituals attracted an increasing number of people and he was soon proclaimed *Phu Mi Boun*, 'the Holy Man', by his partisans. He also became known as Pha Ong Keo or Ong Keo — *Pha* means 'saint'; *Ong*, 'king, prince or a divine person of high rank'; and *Keo*, 'diamond or precious stone'; Moppert (1978: 78) suggested the following translation: "the Saint who possesses the miraculous stone". In April 1901, Ong Keo launched his first spectacular attack on the French local authority in Thateng, in Eastern Province (now Sekong Province). The ambush opened a six-year period of armed action and repression of Ong Keo and his partisans by the French in the mountainous eastern region of the Bolovens Plateau.

Finally, in October 1907, the *Phu Mi Boun* surrendered, following the dispersal of his troops, who had been seriously undermined by various factors including military defeats, epidemics and famine. However, he never really submitted to the French conditions — for instance, he did not relinquish the title of *Chao Sadet* (Great King) that he had bestowed upon himself, and he continued to perform very popular *Bouns*, religious ceremonies combining both Buddhist and Alak rituals (Moppert, 1978: 171). He even implicitly encouraged his disciples, notably Kommandam, to carry on the struggle. Eventually, incensed by his arrogant attitude, the Commissaire of Saravane, Dauplay (who had played a crucial role in the rebellion's repression), decided to get rid of him. He set up a meeting in November 1910 with the clear intention of killing Ong Keo. Debates still surround the circumstances of his murder. Some sources claim that Dauplay himself killed Ong Keo with a gun hidden under his hat (Moppert, 1978; Murdoch, 1974);[7] others argue that it was Dauplay's men who bayoneted Ong Keo to death (Gunn, 1985: 51).[8]

From 'Barbarians' to 'Patriots'

Patricia Pelley, in her study of the constitution of a national historiography in postcolonial Vietnam after the creation of the Democratic Republic of Vietnam in 1945, notes that the presence of ethnic minorities posed a problem in the rewriting of the newly independent state's national history. The treatment of ethnic differences was erratic, oscillating between two extremes: concealment or recognition of ethnic heterogeneity. When the latter option was adopted, Pelley argues, it was done in a way that transformed the ethnic minorities. The metaphor introduced a "new sense of topography and borders" by "converting strange and hostile landscapes into familiar ones and [changing] barbarian others into brothers" (Pelley, 1998: 379).

Likewise, the leaders of the neighbouring communist state of Laos employ comparable metaphors to bind a diverse population into a national community. Kaysone Phomvihane — President of the Lao P.D.R. until his death in 1992 and celebrated at present in the country as the inspirational figure of the regime — poetically claimed that "[e]ach ethnic group has a nice and beautiful culture and belongs to the Lao national community, just as all kinds of flowers grow in a garden of various colours and scents" (Ministry of Information and Culture, 1996: 13). Yet the seemingly egalitarian community and interrelated population remain dominated by the Lao-Thai ethno-linguistic category. The authors of *Pavatsăt lao* [*History of Laos*], published by the Ministry of Information and Culture in the mid-1990s, explain the ethnic order in these terms: "The specificity of the living conditions and the relations between various ethnic groups engender favourable conditions for national harmony thanks to their [ancient] origins in Laos. Those large communities have unified and the population is united. It is the population of Laos, with the Lao-Thai speaking community [that is, the ethnic Lao] as its core, in a multi-ethnic structure" (Ministry of Information and Culture, 1996: 13).[9] The influence of Vietnamese historiography and ethnology is blatant here, as shown in this excerpt by a Vietnamese author:

> The Vietnamese have an important role, being the principal and largest (almost 90%) group in the population of our country, with a long

> historical evolution, and a major contribution to the task of building and maintaining the country. In history, the Vietnamese are the nucleus, the core of solidarity among the fraternal peoples who together have built and protected the Vietnamese fatherland (Lockhart, 1988: 23).

History writing by the state and its agents in Vietnam and Laos necessarily implies the taming of minority/non-national elements and their incorporation into the national body, where they are assigned a fixed place and a muted part. In other words, their destiny is to be led by the ethno-cultural majority, whether they be Kinh (in Vietnam) or the ethnic/lowland Lao (in Laos). The task seems simple enough for the state's historiographers. But this historical discourse contravenes the rhetoric of ethnic equality and solidarity, still an essential component of Marxist-Leninist history writing that cannot suffer accusations of majority chauvinism. The narratives of war that have shaped to a great extent twentieth-century Vietnamese and Lao historiographies have allowed official history writers to reverse the representation of ethnic minorities: from a liability ('barbarians' and 'primitives'), they became an asset when transformed into independent fighters.

Rebellions in the highlands of French Laos have thus been constantly reinterpreted by Lao nationalist historiographers as the pioneering fighting movements for the independence of the country. However, in reality the objectives of these armed revolts were variable: some of the rebellions were millenarian movements; others, more prosaically, were attempts to resist the imposition of French — and to a lesser extent, lowland Lao — administrative and political authority. For Geoffrey C. Gunn, the "shared Montagnard ethnic identity or sense of separateness from outsiders" may explain the insurrections, although he prefers to stress material causes such as colonial tax, *corvée* requirements and the abuses of the *lam kha* (middlemen) (Gunn, 1985: 59). According to François Moppert, though, the main factor behind the revolts is to be found in the form of the traditional dichotomy between "valley peoples" and "hill peoples", the latter having preserved to a certain extent their political autonomy, thanks to the topography of the region, hence retaining a strong sentiment of independence, which was ferociously defended on the ground, through armed resistance if necessary. The French administration neglected this fundamental attribute of the highland peoples and consequently had to face the consequences of their policy (Moppert, 1978: 227).

The material causes of these revolts led by highland peoples against the colonial administration have not been revised in state-sponsored history manuals and school textbooks since these movements serve well the need of the state to fill in the blanks with factual heroic events. Their 'patriotic resistance' against 'foreign domination' is accentuated while their true motivations, as well as the ethnic origins of their leadership, are played down. In other words, local conflicts have been recast as proto-nationalist movements, such as in this article published by the state-monitored English-language newspaper, *Vientiane Times*, which emphatically claims: "[the armed struggles of the people of various ethnic groups] showed the spirit of steadfast and unyielding struggle of the valiant Laotian people who refused foreign domination. They ignited the revolutionary flames of patriotism of the multiethnic Lao people which have continued to burn inextinguishable" (*Vientiane Times*, 8–11 January 1999).

II. Rhetoric of Struggle: Voices from Below

I will focus my analysis on the case of Ban Paktai in Sekong Province in southeastern Laos. The village of Ban Paktai is also called Ban Ong Keo or Ban Vìlàsòn (Heroic Village), as it was the birthplace of Ong Keo, who was turned into a national hero in the official historiography. The sole authoritative informant, Boualiem, had moved to a neighbouring village, Ban Som, to marry. His father was one of Ong Keo's fighting companions. Boualiem was a 75-year old man when I interviewed him in 1999. He introduced himself as a member of the Ngè ethnic group.[10] He looked fit at that time and the tone of his voice was still assertive, although his face was heavily scarred and he had lost an eye. He spontaneously started telling us about his own life as a war veteran and especially of his experience of torture by the "enemy". He started his "revolutionary activities" in 1951 as the leader of a group of skirmishers. Three years later he "sacrificed" (*sàlàkhat*')[11] his family and joined the resistance. In 1957 he was captured by the enemy and was accused of plotting against the government. Despite his protestations to the contrary, he was beaten up. In his own words:

> They arrested me and threatened to kill me. They took me to an isolated place by car, but I refused to get out. I told them that if they wanted to kill me, they might as well do it in the car! Instead, they

> took me back and locked me up in a small hut with just one hole for seven days and seven nights. They used electric shocks, they hanged me upside down. I was so badly beaten up that I fainted and lost one of my eyes [...]. But I was determined to keep the secret and to die for the country (*tay pheua sat*). If I had given information, I would have lost the country (*sia pàthetsat ban meuang*). If I had to die, I would die alone and save the country (*pàthet sat nyàng*). But I was determined.

He was finally freed and carried on the struggle. He would be arrested three times during the war but he felt that his first arrest was by far the worst. Boualiem's narration bears a remarkable similarity to the model stories of 'revolutionary heroes' published in communist propaganda documents. Equally stressed in these stories were values such as integrity, courage, sense of self-sacrifice and patriotism, and they invariably involved too elements of physical and emotional violence. For example, Kaysone Phomvihane told the following 'heroic' story of Sithong, a 'revolutionary model', in his speech during the Saonum Lao Lao Hak Xat (Patriotic Lao Youth) Congress in 1968:

> Comrade Sithong joined the revolutionary path at an early age. While he was doing his work, the enemy arrested him. At the beginning, the latter tried to corrupt him, to offer him money [...]. But Sithong rejected these offers. Having failed in using soft methods, the enemy employed violence. They tortured him with electricity, burnt him [...]. But Sithong remained calm and didn't lose his courage. During his transfer, with other comrades, he escaped, joined the Revolution and pursued his revolutionary struggle (Kaysone, 1975).

On the other hand, the villagers of Ban Paktai also show some elements of a divergent interpretation of the 'revolutionary' life of the 'hero' Ong Keo, which does not follow exactly national or scholarly narrations. Instead, they interweave the thematic of struggle with local traditions. During his interview, Boualiem portrayed Ong Keo as having supernatural powers befitting of a true 'Holy Man':

> One evening, Pha Ong heard the Phi Bang Bot[12] who came down on his horse. But he couldn't see him. He could only hear him. Ong Keo was in the spirit house. He learnt the chants and the prayers from the Phi Bang Bot during three days and three nights. After the third night, Ong Keo saw the candles in the spirit house. He still couldn't see the Phi Bang Bot, only his horse. From then on, Ong Keo had

> the power. If he ordered the buffaloes to fight, they would; if he told people to fight against each other, they would. So everybody, without exception, in Muang Thateng believed that he was a *Pha Ong*, the most powerful, that he could defeat the French. And Ong Keo said that he wanted to defeat the French because they were oppressing the people.

The attribution of special powers to a charismatic leader is a common occurrence, especially in non-Buddhist traditions, as Murdoch explained in his essay on the 'Holy Man's' revolt:

> The panels found in the Saravane area portraying Ong Keo as a *Thevada* suggest the invocation of the proto-Bodhisattva Maitreya[13] tradition. In addition there were repeated references to "Phu Mi Bun" (he who has merit) and "Thammikarat" (Ruler of Law or Ruler of Justice"). On the Lao side of the river [Mekong], and specifically among the non-Buddhist Kha, the more common reference was to invulnerability — as though invulnerability to bullets or personal harm was a kind of "proof" of the "legitimacy" of the Phu Mi Bun and his cause. The tradition of sorcery, spirit-mediums, and invulnerability is particularly strong in the Kha tradition, as has long been acknowledged by the Lao. [...] The background religious elements of the traditions of the Maitreya, the *Phu Mi Bun*, and the invulnerable sorcerer were to be incorporated by the leaders of the rebellion. By drawing on these elements, the rebellion's leaders became focal points for the dissatisfaction of the populace. Without this religiously sanctioned leadership, it would have been far more difficult to have organised the rebellion's followers (Murdoch, 1974: 64–5).

In effect, the tradition of sorcery and invulnerability has remained carved in oral memory, as demonstrated in Boualiem's account of Ong Keo's execution. According to him, the *Phu Mi Boun* was summoned to a meeting by the Commissaire of Saravane, Dauplay,[14] in Vat Tai, Thateng. But as soon as he and his soldiers (there were six of them) entered the room, Dauplay locked the door. The French officer then issued Ong Keo with a deadly challenge: if by dawn he were unable to escape, he would be killed. The next morning, Ong Keo was still entrapped and Dauplay therefore ordered his men to fire at him. But the bullets did not reach him. Dauplay then ordered his men to stab him to death, but their blades could not penetrate his flesh. Eventually, a *sin* (the Lao woman's sarong) was wrapped around a rifle's bayonet. This time the blade pierced his body and Ong Keo died — but there was no blood. Invulnerability was Ong Keo's proof of his legitimacy

(Murdoch, 1974: 64). Only an 'impure' element, the *pha sin*, could remove his power. The official historiography has ignored the magical powers of Ong Keo, but the villagers of Ban Paktai, on the contrary, incorporate them as the central element of their narration while also acknowledging Ong Keo's fight against the French colonialists. They are not challenging the national narration; rather, they are adding to it a mystical dimension that comes from local traditions.

War Genealogy

Reactions in Ban Paktai to the national narrative of Ong Keo have been ambivalent. While the villagers are grateful for the attention he is receiving, they express bitterness at what they feel to be a dispossession. Boualiem had already told his version to some Lao provincial officials and to some foreign scholars. Yet they never heard from these researchers again, nor had they been informed of the results of these investigations. The villagers expressed the wish to have a museum of Ong Keo in the village and insisted that it should be nowhere else.

One night, as inhibitions weakened further, Khamsing, the village's Communist Party representative, clearly drunk, suddenly told me in a surprisingly distinctive and firm tone that Boualiem deserved to be raised to the rank of *vìlàsòn heng sat* (national hero), like Sithon Kommandam (the son of Ong Kommandam) and Ong Keo:

> I agree with your research, but I think that other valourous soldiers, who are still alive, should also be decorated. Boualiem should receive the first-class medal that he never got; all his medals are second-class ones.[15] Boualiem deserves it; he was tortured and he fought for the nation.

In an interview a few weeks later, Khamsing further stressed the leading role of Uncle Boualiem in the shadow of Ong Keo:

> VP: Were there many revolutionaries in Ban Paktai?
>
> K: Yes, there were. To tell you the truth, from the start, it was Uncle Boualiem who trained [*sang*, literally 'build up'] two comrades. Then, it developed from 1954 to 1956. Then, from 1956 to 1960, there were 12 comrades. It was Uncle Boualiem who built them up. He's a true hero. The enemy's barbarity, it's not nice. The tortures he endured, it wasn't nice. He didn't tell you the other day. He was modest. But we, his children, know his actions. He's an authentic hero of the province of Sekong…

VP: All these three comrades are from the same ethnic group?

K: Yes, all three were Nge, from Ong Keo's lineage. They [all] are his children.

VP: They were from Ban Paktai?

K: Yes, all of them!

The villagers of Ban Paktai include Ong Keo in what I term a 'war genealogy'. The figure of the ethnic leader is being reinterpreted to endorse a narration that follows neither the 'national' history nor the story of ethnic rebellions. He is no longer the static and monolithic figure of the national past. Instead, Ong Keo appears to be recast as the ancestral figure of the 'revolutionary' struggle of Ban Paktai. His patriotic figure is reappropriated to legitimate his putative descendants' claim for recognition of their role during the Vietnam/American War, and his story is being retold to support their claims. Indeed, Khamsing's protest that night is a claim for homology between the "great" and the "small fates",[16] that is, Boualiem, like Ong Keo and Sithon Kommandam, is a local hero as much as a national hero.

But sadly for these villagers, their stories do not fit the history of their village, a *Ban Vilason*, as told by the authorities. The title was given on the grounds of their ancestor Ong Keo's so-called anti-colonial struggle against the French administration, and not because of their involvement in the Vietnam/American War. Despite an autobiographical narrative embedded in socialist historical discourse and their assertion of an unbroken revolutionary tradition between Ong Keo and their own fighting, the district and provincial officials disregard these villagers' vision of the past and their claims upon the present official historiography. It is not implausible that this may be for a trivial reason, simply a lack of interest in these 'peasants' and 'minority people'. However, I argue that the indifference is less a matter of prejudice than a consequence of the state practice of the "technology of amnesia" (Watson, 1994: 19, in reference to Eastern Europe and Soviet Union) regarding its war dead and veterans.

III. Heroes and Revolution: The Missing Link

Revolutionary regimes that come to power systematically deploy the techniques of awards and celebrations of exemplary members in an attempt to transform and appropriate the people. The French historian, Benoît de Tréglodé (2002), argues that the production of "New Heroes" in the Democratic Republic of Vietnam (DRV) in the 1950s and the 1960s contributed to the forging of a link between the centre and the periphery. In other words, the celebration of exemplary members played a role in the political unification of the 'national' territory by endowing the figure of the local hero with a 'national' aura. Similarly, Shaun Kingsley Malarney shows that the Vietnamese communists during the American/Vietnam War (1963–1975), in their effort to legitimise the war, developed a new set of definitions for noble and virtuous actions, the critical element of which was the "transcendence of self-interest and the selfless devotion to the collectivity" (Malarney, 2001: 49). Among the tribute policies for those who fought and died and for their families, the most important ceremonial innovation by the government was the creation of an official and secular memorial service for the war dead.

One hundred and forty-eight revolutionary fighters were rewarded with the title of "New Heroes" between 1950 and 1964 by the DRV (Tréglodé, 1999: 21). The hero under the DRV was a very elusive figure, surrounded by an aura of mystery that enhanced his reputation and prestige. He was, in a way, super-human and remained beyond the reach of the masses as an example to follow but probably never to attain. In consequence, it was very rare for villagers to have met or seen a hero during their lifetime; heros' apparitions were carefully orchestrated by the authorities (Tréglodé, 2002: 230).

To my knowledge, there was no such degree of production of heroic biographies, heroes or revolutionary martyrs by the Pathet Lao or the communist regime in Laos during the war or after 1975. Unlike in the DRV, the Lao communists did not attempt — at least not in such a systematic way — to replace class by heroism, through ritual and carefully crafted responses. Although patriotic emulation and revolutionary heroism were very much inscribed in the Lao communist propagandist agenda, there were no such institutionalised practices at the local level to glorify people's sacrifices and for the Lao communist leadership to display in a ceremonial gesture their gratitude and appreciation for those who died for the 'just cause'. When I asked former 'revolutionaries' (*khon pativat*, soldiers, nurses or 'agents on the ground') what the word *vilason* (hero) meant and who deserved to receive such title, I invariably received the same vague and standard answer: "A *vilason* is the fighter who is more courageous than the others, who would volunteer for dangerous actions when no one else would." I would then ask, "Do you know many *vilason* who are still alive?" "Most of them are dead," was the common reply. To be *vilason* does not therefore necessarily mean to sacrifice one's life; nonetheless, to die for the Revolution may be seen as logical since the *vilason* would always take a greater risk than anybody else.

It is somewhat revealing that a National Federation of War Veterans (Sahapan Nakhop Torsu Haeng Sat) was created in Vientiane in September 2003 under the auspices of the Ministry of Labour and Social Welfare. I was told that the late implementation was due to the lack of funding in the past, but also in order to comply with ASEAN standards (Laos joined the regional organisation in 1997). The Federation's representative recently came back from an ASEAN meeting in Vietnam of war veterans' associations from all member countries. Because the creation of the Federation in Laos was so recent, it was granted observer status along with Brunei's and Cambodia's. This association seems to have more welfare-oriented objectives (to provide material support for war veterans from the Army and the Police, widows and orphans) than a commemorative mission. But one of the Federation's senior members admitted that the organisation was still under-funded. "This federation is only just in name given its means," he said, "the title has been chosen, nonetheless, to give it an equal status with the other federations, the Lao Women's Union, the Youth Union and the Workers' Union."

The Federation, unsurprisingly, includes under the category of war veterans those who fought for the 'right side', that is, against the French and the 'Former Regime' (the Americans and the Royal Lao Government), as well as those who help at the present time to 'preserve peace and security' in the country. Yet, a former Pathet Lao colonel (of Khmu ethnic origins) recently observed in his interview that the 'Vientiane side' (that is, the Royal Lao Government and the American) soldiers should also be included in the welfare programmes as he declared in a stunning counter-discourse: "They were also unwilling victims of the war."[16] But this view is still fairly isolated in present-day Laos. Although the Federation welcomed people such as myself who took an interest in their mission and activities, when I asked to come back and interview some *vilason*, they backed down and refused my request. A few days later, while discussing with a Lao colleague about my meeting with the Federation, he strongly advised me not to use the term 'revolutionary activities' (*khieunvay pativat*) in my interviews because "people may think that you want to spy on their past and to find flaws".[17]

This piece of advice is hardly surprising for a regime that still imposes state autobiographical guidelines on individuals' life stories. But it is not the only reason for the persistent mentality of secrecy and paranoia. While the colonial period offers ground for emphasising such values as unity and solidarity, the multi-ethnic narrative undermines, if not omits, certain historical periods that may not appear politically acceptable as they reveal conflicts and divisions among those very people who were supposedly all united against a common enemy. Grant Evans notes that the episode of the so-called 'American war' (1954–75) has disappeared in the 1996 school textbooks, although it was included in the former 1979 edition (Evans, 1998: 164). As he observes, "Laos today is still in search of a convincing national narrative, because 'fratricide' there was not only in the distant past but very recent — and it is still not 'reassuring'. The civil war, which lasted from the late 1950s until 1975, must be borne in mind because it is the process by which the new regime came to power, but it also has to be forgotten as a period of disunity" (Evans, 1998: 188, emphasis in original).

A hardcover book entitled *Pavatsātkwaengsālavan* [*History of Saravane Province*] was published in Laos in 2000. The monograph belongs to the series of historical studies written by the local authorities themselves, the Saravane Provincial Publication Committee. The decentralisation of the production of knowledge has not resulted in independent works and divergent narratives of the country's colonial and post-colonial history, however. Only the geographical scale has been narrowed down to the provincial level, with no variation from the state historical discourse being apparent. It is therefore hardly a surprise that so far only those provinces known for their 'heroic' battles against the 'enemy' have published a version of their recent past. These publications serve mainly to enhance the province's profile nationwide.

History of Saravane offers a particularly interesting case. As a matter of fact, a truer title would have been the *History of Saravane* ***and Sekong*** since events related in the book affected the two neighbouring provinces. But Sekong (a former Saravane province under the old regime) was only created in 1981, as a result of which four districts (Thateng, Lamam, Kalum and Dakchung) were removed from Saravane's administration. The territory of present-day Sekong was a strategic site during the American War as the 'Ho Chi Minh trail' ran through the area. The trail was thus dubbed the 'road of the three nations' as it was possible to reach from Sekong both North and South Vietnam. But the battles differed greatly from one district to another due to the great topographical variations between them. As the road (National Road 16) in the plains going from Saravane to Attopeu (the southernmost province of Laos) and passing through the former Lamam District (now located in present-day Sekong Province) was under the close control of the rightist Royal Lao Army (RLA) posted on the Bolovens Plateau, the Viet Minh and the Pathet Lao used the trails located in the eastern districts of Dakchung and Kalum (Sekong Province), bordering Southern Vietnam. In consequence, these two mountainous and remote areas were heavily bombed from as early as the 1950s. How then does the monograph deal with the civil war in those south-eastern mountainous regions where the fighting was particularly confusing, with the 'enemy' and the 'patriots' sometimes controlling the same villages and people shifting sides between the 'imperialists' and the 'communists'? How does it incorporate the ethnic factor in areas where the majority of the population who suffered from the bombings and the battles were of ethnic minority origins? In a word, how much of the civil war's fragmented past is remembered and how much is forgotten in the *History of Saravane*?

The title of the chapter on the Vietnam/American War — "The struggle against the American imperialists and neo-colonialists from 1954 to 1975 in Saravane Province" — leaves no room for ambiguity. The United States is clearly identified as the "most cruel enemy" from the first page (Saravane Provincial Administration Office, 2000: 70), replacing the French in the role of the villain. The Royal Lao Government, 'the Vientiane side', on the other hand, merely acted on American orders; they were their 'lackeys'. In a way, the book seems to argue, the causes of the civil war were external: the United States masterminded and fuelled the country's political and ideological divisiveness because it "fundamentally aimed at transforming Laos into a new form of colony and a military base" (Saravane Provincial Administration Office 2000: 75). The Lao communists, conversely, were those who fought for the "reunification of the Lao people" (Saravane Provincial Administration Office, 2000: 70). They drew together "tens of thousands" of men, women and children, who formed the forces of the 'patriotic Lao multi-ethnic people' in the two northernmost provinces of Laos,

Huaphan and Phongsaly,[18] while supporting and training those left behind in the 'zones under the enemy's control' to fight for the 'new revolutionary era'. In short, the interpretation of this highly complex period is overly simplified and encapsulated in a Manichean frame.

There is no mention, on the other hand, of the ethnic origins and identity of the communist recruits in the chapter. The content of the state historiography, in general, tends to imply that the communist-led nationalist movement in Laos was based on a genuine popular awakening to anti-colonialist consciousness of the whole population, of which the ethnic minorities formed only one component. This claim leads implicitly to the weakening of the non-ethnic Lao role in the revolution. An article published in the *Vientiane Times* on the fiftieth anniversary of the creation of the Lao People's Army (LPA) claimed that the Pathet Lao soldiers gained the ethnic minorities' confidence, as they did with other sections of the population: "we won the people's support after lengthily explaining them [sic] our goals and showing them the justness of our cause" (*Vientiane Times*, 8–11 January 1999). Ethnic minorities were among the people who happened to be there to support the movement. They, like the rest of the "patriotic people", gave their "sons and daughters" to the revolution. They are no longer presented as key actors in the "revolutionary struggle" as they once were in the early historical representations. For example, 30 years ago, a Neo Lao Hak Sat publication stressed the active participation of ethnic peoples during the war. It was thus asserted: "The multinational character of Laos also reflects itself in the composition of the revolutionary army. In all units, from the biggest down to the smallest, there are men of various nationalities enjoying complete equality of political and other rights. Each nationality has one or several famous names in the army: Si Thoong is of the Lao Loum nationality, That Tou of the Lao Soung, and Thao Kong of the Lao Theung" (Neo Lao Hak Sat, 1966: 25).

Likewise, the crucial support of the Viet Minh, the Vietnamese communist movement, is very much minimized. For the sake of long-term Vietnamese-Lao friendship, it would not have been politically correct to completely erase the Vietnamese from the narrative, in the way *History of Saravane* does with ethnicity in its narration of the Vietnam/American War. On the other hand, the Vietnamese and particularly the Lao leaderships are equally wary of potential accusations of Vietnamese domination over their Lao "apprentices".[19] Historiographies in Laos, in consequence, usually apply sober terms when they describe

Vietnamese aid during the war. The Vietnamese communist armed forces and advisers are thus modestly referred to as "volunteers". Yet it has been proven that the Lao communist leadership and army depended to a great extent on their Vietnamese counterparts for both their military and political training and organisation, as well as for manpower and material supply and logistics.[20]

Christopher Goscha (2004) shows that in the aftermath of the Second World War, the Vietnamese communists began to form and consolidate revolutionary bases, structures and cadres in Laos and Cambodia, whereas before 1945 their efforts to build up and run revolutionary networks in Western Indochina relied almost entirely on Vietnamese locals in French Laos and Cambodia. In a section of his article, Goscha provides a fascinating account of how the Vietnamese spread revolutionary propaganda in the villages throughout the eastern part of Laos. These 'volunteers' learnt not only Lao but upland minority languages as well. They even shared the everyday life of the local population, learning their customs but also teaching them modern hygiene and agricultural techniques. Indeed, these 'communist missionaries' not only campaigned to convert the upland minority population to communism and the revolutionary cause, they also gave those 'backward people' 'civilizing' lessons. Motivated by strategic imperatives and driven by deeply rooted convictions, they tried, sometimes with success, to win the local population's support despite the hardship and relentless efforts this entailed (Goscha, 2004: 154–6).

For these reasons — the civil war, ethnicity and a foreign-sponsored revolution — the state's commemoration of the war dead and support for their survivors has been inconsistent, if not superficial, in Laos. The commemorations of the past in this country could perhaps be better defined as "willed amnesia" than "hyper-mnemosis" (Hue-Tam Ho Tai, 2001: 8), the consequences of which are inevitably to widen the gap between the official narrative and the history 'from the ground', to negate the linkages between the political leadership and the people.

Conclusion

It is a commonplace assertion in the study of nationalism that the construction of national identity necessarily relies on the creation and use of narratives — part history, part myth — which imbue nations and nationalist projects with coherence and rationale. But the connection between the collective discourse and the personal narrative is often missing. Works on nations and nationalism tend to neglect to address individual interpretation. For instance, Fox's comment on Anderson's imagined community is rather valid: "for Anderson, the imagined community of the nation is a mass fiction; it is never clear who, if anyone, imagines particular communities, or if there is any difference in the resulting fictional community depending on who imagines it and how they do so" (Fox, 1990: 7). In a word, "why and how do people invest themselves in nations and nationalism?" (Hearn, 2002: 745). The answer may lie in the ontological desire that guides one's life story, Jonathan Hearn suggests. An individual uses his/her narrative to make sense of his/her own life by attaching it to larger stories, 'public narratives', thus connecting his/her individual identity to the destiny of a collectivity. Hearn writes, "[w]hen a person identifies with a collective narrative, of the nation for instance, they do not simply locate themselves within that orienting story; they invest themselves in and identify with the central protagonist, the collectivity, the nation [...]. It is through an *isomorphism* between the individual and the collective as protagonist that people become attached to narratives" (Hearn, 2002: 749–50, emphasis my own).

The villagers of Ban Paktai seek to legitimise a link between themselves and the nation. Through the logic of an invented line of descent — being Ong Keo's 'revolutionary children' — they try to attach their 'small' fates to the 'great' history. Following the socialist rhetoric, which stresses the deeds of extraordinary individuals as models for others, the villagers of Ban Paktai feel that some of their fellow men and women also have the right to bear the title of 'national hero' for their actions during the Vietnam/American War. Their claims to being 'revolutionary heroes' reflect their identification with a collective identity. More precisely, their narratives reveal the imagining of a nation, born of specific historical, political and ideological contexts: during wartime when the 'enemy', that is, the rightist Royal Lao Government and the United States, served as the contrastive and defining figure of the Other, and when 'being an ethnic person' (*pen khòn sòn phaw*) had the positive connotation of being attached to the ideals of revolutionary fraternity. In other words, these members of minority groups show loyalty to a country where ethnicity and socialist ideals once blended. But in the present-day historiographical agenda of the Lao P.D.R, the 'national' history gives little weight to the history 'on the ground', especially when it is recounted by ethnic minority voices. The latter's narratives are now going 'against the flow':[21] their stories are being alienated from the encompassing narrative, running contrary to the state's historical discourse. As a result, the narrative of Boualiem's anti-colonial struggle is likely to remain on the margins of the 'national' history.

Notes

1. 'Subject' is used here to refer to an individual who is subjected to the actions of an authority.
2. The example usually quoted is the picture taken of the Communist Party's senior members making merit during major Buddhist festivals.
3. In their joint article on Hmong migrations and history (1997), Culas and Michaud describe the dramatic situation of the Hmong in Laos during the Vietnam/American War. According to their estimation, several thousand Hmong participated in the fighting against the Pathet Lao and the Viet Minh Communists, while perhaps as many other Hmong were enrolled in the People's Liberation Army, the Communist armed forces. Even for those who did not want to get involved in the conflict, in order to survive under extremely difficult material conditions, they had to seek help from one side or the other, that is, the Royal Lao Government/Americans or the Pathet Lao/Viet Minh. If they did not, they would be suspected of sympathising with the enemy.
4. 'Kha' is a derogative term that was applied to highland (that is, non-ethnic Lao) peoples. It means 'slave', and hence denotes a class structure rather than a racial hierarchy.
5. It could also mean 'Uncle My' (in Vietnamese, 'Bac' means 'Uncle').
6. According to all three authors: Moppert (1978: 50), Gunn (1985: 43), Murdoch (1974: 55). The Alak ethnic group, like the Ngè, belongs to the Austro-Asiatic ethno-linguistic category.
7. Murdoch quotes from Burchett's book (1957: 242). The latter interviewed the son of Ong Kommandam, Sithon, who gave him this version of Ong Keo's death. Moppert did not indicate his sources, although they are most likely to be the same as Murdoch's.
8. Gunn, in turn, quotes from a report by Dauplay: AOM Aix F6., "Mort de Bac My et capture de ses lieutenants", Dauplay to the Resident Superior of Saravane, 19 December 1910. However, considering the fact that Dauplay was the main investigator into Ong Keo's death, one may question whether his testimony is entirely trustworthy.
9. For an analysis of the origins of the Lao people as narrated in the Lao-language historiography, see Pholsena (2004).
10. The Nge ethnic group belongs to the Austro-Asiatic ethno-linguistic category.

11. Although the expression *sàlàkhat* does not exist in Lao, Boualiem may have combined the words *sàlà* (to sacrifice) and *khat* (to be torn), to stress the magnitude of his sacrifice.
12. A malevolent spirit.
13. In Buddhism, Maitreya (Sri Ariya Maitreya) is the future Buddha who, many of the faithful believe, will come 5,000 years after the death of Gotama Buddha (Keyes, 1995: 90).
14. In the interview, Boualiem pronounced Dauplay's name as "Complay". I surmise that it is a deformation of Dauplay.
15. A villager whom I could not identify at that time mentioned a badly conducted investigation into Boualiem's deeds at the time the medals were awarded.
16. I have borrowed this expression from de Tréglodé (2002).
17. Interview in December 2003, Vientiane.
18. Occupied and administered by the Lao communists and the Viet Minh since 1953.
19. The term is borrowed from the title of a book by MacAlister Brown and Joseph J. Zasloff, *Apprentice Revolutionaries: The Communist Movement in Laos, 1930–1985* (Stanford University, Stanford, California: Hoover Institution Press, 1986).
20. See, for instance, the pioneering studies of Paul F. Langer and Joseph J. Zasloff, *North Vietnam and the Pathet Lao: Partners in the Struggle for Laos*, Cambridge, MA: Harvard University Press, 1970; and MacAlister Brown and Joseph J. Zasloff, *Apprentice Revolutionaries: The Communist Movement in Laos, 1930-1985*, Stanford, CA: Hoover Institution Press, 1986.
21. I have borrowed the expression as used in the context discussed in Hearn's article (2002).

References

Bhabha, Homi K. (1995 [1990]). "DissemiNation: Time, narrative, and the margins of the modern nation", in Homi K. Bhabha (ed.), *Nation and Narration*. London and New York: Routledge, pp. 291–322.

Burchett, Wilfred G. (1957). *Mekong Upstream*. Hanoi: Red River Publishing House.

Connerton, Paul (1995 [1989]). *How Societies Remember*. Cambridge: Cambridge University Press.

Culas, Christian and Jean Michaud (1997). "A Contribution to the Study of Hmong (Miao) Migrations and History". *Bijdragen tot de Taal-, Land- en Volkenkunde*, 153-II: 211–43.

Evans, Grant (1998). *The Politics of Ritual and Remembrance. Laos Since 1975*. Chiang Mai: Silkworm Books.

______ (2004). "Different Paths: Lao Historiography in Historical Perspective", in Christopher Goscha and Søren Ivarsson (eds), *Contesting Visions of the Lao Past*. Copenhagen: NIAS Press, pp. 97–110.

Fox, Richard G. (1990). "Introduction", in Richard G. Fox (ed.), *Nationalist Ideologies and the Production of National Cultures*. Washington D.C.: American Anthropological Association, pp. 1–14.

Gillis, John R. (1994). *Commemorations: The Politics of National Identity*. Princeton and New Jersey: Princeton University Press.

Goscha, Christopher E. (2004). "Vietnam and the world outside. The case of Vietnamese communist advisers in Laos (1948–62)". *South East Asia Research*, 12, 2, June: 141–85.

Gunn, Geoffrey C. (1985). "A Scandal in Colonial Laos: The Death of Bac My and the Wounding of Kommadan Revisited". *Journal of the Siam Society*, vol. 75 (1, 2), January–July: 42–59.

______ (1990). *Rebellion in Laos: Peasant and Politics in a Colonial Backwater*. Boulder, San Francisco, Oxford: Westview Press.

Hall, Stuart (1994 [1992]). "The Question of Cultural Identity", in S. Hall, D. Held and T. McGrew (eds), *Modernity and its Futures*. Cambridge: Polity Press, pp. 273–325.

Hearn, Jonathan (2002). "Narrative, Agency, and Mood: On the Social Construction of National History in Scotland". *Comparative Studies in Society and History*, 44 (4): 745–69.

Ho Tai, Hue-Tam (2001). "Situating Memory", in Hue-Tam HoTai (ed.), *The Country of Memory. Remaking the Past in Late Socialist Vietnam*. Berkeley, Los Angeles, London: University of California Press, pp. 1–17.

Kaysone Phomvihane (1976). "Political Reports presented by Mr Kaysone Phomvihane at the National Congress of the People's Representative in Laos (1 December 1975, condensed)". *Journal of Contemporary Asia*, vol. 6 (1): 110–9.

Kertzer, D. (1988). *Ritual, Politics and Power*. New Haven and London: Yale University Press.

Keyes, Charles F. (1995 [1977]). *The Golden Peninsula: Culture and Adaptation in Mainland Southeast Asia*. Honolulu: School of Hawaiian, Asian and Pacific Studies, University of Hawai'i Press.

Lockhart, Bruce M. *Looking Down from a Tightrope: Ethnology in Vietnam*. Unpublished paper.

Malarney, Shaun Kingsley (2001). "'The Fatherland Remembers Your Sacrifice'. Commemorating War Dead in North Vietnam", in Hue-Tam Ho Tai (ed.), *The Country of Memory. Remaking the Past in Late Socialist Vietnam*. Berkeley, Los Angeles, London: University of California Press, pp. 46–76.

Ministry of Information and Culture (1996). *Pavatsăt lao* [*History of Laos*], vol. 1. Vientiane.

Moppert, François (1978). *Mouvement de résistance au pouvoir colonial français de la minorité protoindochinoise du plateau des Bolovens dans le sud Laos: 1901–1936*. Unpublished thesis, Université de Paris VII.

——— (1981). "La révolte des Bolovens (1901–1936)", in Pierre Brocheux (textes réunis par), *Histoire de l'Asie du Sud-Est: révoltes, réformes et révolution*. Presses universitaires de Lille, pp. 47–62.

Murdoch, John B. (1974). "The 1901–1902 'Holy Man's' rebellion". *Siam Society Journal*, vol. LXII: 47–66.

Pelley, Patricia (1995). "The History of Resistance and the Resistance to History in Post-Colonial Constructions of the Past", in K.W. Taylor and J.K. Whitmore (eds), *Essays into Vietnamese Pasts*. Ithaca, New York: Cornell University Press, pp. 232–45.

——— (1998). "'Barbarians' and 'Younger Brothers': The Remaking of Race in Postcolonial Vietnam". *Journal of Southeast Asian Studies*, 29 (2): 374–91.

Pholsena Vatthana (2004). "The Changing Historiographies of Laos: Focus on the Early Period". *Journal of Southeast Asian Studies*, vol. 35, no. 2, June: 235–59.

Renan, E. (1997 [1882]). *Qu'est-ce qu'une nation?*. Paris: Éditions Mille et une nuits. English translation, "What is a nation?". in A. Zimmern (ed.) (1939), *Modern Political Doctrines*, London: Oxford University Press, pp. 186–205; as well as in H.K. Bhabha (ed.) (1995 [1990]), *Nation and Narration*, London and New York: Routledge, pp. 8–22.

Saravane Provincial Administration Office (2000). *Pavatsātkwaengsālavan* [History of Saravane Province]. Vientiane: State Printing House.

Tonkin, Elizabeth (1992). *Narrating our Pasts. The Construction of Oral History*. Cambridge and New York: Cambridge University Press.

Tréglodé, Benoît de (1999). *"Héros nouveau" et "Combattant d'émulation" en République démocratique du Viêt Nam, 1948–1964*. Published thesis, École des Hautes Études en Sciences Sociales, Doctorat d'histoire et de civilisation, Paris.

——— (2001). *Reflet d'une nation: la figure de Hô Chi Minh dans les biographies du "héros nouveau"*. Symposium paper, Institut d'études politiques de Paris, Groupe d'études sur le Viêt-Nam contemporain, "Le Viêt Nam depuis 1945: Etats, Marges et Constructions du Passé", 11–12 January 2001.

——— (2002). *Héros et Révolution au Viêt Nam, 1948–1964*. Paris: l'Harmattan.

Watson, Rubie S. (1994). "Memory, History, and Opposition under State Socialism. An Introduction", in Rubie S. Watson (ed.), *Memory, History, and Opposition under State Socialism*. Santa Fe, Mexico: School of American Research Press, pp. 1–20.

CHAPTER 4

Truth and Memory: Narrating Viet Nam

Sharon Seah Li-Lian

Memories as Text: The Language of Remembering

The relationship between truth, memory and history is a complex one, with more grey than black-and-white areas. One cannot speak of history without acknowledging that memories — be they officially documented and thus supposedly objective, or openly subjective individual memoirs — form part or parts of history. One also cannot speak of memories, whether oral or written, without venturing into the shadowy area called truth or veracity. Truth claims form reality as we know and understand it to be. To question truth is to challenge reality. Where is reality? It lies within the text, written or oral. Once uttered, the text circulates within the realm of discourse, waiting to be contested.

Text determines our access to the past and directs our understanding of the past as given or as reconstructed. Taking the deconstructionist view of history, the written historical narrative is a re-presentation of historical givens, mediated by language, the medium with which we relate to the past. Language mediation functions like an opaque screen between us and 'reality', constituting what we know as 'truth'. No text can ever maintain its purity, nor clearly represent the reality that we want to arrive at, because language is itself continually being mediated. History embodies the relationship between texts, the past as given, and our present, but the relationship is largely determined by language-use.

The ultimate, definitive truth is beyond us since the world as we know it is soaked in language. Thus unless the world is stripped of the language that it is familiar with, unless a pristine, pure language could be used (Freeman, 1993: 11), there is nothing for us to 'get at', only discourses to deconstruct. The desired end, that is, to arrive at 'reality', is not an impossibility; it is a non-possibility since ultimately language's reference is unto itself (ibid.). In this case, because 'reality' is a non-possibility, the constructions of historical veracity need to be deconstructed to understand the workings of language behind the 'truth'.

Our knowledge of the past is rendered problematic because of language mediation in the text, either as an historian's work, or as archival, documentary evidences such as diaries, photographs, paintings, works of art, official documents, monuments, films and other multi-media devices. An object, whether physical or abstract, falls under the category of text once it fulfils two criteria. The first of these is authorial presence — the fact that the object is the creation of another; the second, the idea that the abstraction, once made public through either the act of utterance or of writing, is henceforth subject to the forces of circulation and production. Since language plays a part in mediating 'reality', the process of 'knowing' is henceforth mediated and the results are therefore a product of mediated reality. Following historian Roger Chartier, all texts should best be seen as the fruit of a constructed production; they do not represent objective access to the reality of the past but are, rather, a re-presentation of the past (Chartier, 1988: 42). The past as given is therefore closed to us, by default because history is packaged as *history-as-known*.

Narration as Reconstruction or Deconstruction

Reconstructionist historians argue that there is discoverable 'truth' within history; they hold to the idea that *the* truth once existed, and that because events and actions correspond to evidences, the truth is therefore discoverable (Munslow, 1997: 39–40). Because truth awaits discovery, reconstructionists are of the opinion that narrative is non-scientific, being of a teleological nature. Using narratives, history becomes a reconstruction of the past that can objectively reveal what happened. The narrative tool is viewed as unproblematic even though it functions to translate meaning.

Yet it is simplistic to suppose that the translation of the past into history by means of narrative can be taken to be an excavation of the truth. This approach does not take into consideration the fact that language has an important function in narrative, that "there is no access to knowledge except through the murky and dangerous waters of language" (Munslow, 1997: 58). The greatest critic of the idea of recoverable truth is Foucault, who has been seen by mainstream historians as anti-historical. Foucault argues that written history is an act of creation via the employment of data, and that this act is the ideological product of the age. In his essay, "The Discourse of History" (1996), Barthes likewise challenges history's dependence on the correspondence between evidence, the designation of historical facts and the reality of objective history as created by the historian. Barthes sees written history as only another narrative; he is critical of the historian's habit of distancing the self so as to create a sense of objectivity and realism. To Barthes, this creates an illusion by which "history seems to be telling itself on its own" (1996: 7). Allowing historical events to speak on their own without any signs of the utterer, gives rise to what Barthes terms the "referential illusion". Narration functions as the "privileged signifier of the real"; once we take a critical approach to the role of narrative, we see that history is at best performative and is inevitably ideological.

Language is the foundation stone of narration, and it is never innocent; it is ideological, an invention of power. Production of meaning depends on language-use; meaning-production corresponds to reality-production. Reality-production translates into the will to power. Power and ideology are two concepts so closely linked that it is difficult to tell them apart, for the ideology rests on power for its maintenance while power relies on ideology to strengthen its grip. Ideology can be loosely defined as a mode of thinking relating to the hierarchy and distribution of power. Language carries with it an ideological function pertaining to reality and power distribution. The archaeology of 'truth' is about searching for the will to gain power. The currency of the narrative is power (Foucault, 1972). Foucault views narrative as a discursive formation that exists in the present, making a complex reference to the past. In constructionist/reconstructionist approaches, narration directly translates into 'truth' and 'reality'. This is rendered problematic by deconstructionists who question language-use in narration. Narration's claim to be representative of reality is suspect because it is an imagined story form. Narration is someone's reconstruction of his/her own experienced or imagined past, but it is always already problematic because of the language-ideology-power relationship. In the following pages, I show how the state plays a dominant role in constructing a master narrative that suppresses alternative narratives.

Figure 1. Statue at Kham Thien Street, Hanoi.

Marking 'the Other' from Without

War monuments and statues are erected to embody local communal identity. After its numerous wars, Viet Nam has become almost a memorial ground in itself. Cemetery monuments,[1] statues, civilian and military museums, and temple pagodas add to the memory-triggering kaleidoscope of Viet Nam's history.

In Hanoi's Kham Thien Street, a statue of a woman carrying a lifeless child was erected to commemorate the residents who perished in the 1972 bombing by the United States (see Figure 1). The present compound stands in the place of houses numbered 47, 49 and 51, which were flattened by US bombs in 1972, wiping out the families living there. When asked about the choice of this statue, one war veteran's answer was that this household deserved commemoration because it brought out the senselessness in the American bombing. Another reason was that this compound was the worst hit in the entire street. In 1995, the place was marked as a historic site by the Vietnamese government.[2]

The woman and child who inspired this sculpture were from a Chinese family by the name of Lai; her name is Nguyen Chi Sam and the child was her 15-day-old baby. One leg propped on a piece of bomb shrapnel, the woman stares ahead of her with intense hatred and anger. The child she carries in her arms reminds us of the senselessness of war, which spares no-one, not even the innocent.

The statue of the woman and baby is instantly recognizable in Vietnamese iconography. As observed by Vietnamese writer Huu Ngoc (1998: 49), there are many war monuments featuring the same mother-and-child figure. This figure expresses the pain of women waiting for their men at home, reminding us that war hurts the women and children most. It forms an essential part of the narration of the nation's history, appearing in myths, statues, monuments and museums.

From ancient myths to modern-day heroes, from the struggles of old to the most recent wars, the woman in Viet Nam has her place in history. Examples include Lady Au Co,[3] Lady Trieu,[4] and in the eighteenth century, Bui Thi Xuan, the brilliant general of the Tay Son resurrection. There is also the legend of the Trung sisters who fought the Chinese aggressors. During the American war,[5] legendary figures include Me Suot (Mother Suot), who rowed many troops across the river, and also the ten legendary Dong Loc girls who sacrificed their lives to keep the Ho Chi Minh Trail open.[6]

The women's anger at that time was very strong. One resident informed me that, "The women at that time wanted to take up arms against the aggressors." In 1975 when Henry Kissinger visited Kham Thien Street to verify if it was a military target, emotions ran high. As another resident recalled: "I was there myself. The people were very angry with the Americans. If he had said anything then, the people would have killed him." Indeed, in 1977, the newspaper *Viet Nam* (225) published a report on Kham Thien Street, in which the Party Secretary of the Kham Thien branch was quoted as saying: "Scarred by their irreparable loss, Kham Thien people have not lost a deep hatred for the enemy..."

Behind the statue is a pillar engraved with the date "26.12.1972" and the phrase "*Khac Sau Cam Thu Giac My*". The words "*Khac Sau*" mean 'to engrave', "*Cam Thu*" mean 'to feel a vindictive hatred for', and "*Giac My*" refer to the American enemy, exhorting the people not to forget their hatred towards the Americans. Before the statue is a Chinese porcelain urn containing prayer joss sticks and offerings when people come to pay their respects to the dead. Clearly, in this instance, the Americans are identified as 'the Other'.

Museums: Contested Spaces

In the museum, 'the Other' is picked up in the narrative discourse generated by selectively chosen displays. Museums are deliberate orchestrations intended to preserve as well as provoke collective memories. A museum holds the right to the authorship of history, and is recognized as presenting the most accurate version possible of history. The War Remnants Museum in Ho Chi Minh City was formerly named the Museum of American War Crimes, constructed to put America on trial through its choice of exhibits. It was later renamed so as not to cause problems for tourism, particularly the need to attract American dollars.

Walking into the museum, one sees an array of bombs, weapons, aircraft, anti-aircraft machinery and tanks. An explanatory note accompanies each display, informing the visitor, if it is an American bomb, how many lives it took and how many tonnes were dropped, and if it is a Vietnamese weapon, how many enemies were destroyed. There are several sections in the museum devoted to various themes. Setting the context is an exhibit of the Declaration of Independence of the Democratic Republic of Viet Nam, 2 September 1945, which asserts in the words of President Ho Chi Minh:

> Viet Nam has the right to enjoy its freedom and independence, and it has indeed become a free and independent country.

The rhetoric of freedom and independence in the Declaration is inspired by the American Declaration of Independence of 1776. Another excerpt, "[W]e hold these truths to be self-evident...", reminds visitors that the Vietnamese people are deserving of the rights that Americans themselves enjoy.

Curiously, in this section, McNamara's book *In Retrospect: The Tragedy and Lessons of Viet Nam* and its translated version are also on display. A quote from McNamara's book, "Yet we were wrong, terribly wrong. We owe it to future generations to explain why", is the first thing visitors see on the museum brochure, which ends with a photograph of McNamara taken from the jacket of his book. Clearly, this is an obvious suggestion of American atrocities committed in Viet Nam.

The next section is devoted to the My Lai Massacre and the effects of Agent Orange during the war. Against a backdrop streaked with bloodlines and footprints — presumably of American GI boots — are photographs of the massacres, as well as victims' belongings such as a food tray, a bamboo pole, a pair of slippers, clothes and other daily necessities. The most startling exhibit is a human-size sculpture made of bomb fragments entitled 'Mother', the shell of a human skeleton ravaged by the effects of war, blackened and stripped of her dignity and her humanity (see Figure 2). Here again, we see the icon of Mother Viet Nam representing the sufferings of her people.

One of the most haunting and provocative exhibits are fetuses contaminated and deformed by Agent Orange kept in bottles and displayed in a very clinical manner (see Figure 3). This is a display difficult to ignore. The day I visited, one American lady was in near tears when she saw it, whilst a young Vietnamese boy stared in fascination as his father pulled him away. It is a very stark and unambiguous reminder of the American atrocities visited upon the Vietnamese people.

It is the choices made in the selection of potential exhibits and the manner of display that needs further examination. Not only does war kill the living, but the unborn are also affected — the future generation of Viet Nam has been destroyed, wiped out. The bottles of Agent Orange-deformed fetuses are not there for aesthetic purposes; these are objects inscribed with a heavy historical and moral subtext. They have been translated into historical objects, authenticated by the museum's authority, taken out of everyday life, detached, encased and put on display. The choice of the aborted deformed fetuses as an exhibit is calculated to shock and bring the reality of the effects of war closer to the heart.

In the War Remnants Museum, the *already-said* is in a real sense the *never-said*, in the Foucauldian sense. Putting the American nation on trial for its war crimes therefore places the Vietnamese people and nation in the judge's seat, granting them the right to decide on the

Figure 2. Sculpture entitled 'Mother', War Remnants Museum, Ho Chi Minh City.

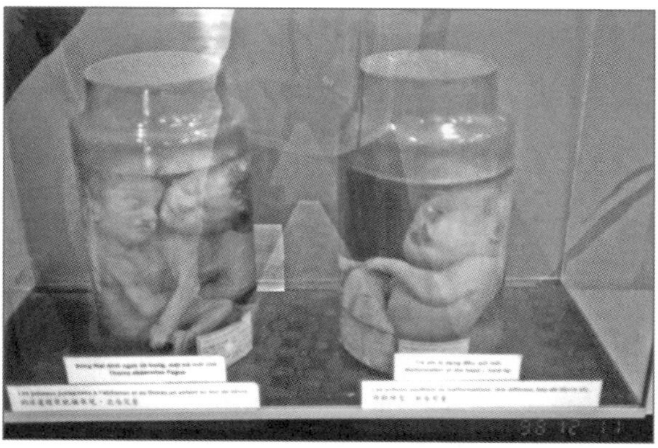

Figure 3. Exhibit of fetuses affected by Agent Orange, War Remnants Museum.

verdict. The message that the guilt and shame ought to be borne by the perpetrators hides the self-righteousness of the state, implying at one level that the Communist government would not commit such atrocities against its own people, and at another level, that the war was one waged against a foreign enemy. It was not a civil war in which one brother fought another. The real enemies are here the Americans, the imperialists, not the Vietnamese themselves.

'The Other' Within

'The Other' within is identified as those who do not agree with the government. They are rendered visible by certain displays and exhibits in the museum. The re-creation in the War Remnants Museum of the jails on Con Dao island, notoriously known as the Tiger Cages, complete with wax figurines, a guillotine, cramped cells and vivid descriptions of how prisoners were tortured, marks the southern regime out as enemies of the revolutionaries who were caught and tormented. The Diem regime was known for its cruelty and oppression against revolutionaries working for the northern government. An entire section of the War Remnants Museum is devoted to what the state terms 'hostile forces', both inside and outside Viet Nam. The counter-revolutionaries were those who set themselves up against the Communist government. Many of these were *Viet Kieu*, or overseas Vietnamese, who were ideologically opposed to Communism.

From 1975, Vietnamese who opposed the Communist Party went into exile. Strong anti-Communist elements living outside the country sought to organize counter-revolutionary activities to undermine the Communist government. Others who remained were sent to reeducation camps, had their jobs taken away and suffered other kinds of mistreatment. The *Viet Kieu* community is strong and has grown since 1975.[7] Works by writers, poets, novelists and other intellectuals living outside Viet Nam are termed 'literature in exile', a phrase coined by poet Do Quy Toan. He wished to distinguish between those who were still creating literature under the "dictatorial regime", whom he viewed as living "in exile in their own fatherland" (Nguyen Hung Quoc, 1994: 144), and the *Viet Kieu* community, whose work he saw as authentic and orthodox. Literature in exile contains the three elements of politics, opposition and freedom (ibid.: 148). A clear line is drawn between the *Viet Kieu* and the Communist government; within Viet Nam the *Viet Kieu* are seen as 'the Other' because of their opposing position.

Figure 4. Tiger Cages, War Remnants Museum.

Figure 5. A section devoted to counter-revolutionary activities, War Remnants Museum.

'The Other' from within, whether living in Viet Nam or abroad, has been characterized as a marginalized and demonized misfit in the national narrative. It has been taken out of the national narrative and rendered obscure. The memory of the southern Army of the Republic of Viet Nam (ARVN) soldiers has been erased, deemed undeserving of commemoration and silenced. Collaborators with the American imperialists are demonized as cruel despots, jailers who tortured the brave revolutionaries in the Tiger Cages. The supporters of Diem and other despots after him are portrayed as traitors to the Vietnamese people. The problem of 'the Other' living outside Viet Nam is trickier because of two factors — the amount of remittances sent home and investments trickling in.[8] The government has taken a more reconciliatory stance towards them in recent years, making it more attractive for them to set up businesses. However, those who are still living in the country are easily silenced by the master narrative.

Complexities in Memory

After 1975, Viet Nam's economy underwent nationalization and collectivization programmes. From 1976–1980, industrial production increased a mere 0.1–0.6 per cent (Tran Van Hoa, 1997: 8). Economists cited several factors, one of which was the prolonged war that resulted in severe shortage of manpower skills, capital and infrastructure. The other was a serious shortcoming in management and leadership; among other problems were bureaucratic inertia and administrative inefficiency. The government introduced a series of Five-Year Plans and microeconomic reforms, but structural problems remained unsolved.

In 1986, the Doi Moi or renovation period began. This period was commonly cited as the turning point for economic success in Viet Nam. With Doi Moi, the country opened its doors to foreign investment and the world economy, taking steps to integrate itself in the region. In 1994, Viet Nam officially applied for admission to ASEAN and became the association's seventh full member on 28 July 1995. With the economic crisis of the late 1990s, American investors were much needed in the country to open up the job market, since the rest of the region was at a standstill.[9] The US-Viet Nam bilateral trade pact of 2000 marked the beginning of a period of increasingly rapid development which has already done much to transform the Vietnamese economy and raise living standards.

Viet Nam's economic growth has brought many foreign investors into the country, among them Americans. American influence is felt too at the level of popular culture as more Hollywood movies, songs and books are being consumed.[10] Today, no one talks about the war anymore and the resentment towards America is hard to find. In the documentary film *Rising Above: Women of Viet Nam*, the American pilot who was famously shot down and taken prisoner by a woman soldier, Kim Ly, returns to visit her after more than 20 years. In the film, Kim Ly talks about the government's policy of opening up, and says that since there's no more hatred towards the United States, why should she not welcome him back?

The thorny questions of the past, present and future plague the Vietnamese today. How should they behave towards past aggressors? In the government's viewpoint, the Americans should be welcomed because they bring exciting ventures and tourist dollars. But this contrasts sharply with the processes of memorialization in the country — the building of monuments, the marking of historic sites and the preservation of war relics. Some of the projects are becoming part of tourist attractions, with companies offering DMZ tours, a visit to the Cu Chi Tunnels and other war sites.[11] But what about official history, as well as popular memories relating to the Vietnamese experience, which ought to be preserved? Reconciliation between history, memory and reality is tricky for many people across the spectrum.

In the interplay between personal memories and official discourse, people struggle to make sense of the realities around them, especially the indispensable American presence that provides employment and badly needed investment. As one veteran puts it:

> I have no hatred towards the Americans. There are many in Viet Nam now setting up good relations. There was a point in time when people had to take sides and fight. Human beings are human beings, so I have to take sides.

The Vietnamese must deal with ambiguous feelings towards their former enemy. Luu Doan Huynh (1993: 243) soul-searches thus:

> ... since we considered the American people to be our friends, how can we talk about defeating them? Therefore, one can only say Vietnam defeated a war of aggression waged against it by the US government, by US imperialism.

The best way out of this dilemma is to claim that they fought a war of resistance against US imperialism, *Khang chien chong My*, rather than against the Americans, similar to what one resident of Kham Thien Street said earlier about fighting American colonialism, not American people. Huynh sees no reason for Viet Nam to consider the United States as the enemy because there is no contradiction in terms of national interest between the two nations (1993: 245).

To mark the Americans as 'the Other' is far easier than to cast the South — fellow Vietnamese — in the same light. The memorialization of the war against the Americans is an *already-said*, whereas the memory of the losing side is a *never-said*. The national narrative simply states that the Vietnamese nation triumphed. The loss of the South is never mentioned partly because as it is alleged that all Vietnamese, be they northerners or southerners, stood for the ideology of the north, nothing was lost. In the memorialization of war, the nation is dismembered.

Excavating Veracity, Re-creating Meanings

The claim of 'historical truths' begs the question of whether there are also historical un-truths or historical lies. Who tells the truth? And to whom? Can we consider that truth is constructed for the benefit of some and to the detriment of others?

The matter of historical veracity is a tricky one, subject to the mediation of language in historical discourses. In the analysis of collective memory, provisionality is necessarily problematic, an engaging issue at every level (Wagner-Pacifici, 1996: 306). Historical-social meanings are subject to contextual and situational changes because of the focused backward gaze imposed upon historical events and personalities. History is therefore always retrospective — the present and the future cannot constitute history as yet. In conventional linear time, the past, present and future occur in a chronological manner. The past cannot be constructed unless the present has passed, and the future remains expected. The past is constructed and continually re-created in the paramount reality of the present. Following Mead's conception of time (1959: 111), while the present is viewed as real, the past and future can only be ideational and representational.

The complexes of meaning engraved in the narration of the life history of a nation often go unnoticed in everyday life. In themselves they carry further subtexts of meanings. In the memorialization of

Viet Nam People's Army (PAVN) soldiers, the sorrow and grief of families standing on the other side of the fence is passed over, taken out of public view and relegated to an obscure corner of history. The life history of the nation must not contain historical facts that oppose the dominant narrative, but it can still contain subtexts. In 1968 when the Viet Cong seized control of the imperial city of Hue during the Tet Offensive, house-to-house searches were conducted to arrest people who were even vaguely connected to the southern regime. A few years later, nearly 3,000 corpses were exhumed from nearby riverbeds and jungle clearings. These were victims who had been either shot, clubbed to death or buried alive. This historical fact is buried, along with other inglorious incidents of Communist history. Top generals in the Communist Party denied these killings, calling it a fabrication, even to the extent of claiming that the bodies were mostly Viet Cong cadres and sympathizers killed by the South Vietnamese army (Karnow, 1991: 543–4). Which is the 'historical truth', and who determines what this 'truth' is?

The translation of *events-as-such* into *history-as-known* needs to be deconstructed. The translation must be reversed in order to understand the encoding of meanings. Complexes of meanings that are perpetuated in official memories and inscribed in popular memories are not static; rather, they are subjected to manipulation and the shifting currents of the times. The meanings of events, histories and personages are carried within the collective memories of any one society. An obstacle-free recollection not fraught with contradictions or conflicts is dependent on the degree of veracity achieved by sites of authority in the writing of the narrative text. The narrative text then stakes a claim as the single representation of history in collective memory.

One mechanism through which societies remember the past is the museum. Museums construct an articulated space, designed to house artefacts of national importance and to preserve the relics of historical events and significant documents. As such, museums are used as spaces within which to stage 'historical truths' pertinent to nation-building and identity. They range from rudimentary huts set up by the local community to remember local history, to state buildings built specifically to house national history. The availability and accessibility of this public space makes it easy for the authorities to capitalize on and harness the museum for national education. The problem of historical selectivity makes its way into museums as curators choose to preserve

Figure 6. "Historic Truths" Section, War Remnants Museum.

some items and discard others, in an effort to create 'the truth'. One of the sections in the War Remnants Museum is labelled 'Historic Truths'. The title itself appears to eliminate alternative truths, making the claim to present 'the truth'.

Again, the implication is the notion that only one version of 'historical truths' is valid. The label 'Historic Truths' sets the record straight, implying that whatever one sees in the museum is the correct representation of *events-as-such*, attesting to the correspondence principle, that is, past events may be regarded as true as long as they correspond to one or more sets of truth conditions (Munslow, 1997: 38–41). 'Truth' is assumed to be unproblematic, a reality that possesses objectivity, a tangible abstraction. In the correspondence principle, *history-as-known* equates with *events-as-such*.

The nation is thus documented by collected objects (Prosler, 1996: 35): the territorial origin of the state, and its spheres of political influence, are represented collectively by displays of authentic objects testifying to real historical events happening in real time. The museum, as an articulated space, becomes a manipulable terrain that can be used by the state to narrate the official version of history, effectively moulding popular memory in its favour. The official story may contradict personal and popular memories of history, but faced with an onslaught of what is officially correct, citizens find themselves forgetting their real experiences and retaining instead official rhetoric. It is possible that the museum functions as a tool for the erasure of alternative histories and counter-memories. The reinvention of the state and of national life depends on the control, production and circulation of official rhetoric. National revival relies on the production of 'truth', one that necessarily eliminates obstacles in the path of the narration of a believable life history of the nation. What is 'true' is beneficial to the state and its advocates for 'truth'. Thus the museum is instrumental in the re-creation of truth and veracity, taking on the "form of a complete microcosmic representation of the sovereign nation state" (ibid.).

When confronted with an overwhelmingly dominant discourse on history and a strong collective memory based on the national narrative, there emerge within the 'We' of the nation, several modes of response. Taught to believe in the national narrative, the 'I' within the nation may convert to become a true believer in the truth propagated by powerholders. Completely drawn into the national narrative, the true believer accepts and does not question the dominant discourse. One may also be an innocent believer, out of ignorance of other truths that may be present but never discovered. Another response to the national narrative may be one of resignation, an unwilling acceptance; or a point may be reached at which the individual becomes, covertly or otherwise, an unbeliever in the truth.

Alternating between rejection and acceptance, apathy towards the dominant discourse may set in, so that there is neither acceptance nor rejection of what is offered as truth. There is no longer a need to talk about history, and showing no interest in the subject is apathy in itself, perhaps a form of resistance to the onslaught of historical 'truths'. As a Vietnamese friend said, "Probably people will talk about it if the government didn't put it on TV so much all the time."

Historical selectivity determines the final picture, like pieces of a puzzle fitted together to form a whole. Historical events that are woven together do not come by chance, but are carefully selected to construct *history-as-known*, such that what we know as history is no longer challenged or questioned. It becomes taken-for-granted, knowledge that is processed for the benefit of some. Alternative forms of knowledge are consistently rejected in the face of the dominant telling and retelling of the story. At times like these, rejection turns into apathy. As a Vietnamese friend tells me:

> At some point when I was little, I decided not to know anything about the war, so I avoided all the literature and films about the war. Also there wasn't anything to watch except propaganda. Everybody must echo what the leaders say.

In these circumstances, 'objectivity' appears suspect and unattainable. There is a concern with narration and truth-value, but is there one truth to be unveiled? Should we assume that history should contain only one truth, and that there is no room for alternatives? Perhaps another approach would be to conceive of the narrative process as simply a 'knowing' process, not a truth-search. By turning the truth-search into a 'knowing' process, one enables the representation of many otherwise neglected and unknown voices in history, making room for deeper comprehension of the complexities of 'historical truths'. That history is not black-and-white but a complex composite of many grey areas, is an idea that has yet to be accepted.

Notes

1. The cemetery monuments I am referring to are called *nghia trung liet si*, and are situated in nearly every province, district and commune. The term is translated as 'revolutionary martyrs' cemetery'. The term *liet si* has become politically charged, though it originally meant simply 'war dead'. The cemetery monuments contain the graves of soldiers who have fought in any of Viet Nam's wars, from the American war to the Cambodian border wars. There is a standard obelisk-shaped monument commemorating the merits of these soldiers within the cemetery grounds.
2. A tiny museum occupies the same compound as the statue. Displayed on its four walls are some pictures of the 1972 bombing, pictures of several captured pilots, Vietnamese who died in the bombing raids, as well as more recent pictures of the 1995 ceremony marking the place as a historic site. Tiny and modest though it may be, the museum seeks to explain the bombing with statistics of bombs dropped and casualties.
3. An immortal who married King Lac Long Quan. Together they gave birth to 100 eggs from which 100 beings were hatched, who subsequently became the ancestors of the Vietnamese.
4. Lady Trieu is a legendary figure who fought off the Chinese aggressors in the third century.

5. I did not use the term 'Viet Nam War' because my respondents referred to it as the 'American War', and it did not seem appropriate to be writing about master commemorative narratives using references from outside Viet Nam.
6. A documentary film was made about the ten Dong Loc girls. Dong Loc is where the girls spent their youth contributing to the war effort by repairing roads and defusing bombs. In October 1968, bombs buried ten young girls from the Fifty-Fifth Volunteer Corps as they filled craters to keep the road open (Turner, 1998: 20). During the war, many units of women volunteers either fought or worked on the trail. Each unit consisted of about ten girls, and countless women sacrificed their lives for the country. The ten Dong Loc girls have become a reference for the courage and bravery of all these women.
7. In 1975, millions fled Viet Nam to become refugees in other countries.
8. According to the country report, *The Economist Intelligence Unit,* 1st Quarter 1995, the overseas Vietnamese community was estimated at 2 million strong with a post-tax income of 15 billion. Remittances home reached US$600–700 million a year. By 2010, the overseas community was estimated at 3 million strong and was remitting US$8 billion per year (Source: *Viet Nam News,* "Viet Nam: Remittances to rise again this year", <http://www.remittancesgateway.org/index.php/press-clippings/industry-news/1000-Vietnam-remittances-to-rise-again-this-year> [accessed 17 October 2011]).
9. "Can Vietnam Forget?", *US News & World Report,* 10 Aug. 1998.
10. The movie *Titanic* was being shown at the time I was in Viet Nam, and conversations with young Vietnamese revealed much about their changing tastes.
11. In 1954, the Ben Hai River was used as a dividing line between the Republic of Vietnam (South) and the Democratic Republic of Vietnam (North). The DMZ (Demilitarized Zone) consisted of a 5-km land area to either side of the river. It was declared as a temporary measure before the promised 1956 national elections.

References

Barthes, R. (1978). *Mythologies.* New York: Hill and Wang.

——— (1996). "The Discourse of History", introduced and edited by Keith Jenkins. *The Postmodern History Reader.* London: Routledge, pp. 120–3.

Chartier, R. (1988). *Cultural History: Between Practices and Representations.* Cambridge: Cambridge University Press.

Foucault, M. (1972). *The Archaeology of Knowledge.* London: Tavistock Publication.

Freeman, M. (1993). *Rewriting the Self: History, Memory, Narrative.* USA: Routledge.

Huu Ngoc (1998). *Sketches for a Portrait of Vietnamese Culture*. Hanoi: The Gioi Publishers.

Karnow, S. (1991). *Vietnam — A History*. New York: Viking.

Luu Doan Huynh (1993). "The American War in Vietnamese Memory" in J.S. Werne and Luu Doan Huynh (eds), *The Vietnam War: Vietnamese and American Perspectives*. New York: M.E. Sharpe, pp. 243–7.

Mead, G.H. (1959). *The Philosophy of the Present*. La Salle: Open Court.

Munslow, A. (1997). *Deconstructing History*. London: Routledge.

Nguyen Hung Quoc (1994). "Vietnamese Literature in Exile (1975–1990)", in Nguyen Xuan Thu (ed.), *Vietnamese Studies in a Multicultural World*. Melbourne: Vietnamese Language & Culture Publications, pp. 144–57.

Prosler, M. (1996). "Museums and Globalization", in S. Macdonald and G. Fyfe (eds), *Theorizing Museums*. Cambridge, Mass: Blackwell Publishers, pp. 21–44.

Srour, Heiny (1995). *Rising Above: Women of Viet Nam*. Documentary film produced and directed by Heiny Srour. Netherlands: Television Trust for the Environment. 52 mins.

Tran Van Hoa (1997). "Vietnam's Recent Economic Performance and Its Impact on Trade & Investment Prospects", in Tran Van Hoa (ed.), *Economic Development and Prospects in the ASEAN*. United Kingdom: Macmillan Press, pp. 1–43.

Turner, K. (1998). *Even the Women Must Fight*. New York: John Wiley & Sons.

Viet Nam (1977). Vol. 225: 9.

Vietnam Economic News (1998). No. 52: 6–8.

Wagner-Pacifici, R. (1996). "Memories in the Making: The Shapes of Things that Went". *Qualitative Sociology* 19(3): 301–21.

Chapter 5

Textual Construction of a Nation: The Use of Merger and Separation

Dayang Istiaisyah bte Hussin

Introduction

In 1996, the Singapore government became alarmed by the growing number of younger Singaporeans who were ignorant of their own country's history. They might know who the 'founding father' of Singapore was, or the country's first President, but many were unsure about the causes of the 1950 Hock Lee bus riots and knew nothing about the State of Emergency that had prevailed in Singapore from 1948 to 1960. These were the startling results of a survey of 2,525 students conducted by the Ministry of Education. Here we can already see that history is the prerogative of the state, insofar as the state has the capacity to 'authorize' which events are selected as significant, and which version of the past is to prevail as legitimate or correct. The obvious reason for the concern over historical apathy among the younger generation is that history, as perceived by Singapore's political leaders, serves as a cultural-symbolic construction of the Singapore nation. History, or to be more precise, that version of it selected by the state, is perceived as the source of Singaporean identity. That is why the Deputy Prime Minister, Lee Hsien Loong, regarded the status quo as an indication of a "serious gap" in the people's education (*The Straits Times*, 22 July 1996).

Later in the same year, the history syllabus in secondary schools was modified. Prime Minister Goh Chok Tong unveiled the National Education Programme (NEP), which aimed to instill in young Singaporeans a shared sense of nationhood through recurrent themes in Singapore's history: constraints and vulnerabilities; crisis and survival.

These themes were neatly conceptualized into "The Singapore Story: Overcoming the Odds", a National Education Exhibition on the history of Singapore held at Suntec City in 1998.[1] The period highlighted was "merger and separation" (1963–65), and the events during this period were regarded as major symbolic texts in pioneering the ethos of national ideology.

The primary objective of this chapter is to show how the Singapore 'nation' is discursively constructed through the continued focus on 'key' events such as the racial riots which occurred during the 1963–65 period of merger between Singapore and the Federation of Malaya. The 1964 Sino-Malay racial riot is continually invoked to sanctify the policy of multiculturalism, one of the founding myths in the construction of the Singapore nation. My point of departure from other works lies in the methodology employed — using newspaper texts to examine how the construction process has been sustained. Empirical studies have yet to be developed to demonstrate the process of articulation of history in the political discourse of the construction of a nation, even though the relationship between history and nation-building is very obvious in the context of nation-states. In the case of newspapers, their familiarity as a source of information often means that they are taken for granted by their readers. 'Defamiliarizing' the familiar through textual analysis will reveal the ideological messages that contribute to the construction of the imaginary community called 'Singaporeans'.

"Imagined Community", Ideology and Historical Discourse: The Nation as an Imaginary Community

Anthony Smith (1996) defines a nation as "a named human population sharing an historic territory, common myths and memories, a mass, public culture, a single economy and common rights and duties for all members". He clearly elucidates the concept of nation as a social, cultural and territorial community with a shared history. The elements of commonality and shared entities represent the essentialist characteristics of a nation. Members of the population need not all experience the same events to acquire a form of collective memory, and hence a common identity. Commonality can be constructed and 'universalized' through the process of repetition. Repetitiveness engenders continuity with the past (Hobsbawm and Ranger, 1989: 1), which furnishes the community with a sentiment that can command allegiance and solidarity (Smith, 1964: 233). Repeated presentation of the past in narrative form produces the discursive formation of the nation, because the narrative space functions as the site for self-construction (Miller, 1994: 160) through the mediation of language. Narrative history is thus an ideological tool in the discourse of the construction of the nation.

The word 'nation' comes from the Latin word '*natio*', which means 'tribe, stock or breed', implying an apolitical human grouping based on kinship. However, the contemporary usage of the word connotes a political dimension. Whereas the "Roman nation" was conventionally referred to as "the race of Aeneas", today a "Singapore national" means "a citizen of the state (nation-state) of Singapore" (Chieh and Tong, 1997: 13). Anderson (1983) defines the nation as "an imagined political community" — a short and simple definition that I have adopted as the conceptual framework in this chapter. That the community is "imaginary" does not mean that it is a fabrication, falsity or distortion of reality. Cornelius Castoriadis contends that "the imaginary is what renders possible any relations of object and image" (Thompson, 1984: 23). As applied to this chapter, the "object" refers to the people of Singapore, while the "image" implies the Singapore nation. According to Anderson (1983: 15), despite the members of the nation not knowing each other, they share the image of a communion in their minds. The "imaginary" refers to the way in which people are oriented towards living together harmoniously and are willing to identify themselves as Singaporeans.

The process of the imaginary entails three aspects: the nation is imagined as limited, sovereign and a community (Anderson, 1983). Prior to 1965, the people of what are today Malaysia and Singapore identified themselves as people of Malaya. Geographically, Malaysia and Singapore are merely separated by the Straits of Johor, and the people residing on either side did not regard themselves as nationally distinct. Hence, the concept of limitation is not primarily determined by physical geographical features but is ideologically constructed. The moment of construction of the Singapore nation is officially marked as 9 August 1965, although self-government had been attained in 1959. Since 1965, Malaysia has been regarded as a separate nation from Singapore, thus limiting the respective populations' identification through the newly demarcated boundaries.

The construction of a modern nation necessitates imaginary sovereignty. The modern nation-state neither has an absolute autonomy nor is a self-contained entity, but is integrated into the extensive regional and global capitalist economy. Consequently, it has to assert sovereign power by enacting laws to regulate immigration and control the entry of 'foreigners' by systematizing requirements for passports, identity cards and visas, all of which are significations of the imagined sovereignty of the nation-state (Levine, 1996).

Ernest Gellner's conception of nation enhances Anderson's theory of "imagined political community". Two criteria set by Gellner (1983: 7) for the emergence of a nation are: that everyone shares the same culture, where "culture" means a system of ideas, signs, associations, ways of behaving and communicating; and that individuals recognize each other as belonging to the same nation. However, primordial ties are not the determining factor, since the process of recognition can be politically imposed and naturalized through socialization and education. In the Singapore case, nation-building is an obvious political construction. With the attainment of independence, recognition shifted from a Malayan identity to a Singaporean identity.

One should note that the concepts of 'nation' and 'state' are interrelated but conceptually non-interchangeable. The state is basically an agency within society that possesses the monopoly of legitimate violence (Gellner, 1983: 3); it refers to a central political authority and not to a community. Thus the process of imagining a community takes place within the framework of the nation, not the state. State-formation can also precede nation-formation. For example, Singapore had been administered differently from Malaya ever since the colonial era, but the concept of a Singapore nation did not exist until its political construction after 1965. Singapore came into being as a nation-less state — a body without an identity.

Discourse and Ideology

Assimilating people of different historical, cultural and religious backgrounds and inducing them to pledge allegiance to a nation is a demanding and arduous task. The process of orientation towards an imagined identity can be achieved through the constitution of a world of signification, that is, symbols and myths through which a society represents its present and past (Thompson, 1984: 24), which are then universalized and socialized through the process of education. But the choice and creation of symbols and myths cannot be random; they are ideologically motivated. Excavating the meaning underlying a social imaginary that serves to sustain asymmetrical relations of domination thus calls for a study of ideology.

Ideas do not drift through the social world without any mediation. They circulate as utterances, expressions and words that are spoken or inscribed via language. Language, however, is not merely a matter of the linguistic structures used in communication but a social phenomenon. Being social, language is enmeshed in relations of power, in situations of conflict, in processes of social change and other activities in the social world (Thompson, 1984). Language is ideological when the dominance of the connotative over the denotative dimension of language reveals the process of sustaining an asymmetrical organization of power, either by establishing the legitimacy of a state, or by putting the legitimacy of other states in question. For example, the statement, 'The 1964 racial riots in Singapore caused the deaths of 22 people', is factual and non-ideological. However, when expressed as: 'The 1964 racial riots, which were instigated by UMNO (United Malays National Organization),[2] caused the deaths of 22 people', the statement displays an ideological intent to demonize UMNO and attribute the blame for what happened to them. This argument is supported by Thompson (1984: 2), who explains that we can observe the traces of ideology in language by focusing on how expressions serve as a means of action and interaction, and the ways in which meaning (signification) serves to sustain relations of domination. Thus, ideology is not only to be found in the discourses of ideologues but also in daily communication, since the principal focus of ideology is the language of everyday life itself.

The imaginary and ideology are not illusions but are constitutive of society, and are materialized through the operation of language. By means of language, discursive objects such as the nation, Singaporean identity and Singapore society merge into reality. Let us consider the Singapore nation as a discursive object. In *The Archaeology of Knowledge*, Michel Foucault (1973) lays down the rules for the existence of objects of discourse. Firstly, we need to map the surface of the object's emergence — when is the defining moment at which the nation emerges? Secondly, the authorities of delimitation must be described — who is the major authority in the society that defines the boundaries of a nation? Thirdly, grids of specification must be analyzed — what are the different types of classifications or categorizations used in defining the nation that will serve to contrast it with other nation-states? In application, the Singapore nation is defined as being 'born' in 1965 (although nation-building had started prior to that) with the PAP government as the ruling authority. In the *Proclamation of Singapore* (Fletcher, 1969), Lee Kuan Yew, the then Prime Minister of Singapore, declared that on

9 August 1965, "Singapore shall become an independent and sovereign state and nation separate from and independent from Malaysia and recognized as such by the Government of Malaysia." What are the grids of specification of a Singapore nation? Lee defines them as "the principles of liberty and justice and ever seeking the welfare and happiness of her people in a more just and equal society" (Fletcher, 1969: 98). Thus a Singapore nation is real when it is spoken of and defined in the above terms.

There is one more grid of specification that contributes to the construction of the Singapore nation. Singaporeans can be contrasted with others such as Malaysians or Indonesians. All three nations have different national anthems, symbols and myths that endow the community with a national identity (social imaginary) distinguishable from others (Thompson, 1984: 24). In short, the Singapore nation and Singapore identity are social constructs, and the process of imagining a nation is ideologically mediated through language.

Facing up to Capitalism and Globalization in the 1990s

The existence of a nation is dependent on a socially bounded and united group of people. As Gellner (1986: 7) stresses, it is mutual recognition that constitutes a shared membership, resulting in the production of a nation. However, the solidarity of the imagined community is threatened by the value of individualism, which emphasizes difference (Chua, 1996: 26). Capitalism, which forms the basis of Singapore's economy, unintentionally generates individualism. Differences corrode commonality and the spirit of self-sacrifice for the social good, and hence will upset the process of nation-building. The PAP government cannot afford to lose to individualism although it cannot give up its capitalist economy.

Another threat to the process of nation-building is globalization. Jan Aart Scholte (1997) conceptualizes globalization as "transcendentalization",[3] a trend that sees social relations becoming less tied to territorial frameworks (1997: 431). One of the manifestations of globalization occurs in the dimension of *consciousness*, such that people conceive of the world as "a single place, [and] affiliate themselves with communities (e.g. religious faith, race) that transcend borders" (1997: 432). There is much historical evidence in Singapore to confirm this argument, such as the affiliation of migrant Chinese here to China in the 1950s and 1960s, as well as the contribution of the Iranian Revolution in 1979 towards Islamic resurgence, and its effects on the Muslims in Singapore.

The government, aware of the absence of cultural unity among the originally immigrant population of Singapore, realizes the potential threat that globalization poses to nation-building.

Solidarity and unity, therefore, have to be established upon something that has psychological and emotional bearing on individual Singaporeans. The search for a common symbolic core in the post-independence period ranges from the expounding of 'Asian Values' in the mid-1970s, the short-lived Religious Knowledge programme in secondary schools from 1984–89, the promotion of 'Family Values' in 1994, and finally to the extensive historical discourse built into the National Education Programme in 1996. These moves represent a continuous attempt to align society, with its overarching policy of multiculturalism, with a collective orientation, and to institute social discipline as a bulwark against the invasion of individualism and globalization.

Narrative history is not just any account of the past, nor is it merely about the presentation of historical facts. Historical 'facts' do not exist naturally but are defined as such by historians and other writers (Carr, 1973: 11). Through the mediation of language, and the role of the author of the narrative history, a selected version of historical fact may prevail as legitimate. As such, narrative history is a potent ideological mechanism in the work of nation-building. Important questions such as 'Whose past is highlighted?', 'What kind of past is to be presented?', 'How is the past talked about?' and 'For what purpose?', all illustrate the intimate relationship between language, ideology and history.

I am proposing, therefore, a view of history as a textual ideology. Furthermore, command of the dominant narrative of the nation's history is the prerogative of the ruling elite. 'Credible and authorized' narrators of this history will therefore be members of the ruling elite, and their work will obviously serve to justify and legitimize the ruling hegemony. The merger and separation period is strategically appropriated in Singapore's story as a means of justifying the policy of multiracialism.

Textual Analysis of Newspapers: Newspapers as Data

Newspapers are a crucial source of data, both because they are a regulated medium of information and because they command an extensive readership. Then Prime Minister Goh Chok Tong explicitly stated that the media plays an important role in nation-building (*The Straits Times*,

7 September 1998). Thus if any of the local newspapers were found to be relaying messages judged as "threatening national security", their production would be stopped.[4] Despite being owned by a public listed company, Singapore Press Holdings operates under restrictive legislation so that its consistency with government policies is ensured. In turn, all newspapers in Singapore exercise restraint and avoid sensitive issues that may lead to racial, linguistic and religious conflict (Chew and Lee, 1991: 304), resulting in selectivity of information in the newspapers. Notwithstanding the restrictions, the newspaper industry has developed considerably, partly because of the great demand for information and the high literacy rate (84 per cent in 1980, a figure which has risen to 93 per cent of adults by 2000, and 95.9 per cent by 2010),[5] making newspapers one of the main sources of information for the Singaporean population.

Being produced daily, easily accessible and inexpensive, the newspaper is often viewed as a mundane printed document and hence taken for granted and not considered as ideological. Many readers will therefore regard the 'information' in the newspaper as technical data. With regard to history, newspaper texts will conventionally be read simply as a presentation of historical narratives, rather than as ideological texts with the potential to mobilize readers to a particular way of thinking, and eventually social behaviour.

Two local newspapers,[6] *The Straits Times* (TST) and *Berita Harian* (BH), are chosen as sources of data for this study. *The Straits Times* is the most widely circulated English newspaper, while *Berita Harian* is the only Malay newspaper available in Singapore.[7]

The two newspapers convey different ideological messages. Compare these headlines covering the 1964 racial riots on the same day.

TST 1: "UMNO instigation sparked race-riots"

BH 1 : "Role of Tun Razak behind riot"
"Syed Ja'afar — The 'hit man' of UMNO leaders who hated Singapore"
"Tunku, the Prince, who knows how to use power"

Clearly the emphases are different although the subject matter is the same. In TST 1, UMNO is mentioned merely as a Malay political party. In BH 1, however, the emphasis is on the various personalities of the Malaysian political leaders. A leader is a representative of the whole party. Hence, reviling the credibility of the leaders of the country (Tunku Abdul Rahman as Prime Minister of Malaysia, Tun Razak as

Deputy Prime Minister) is tantamount to tarnishing the good name of Malaysia as a sovereign nation while enhancing respect for Singapore.

Methodological Explanation

In the discourse analysis of newspaper texts, we are explicating the ways in which the meaning or ideas located in language sustain an asymmetrical relation between the reader and the author of the text. Alvin Gouldner's theory of ideology as rational project argues that ideology cannot be treated as a mere "thing-out-there" to be observed, but rather as *media*-ted by the news (Thompson, 1984: 83–90). Ideology is also expressed in a language (written) that is critical, rational and empirically plausible. The concept of discourse opens an avenue for the investigation of the relation between language and ideology.

Discourse analysis is concerned with naturally occurring expressions such as everyday communication in the form of written texts (for example, newspapers), and not with what is grammatically ideal. It is also interested in the relations between linguistic and non-linguistic activity — the ways in which language is used in specific social contexts, thereby serving as a medium of power and control that can influence social behaviour (Thompson, 1984: 98–9). Thompson adds that another common feature of discourse analysis is the preoccupation with linguistic units that exceed the limits of a single sentence. It is through this last feature that textual analysis, as proposed by Roland Barthes (Young, 1981), provides the technical operationalization for discourse analysis.

Textual analysis applies exclusively to written narrative and is not concerned with the structure of the work. It explores "avenues of meaning", rather than locating all the meaning in the text that allows for its interpretation. A "work", as defined by Barthes, denotes a finished object (Young, 1981: 31) that conveys the idea of "totality" and "unity", as compared to the conception of "text". "Text" itself is not a finished or closed product but is "plugged in" to other texts in an inter-textual relation (Young, 1981: 135). Hence one newspaper text (for example, an article or a report) must not be taken as a 'complete story' but as being interrelated with other newspaper texts. We are dealing with a plurality of texts. In addition, the newspaper text is articulated against a particular socio-historical background, and it is through such inter-textual relations that the imaginary community — the nation — is constructed and reproduced.

The technical procedures in textual analysis involve cutting the text into segments, each consisting of one, or at most three or four sentences. The process is dictated by convenience rather than theory (Young, 1981: 136). The second task that follows is to observe the meaning and its distribution within each segment (Barthes, 1981: 134). This is where the analysis of the relations between language and ideology takes place. The connotative meaning of the text is derived via the process of interpretation.

As proposed by Thompson (1984: 133) the object of interpretation, discourse — language realized in writing — is already an interpretation. Thus each newspaper text must be seen as an already interpreted text, and the analysis of discourse entails the interpretation of an interpretation. The interpretation may also involve synthetic construction of a possible meaning (Thompson, 1984). To do so, we adopt "split reference", a technique introduced by Ricoeur (Thompson, 1984: 137) as the interpretive method involving the suspension of ostensive denotation and the realization of the connotation that cannot be disclosed directly. This will reveal how the newspaper text explicitly refers to or talks about one thing, but implicitly refers to another (the possible meaning). The connotative referent serves to sustain the asymmetrical relations of power (Thompson, 1984: 138). Below is a brief illustration of how the split reference procedure works.

(Analysis)	**(Segments extracted from original text)**[8]

TST 2: "Don't Let External Woes Hit Race Ties"

At the denotation level, the minority Malayalee community is praised for its deep attachment to culture despite being a migrant stock (Segment 6). Deputy Prime Minister Lee did so not out of a great interest in the Malayalee culture, but because culture and race have always been very important components of the PAP government's rationalization of its multiracial policy. Thus in Segment 7 the DPM reiterates that Singapore must always maintain itself as a multi-racial society (connotative referent).

Segment 6
He [Brigadier-General (NS) Lee Hsien Loong] praised the Malayalee community as one which was exemplary of a migrant community with deep cultural roots as well as strong support for Singapore.

Segment 7
Noting that Singapore had worked at building social cohesion over the last 33 years, he said that the country had never tried to merge the various racial groups in one "melting pot".

"Singapore will never be a homogenous society. We have to accept this, and turn diversity to our advantage," he said.

The praises are not accidental. "Attachment" of the community to its cultural roots justifies the existence of multiracialism in Singapore. The Malayalee community is used as the 'sign' or the text to illustrate the success of the multiracial policy, and hence to justify the legitimacy of the ruling authority. This is the ideological message contained in the connotative referent.

The Past from the Perspective of the Present: History Shifts from being 'Useless' to 'Useful' Knowledge

In Singapore, the construction of a national history was a very low priority in the 1960s and 1970s. The leaders believed that they had to "examine the present, think of the future and forget the past" (Ong, cited in Lau, 1992: 50). The urgent issues of nation-building and national survival then were the expansion of industrialization for economic growth, and consolidating the population by providing for immediate needs such as housing and employment. Unfortunately, Singapore's post-1940s history had been 'tainted' with racial and religious conflict. Invoking such a historical past in a loosely integrated and economically weak society could create a bloody battleground for endless racial and communal conflicts. The past was seen as so problematic that the subject of history was simply omitted from the educational syllabus. One cabinet minister said:

> History has no immediate practical use. It does not tell us about the future. It does not help us compute our way through life. Thus in schools, history together with geography, is being pushed out of the curriculum to make room for more immediately attractive and *useful* studies (Ong, cited in Lau, 1992: 50; emphasis added).[9]

"Useful" knowledge then is defined as that generating direct vocational benefits which meet Singapore's economic and industrial needs, such as mathematics, science and the technical subjects.

The 1980s marked a pivotal shift toward a favourable treatment of history. Since then, history has been deliberately used as the cultural-symbolic content in the construction of a Singaporean identity. The Singapore government has adopted a pragmatic approach in much of its policy-making. Prior to the 1980s, the "imagined community of Singaporeans" was aligned on the ethos of hard work and a disciplined workforce, required to meet the economic needs of the developing country. But economic success is a double-edged sword — while citizens benefit from economic stability and the government gains legitimacy to demand greater participation from the individuals toward nation-building, it does not guarantee a long-term collective identification with the nation. The next challenge faced by the leadership was that of a state which had remained identity-less ever since independence and which consisted mainly of migrant stock. A common history, culture and religion can create a deep psychological and emotional attachment for the believers. However, culture and religion were the least favourable factors to deploy in the Singapore context, since the Sino-Malay riots of 1964 had confirmed to the leadership that both variables were too potently divisive, with the potential to undermine the overarching policy of multiracialism. A deliberate 'return' to history is now possible, however, due to the legitimate standing of the state over a socially disciplined community, in spite of the bloody nature of some historical events.

By the 1990s, public ignorance about national history was being articulated as a sign of the development of an identity-less and directionless Singaporean. Deputy Prime Minister Lee Hsien Loong expressed it thus:

> [The] lack of awareness and understanding of Singapore's history was a "serious gap" in the education of the people.... To know who we are, and where we are going, we must know where we have come from and why we are here (*The Straits Times*, 22 July 1996).

Not all historical 'facts', however, are of equal importance. The key events of Singapore's national history are officially presented as the merger and separation and the 1964 racial riots. Why would the 1964 riots be marked as 'historical landmarks' by the state? A landmark is a building or place used by an individual to judge his location, so as to know the direction he has to take. 'Historical landmarks' then denote signs by which citizens may orient themselves in order to understand the direction in which Singapore is heading. Textual investigation of these events, presented in the left column in the following section, unveils the ideological messages that mobilize the population of Singapore in a direction steered by the government.

Historical Landmark 1: The Racial Riots of 1964

The 21 July 1964 riots were not the first bloody riots in Singapore. Prior to this were the Maria Hertogh or Nadra riots[10] of 1950, which involved the Malays and the British. However, the Nadra riots are not given as wide a coverage or publicity as the 1964 riots. Hence, the significance of a historical event does not necessarily lie in the occurrence of an outbreak but, in this case, in the actors involved in the event. Unlike the Nadra riots, the 1964 riots involved the Malays and Chinese, who still represent respectively the minority and dominant groups in Singapore today.

BH 2: "Leaflet Instigating the Malays Distributed During Procession at Padang"

Readers are led to feel the atmosphere of heightened racial sentiments via the usage of quotations (Segments 5, 7, 13) that highlighted the intense hatred existing between the two groups.

To present both parties as being equally wrong would have put the legitimacy of the current PAP leadership in question since the attack by the Malays was specifically directed at the Chinese PAP government (Segments 5, 7). The need to sustain in the reader's mind the image of the Malays as racially more intense — and hence the culprit behind the riots — is therefore important. Thus only the 'racial' speech of a Malay leader from SUMNO was included in the text (Segment 8), and none from the Chinese side. It was not only a 'racial' speech but also a 'religious' one since terms like "Allah", "Muslims", "non-Muslims", "religion" and "Islam" were being invoked. The reader is led to associate the Malay racial sentiments with a religious call and conclude that people do not, under normal circumstances, go around shouting and killing each other; however, when religion is involved, even a docile individual can become ferocious. The inclusion of this speech thus serves to illustrate the seriousness and realness of the threat posed by the Malays (Segment 7).

Segment 5

It was not a good sign when inflammatory leaflets, allegedly issued by *Kesatuan Kemajuan Islam*, were reportedly distributed in the vicinity of Geylang and Joo Chiat in the early afternoon of 21 July urging Malays to unite and crush "the dictatorial Chinese PAP Government" led by Lee Kuan Yew.

Segment 7

Inflammatory leaflets, issued by a group calling itself *Pertubuhan Perjuangan Kebangsaan Melayu Singapura*, had been distributed among the crowds at the Padang. These called on Malays to "destroy" the "Chinese" PAP government. Another warned of Chinese "planning to kill Malays" and urged Malays to unite and "wipe out the Chinese from Singapore soil because if we leave them alone they will make fools of the Malays.... Before the blood of Malays flows on Singapore soil it would be better to see the blood of Chinese flooding the country. Let us fight to the last drop of our blood!"

Segment 8

SUMNO's Secretary-General, Syed Esa Almenoar, also spoke in the same vein:

"It is clear that Allah does not stop Muslims from being friendly with non-Muslims as long as they do not drive them out of their homes and disturb their religion... but in everything that we do, there must be a limit and if it has come to that limit that such people who are non-Muslim have disturbed our religion and have driven us from our homes then Islam says that such people are cruel wrong-doers ... patience and understanding cannot stand the limit when people have come from within or from without, to disturb our castle, our home and our religion. If it comes to such a point, it is the duty of all Muslims to sacrifice their lives and properties for the sake of safety and for the sake of the country.

The duty to the country and the duty to one's home is sacred and if any people, Muslims or non-Muslims alike, work towards disintegration and disruption of the country and our home such people will be treated as traitors. This is the teaching of Islam."

Segment 13
Othman Wok, who was leading the 500-strong PAP contingent, observed that as his group turned into Victoria Street from Arab street, "a number of Malay youths on the left side of the road on seeing our PAP flags shouted in Malay, "Hidup China, mati Melayu" (long live the Chinese, death to the Malays).

The 1964 riots are deemed a good example of what intense racial sentiments can lead to. To illustrate how catastrophic the riots were, figures of the injured and dead were quoted: 23 dead and 454 injured (TST 1, Segment 7). By continually invoking the 1964 racial riots as the worst incident of racial conflict, the fear of such riots is instilled in Singaporeans till this day. They are reminded of the necessity of racial harmony, hence justifying the need to discipline the different ethnic groups in Singapore to form one 'harmonious community of people', and the government's multiracial ideology.

A Morally Right Leadership

The 1964 riot was not merely about the death of 23 people and the injury of 454 others; it was the first time such an event had occurred in Singapore, and it took place during the period of merger with

Malaysia. With its leitmotif of good versus evil, it was turned into a cautionary tale, and by blaming others for the outbreak of the riots, the ruling authority (the PAP government) appears innocent and thus maintains its legitimacy.

TST 1: "UMNO Instigation Sparked Race-Riots"

The opening line (Segment 1) establishes unambiguously the culprit such that the reader need not even complete the whole text. The rest of the text serves mostly to illustrate and justify this claim.

Segment 2 serves to dissociate the Singapore government from the 'evil-doers' and stakes its innocence right from the beginning. Through these two segments, the reader is led to conclude that the Malaysian government was the culprit of the riot while the Singapore government was the innocent victim.

Segment 3 reinforces the good image of the Singapore government. It is just, calm and duly worried for the welfare of the people: "what or who started this situation is irrelevant at this moment … right now our business is to stop this stupidity."

Killing is an immoral act. As racial incitements resulted in the death of individuals, the author establishes racial passions as manifestations of immorality (Segment 6). The Malays, being the attackers, consequently emerge as the wrongdoers who have done the Chinese such an injustice that the "secret society gangsters had stepped in to protect the Chinese and exact revenge" (Segment 7).

It is crucial to drive home the point that the Malays were the instigators of the riot. The truth of this claim is unimportant for it is consistent with the opening

Segment 1
The race riots that hit Singapore on July 21, 1964 did not happen out of the blue but were backed by key players in Kuala Lumpur.

Segment 2
I [Lee Kuan Yew] had just finished my round of golf at the Royal Singapore Golf Club at about 6.20 pm on July 21, 1964, when the police alerted me that Malay-Chinese riots had broken out during the Prophet Muhammad's Birthday procession and the trouble had spread. I dashed home to change and went to police headquarters at Pearl's Hill, where Keng Swee and I were briefed by John Le Cain, the police commissioner, and George Bogaars, the director of Special Branch.

Segment 3
I urged a return to sanity: "What or who started this situation is irrelevant at this moment. All the indications show that there has been organisation and planning behind this outbreak to turn it into an ugly communal clash. But right now our business is to stop this stupidity. Rumours and wild talk of revenge and retaliation will only inflame men's minds."

Segment 6
But racial passions had been aroused and mayhem broken loose. The news, distorted and exaggerated, soon spread by word of mouth. All over the island, Malays began killing Chinese, and Chinese retaliated.

statement that the Malaysian government was the chief perpetrator of the riot. The riot is described as a "planned" one (Segment 1), and the 'evidence' is shown in Segments 9–12 and Segment 15.

To further demonize UMNO, their purported aim was "to reestablish the political influence of UMNO among the Singapore Malays.... [Their] objective was to use the Singapore Malays as pawns..." (Segment 13). This was necessary so that whatever allegations UMNO made against the Singapore government would be seen as valueless in the mind of the reader. Thus accusations against the Singapore government could be easily denounced (Segment 14).

British officers' reports are included (Segments 16 and 17) to reinforce the validity of the narrative and the culpability of UMNO. Europeans, being the 'neutral' party, boost the non-racist and equitable position of the Singapore government.

To assure the reader without any reasonable doubt that Malaysia was the culprit, any other possibilities are ruled out. The cross-examination of a witness (Segment 27) is published as textual evidence.

To further enhance the perception that the Singapore leadership was non-racist, Segments 29–33 describe how PAP officials tried in vain to prevent the possibility of a racial outbreak. On the other hand, UMNO was established as the racist party and was accused of being responsible for the outbreak (Segment 32). This perception is sealed in the

Segment 7
The casualties came to 23 dead and 454 injured, and when the body count was made at the mortuary there were as many Malay as there were Chinese victims. Secret society gangsters had stepped in to protect the Chinese and exact revenge, not least for the harsh behaviour shown towards them by the men of the Malay Regiment and the Federal Reserve Unit, who were mainly Malay.

Segment 9
Later the government published a memorandum setting out the events that had let to the riots. It read: "It is the submission of this memorandum that, unlike in the past, influential political leaders and newspapers were allowed to carry an open and sustained communal and political propaganda for many months.

Segment 10
The purveyors of communal propaganda were not obscure fanatics with little resources and facilities to spread their message. This time, the propagandists of aggressive communalism included people and newspapers closely associated with the central government and with the ruling party of Malaysia.

Segment 11
The memorandum concluded that at no time did those in authority in Kuala Lumpur restrain those indulging in inflammatory racist propaganda. Nobody put a stop to it and nobody was prosecuted for sedition as they could so easily have been.

Segment 12
The evidence produced clearly showed that the riots were not a spontaneous and unwilled manifestation of genuine animosities between the races.

concluding line (Segment 34): "Razak was involved in it and it was clearly his intention to remove Mr. Lee from office". That was the assured purpose of "Albar's campaign", consistent with the opening line (Segment 1).

Segment 13
The purpose of the campaign was principally to reestablish the political influence of Umno among the Singapore Malays. An even more important objective was to use the Singapore Malays as pawns to consolidate Malay support for Umno in Malay [sic] itself.

Segment 14
By placing the blame for the riots on our government and depicting it as oppressing the Malays of Singapore, the perpetrators hoped to frighten those elsewhere in the Federation into rallying around Umno for protection.

Segment 15
A week after the riots, Othman Wok, who had been deputy editor of the *Utusan Melayu,* was told by a senior reporter of *Utusan* in Kuala Lumpur that at 2 pm on July 21, he already knew something was about to happen. Othamn asked: "But the riots did not start till 4 pm, how did you know beforehand that riots would take place?" The *Utusan* reporter replied: "We knew beforehand. We have our sources." **Those responsible wanted to reserve the front page for the big news.**

Segment 16
The diplomats, both in Singapore and Kuala Lumpur, reported back home what had happened. Britain's High Commissioner in Kuala Lumpur, Antony Head, told London he had "no doubt that this extreme element of Umno played a considerable part in stirring up the first communal riots which took place in Singapore."

Segment 17
The British High Commissioner in Kuala Lumpur reported: "The riots had a political rather than a religious origin; there had been a similar, but less serious, outbreak the previous week in Penang state. Communal tension has been sharpened during the

past few months by a propaganda campaign (conducted primarily by the leading Malay newspaper, *Utusan Melayu*) accusing the PAP government in Singapore of unfair treatment of Malays there.

Segment 27
All of them firmly denied that Indonesia was in any way connected with the disturbances. The cross-examination of a star witness ran as follows:

Question: If during the months of May, June, July we have all these various things that I have just been telling you — this propaganda, which is opened and sustained, would you agree that the feelings of the Malays would have been very high?

Answer: Yes.

Question: And it was so on the day of the riots that this highly charged propaganda was the factor with regard to the riots?

Answer: Yes.

Question: Would you agree that this highly charged propaganda was the factor with regard to the riots?

Answer: Yes.

Segment 29
Razak told him that he saw a way out. He was willing to set up a national government of Malaysia in which the PAP would be represented in the Federal Cabinet — on condition that I resigned as prime minister of Singapore; I could take up a post at the United Nations and make an effective contribution from there. After two or three years, the position might be reviewed. Keng Swee asked whether, as a quid pro quo, Albar would be removed.

Razak answered: "No."

Segment 30
Razak was emphatic when he told Keng Swee that he had Albar and the *Utusan Melayu* completely under his control and gave a clear undertaking to Keng Swee that he could control *Utusan*.

Segment 31
Keng Swee made a note immediately after the meeting: "Razak admitted that his opinion was sought whether or not trouble would break out in Singapore and he had given as his opinion that trouble would not break out. He admitted that he had made an error of judgement. Had he forseen it, he would have taken action."

Segment 32
Keng Swee recorded in his oral history in 1982: "Now, this amounts to an admission that he was involved in this whole campaign to whip up Malay racist and religious feelings in Singapore. And Albar's entry into Singapore and his campaigning in Singapore and the support given to *Utusan Melayu* had the full backing of Razak.

"It could not have been otherwise." "Now when Razak said that in his opinion, trouble will not break out, I mean, that's ... I frankly don't accept that.

Segment 33
"No one in his senses would have believed that this shrill racist campaign coupled with a well-organised procession of the Malays in which the *bersilat* (martial arts) groups came out in force, no one could have believed that. The outcome must be racial riots. In fact, some days, perhaps more than a week before the riots broke out, I remember Mr Lee was extremely worried and felt in his bones that there was going to be race trouble. Discussed it with me. I was too engrossed on economic and financial matters. I was not fully informed and appeared quite sceptical about this. Again, this is a matter of political judgement — getting the feel of the situation — which I had not."

Segment 34
"When I questioned Mr Lee very closely, he just sighed and changed the subject. He must have thought that I was very dense on these matters. And indeed I was. Well, whatever the outcome was, the riots took place, Razak was involved in it and it was clearly his intention to remove Mr Lee from office. That was the purpose of Albar's campaign."

The continuous negative representation of the Malaysian government is meant to diminish Malaysia's legitimacy in the eyes of Singaporeans. Although the racial riots occurred in Singapore, the image of the PAP government must remain consistently non-racist and morally irreproachable. The Singapore government must be seen to remain impartial, in order to legitimize its multiracial policy, which claims to accord equal treatment to all the races in Singapore, and to assure Singaporeans that they have not made the wrong choice in continuing their support for the government and in being Singaporeans.

Historical Landmark 2: Separation from Malaysia: Construction of an Unjust Breakup

Singapore had always pushed for merger despite the hesitation shown by the Malaysian government. However, the Singapore leaders' insistence on unification ultimately resulted in separation. To justify that Singapore is and has always been on the 'right side' and to deflect any blame for the separation, the separation from Malaysia had to be portrayed as an unjust break-up.

TST 4: "Suddenly Singapore is Independent"

Firstly, to dissociate itself from any responsibility for the separation, Singapore has to occupy the position of the 'victim'. The separation is construed as an unanticipated and impulsive act by the Malaysian government, as shown by PM Lee Kuan Yew's remarks: "Separation! What I had fought so hard to achieve was now being dissolved. Why? And why so suddenly?"

To enhance the image of Singapore as the 'victim', the "sudden" separation must also be a permanent one. The analogy of "*talak*" (divorce) was used as a metaphor for the separation (Segment 6), down to the three readings in the two chambers of parliament mentioned in Segment 5. The usage of the term

Segment 3

Separation! What I had fought so hard to achieve was now being dissolved. Why? And why so suddenly? It was only two years since the island of Singapore had been part of the new Federation of Malaysia (which also included the North Borneo territories of Sarawak and Sabah).

Segment 5

The House listened in utter silence. The Tunku was speaking at the first reading of a resolution moved by Tun Abdul Razak, the deputy prime minister, to pass the Constitution of Malaysia (Singapore Amendment) Bill, 1965, immediately. By 1.30 pm, the debate on the second and third readings had ended, and the bill was sent to the Senate. The Senate started its first reading "*talak*" is not accidental. The pronouncement of *talak* thrice by a husband results in the permanent annulment of a Muslim marriage with no chance of reconciliation.[11] This presents to the reader the image of the separation as a heartless and unjust one. Since the pronouncement of *talak* is also one-way, imposed by the husband upon the wife, Singapore is positioned as the helpless victim in the hands of the Malaysian government, which announced the separation. The separation is connotatively read as an immoral imposition.

The image of a victim would be incomplete without emotions. Segment 13 presents the emotional breakdown of the PAP leader, Lee Kuan Yew, towards the separation, reifying the 'victim' position of Singapore. Nonetheless, the defeat is dignified, as reflected in Lee's concern that he had let down not only the people in Singapore and Malaysia (Segment 18) but also the allies and supporters who formed the Malaysian Solidarity Convention (Segment 19).

To further assert the rectitude of the Singapore government's position, sympathy from Western leaders was mentioned (Segments 16, 32 and 33), asserting that had the British administrators of Singapore known about the intention to separate, actions would have been taken to prevent it (Segment 42).

at 2.30 and completed the third reading at 4.30. The head of state, the Yang-di-Pertuan Agong, gave his royal assent that same day, concluding the constitutional formalities.

Singapore was cast out.

Segment 6

Under Malay-Muslim custom, a husband, but not the wife, can declare "*Talak*" (I divorce thee) and the woman is divorced. They can reconcile and he can remarry her, but not after he has said "*Talak*" three times. The three readings in the two chambers of parliament were the three *talaks* with which Malaysia divorced Singapore.

Segment 13

I recounted my meetings with the Tunku in Kuala Lumpur during the two previous days:

"But the Tunku put it very simply that there would be a great deal of trouble if we insisted on going on. And I would like to ask… You see, this is a moment of … every time we look back on this moment when we signed this agreement, which severed Singapore from Malaysia, it will be a moment of anguish because all my life I have believed in merger and the unity of these two territories. It's a people connected by geography, economics and ties of kinship… Would you mind if we stop for a while?" At that moment, my emotions overwhelmed me. It was only after another 20 minutes that I was able to regain my composure and resume the press conference.

Segment 16

Among Chinese, it is unbecoming to exhibit such a lack of manliness. But I could not help myself. It was some consolation that many viewers in Britain, Australia and New Zealand sympathised with me and with Singapore. They were interested in Malaysia because their troops were defending it against armed "Confrontation", the euphemism President Sukarno of Indonesia used to describe his small-scale undeclared war against the new and expanded "neo-colonialist" Federation.

Segment 18
I felt I had let down several million people in Malaysia: immigrant Chinese and Indians, Eurasians and even some Malays. I had aroused their hopes, and they had joined people in Singapore in resisting Malay hegemony, the root cause of dispute.

Segment 19
I was ashamed that I had left our allies and supporters to fend for themselves, including party leaders from other states of Malaysia — Sabah, Sarawak, Penang, Perak, Selangor and Negri Sembilan. Together we had formed the Malaysian Solidarity Convention which had been meeting and coordinating our activities to mobilise the people to stand up for a non-communal society.

Segment 32
In truth, I had a heavy heart throughout. Head's bearing impressed me. His demeanour was worthy of a Sandhurst-trained officer in the Life Guards. He had been defence minister at the time of the Anglo-French invasion of Suez in 1956, and had resigned along with Anthony Eden, accepting responsibility for the debacle. He was British upper class, good at the stiff upper lip.

Segment 33
He had tried his best to prevent this break. He had done his utmost to get the Tunku and the Federal government to adopt policies that could build up unity within Malaysia.

Segment 42
But if I had told Head that the Tunku wanted us out of Malaysia, although what I wanted was a looser federation, he would have found a way to stop the Tunku as it was against British interests to have Singapore separated and independent.

Construction of the Champion of Racial Equality

After establishing Malaysia's guilt, it was relatively easier to present all actions of the Singapore government during merger as morally right. This is important because the concept of a 'Malaysian Malaysia', advocating equal status and treatment for all races, which the PAP government propagated, was unpopular in Malaysia. To justify its 'Malaysian Malaysia' position, Singapore's image as the champion of racial equality had to be constructed.

TST 5: "The Crucial Speech ... Which Split the Nation"

In the construction of its image as the champion of racial equality, Malaysia had to be portrayed as racist, hostile and particularly discriminatory towards the Chinese right from the beginning. This is asserted in Segment 3. On the other hand, Singapore had to acquire a non-racist image (particularly not pro-Chinese), to justify its 'Malaysian Malaysia' concept. Thus Lee had to dissociate himself from any race and identify himself as Malaysian (Segment 10). Lee spoke fluently in the Malay language and made a good impression on the Malay speakers (Segments 11, 28). He also showed concern towards the well-being of the Malays (Segments 12 and 13) despite his Chinese ethnicity.

Special privileges/rights for the Malays were depicted as non-justifiable and irrational, and even counter-productive (Segments 11, 12 and 20). That Malays had special rights but were still economically backward substantiated Lee's argument that special rights were unnecessary. This thus justified Lee's call for equality in all spheres for all the races.

The impact of Lee's speech propagating the 'Malaysian Malaysia' concept was so effective as to be stunning (Segment 26).

Segment 3
I made my most important speech in the federal Parliament to a hostile and tense audience, including a large number of Malay MPs who had been fed daily with anti-PAP, anti-Lee Kuan Yew and anti-Chinese propaganda by the *Utusan Melayu* over the past year.

Segment 10
On the contrary, I kept on reminding people: "I am a Malaysian, I am learning Bahasa Kebangsaan (the national language) and I accept Article 153 of the Constitution (on the special rights of the Malays)."

Segment 11
Having reached the most sensitive part of my speech, in which I would expose the inadequacy of Umno's policies, I decided to speak in Malay. Although my Malay was not as good as my English, I was fluent compared with other non-Malay MPs.

Segment 12
I said that while I accepted Malay as the sole official language, I did not see how it could raise the economic position of the people.

Would it mean that the produce of the Malay farmer would increase in price, that he would get better prices? Would he get improved facilities from the government? I added that if the Alliance did not have real answers to current economic problems, it should not stifle the opposition.

This was 'proof' that this concept was rational and ought to be implemented.

Segment 13
Because we had an alternative, and it would work: "In 10 years we will breed a generation of Malays, educated and with an understanding of the techniques of science and modern industrial management."

Segment 20
"If we delude people into believing that they are poor because there are no Malay rights or because opposition members oppose Malay rights, where are we going to end up? You let people in the kampungs believe that they are poor because we don't speak Malay, because the government does not write in Malay, so he expects a miracle to take place in 1967 (the year Malay would become the national and sole official language). The moment we all start speaking Malay, he is going to have an uplift in the standard of living, and if it doesn't happen, what happens then?..."

Segment 26
My Malay Cabinet colleague, Othman Wok, was in the chamber. He recalled: "The chamber was very quiet and nobody stirred. The ministers of the central government sunk down so low in their seats that only their foreheads could be seen over the desk in front of them. The backbenchers were spellbound. They could understand every word. That was the turning point. They perceived Lee as a dangerous man who could one day be the prime minister of Malaysia."

Segment 28
The Malays present did not expect me, the supposed anti-Malay Chinese chauvinist out to destroy the Malay race, to speak in Malay with no trace of a Chinese dialect accent that most Chinese would have. I had been born and bred in Singapore, speaking the language from childhood. I could trace my ancestors for three generations in Singapore. They had made as big a contribution to the country as any Malay in the chamber. And I was on their side, not against them. I wanted to improve their lot.

By emphasizing the rationality of the 'Malaysian Malaysia' concept, the PAP government would be seen as the champion of racial equality, and the Malaysian government, on the other hand, as racist or Malay communalist. This construction is imperative as it justifies multiracialism, one of the founding constitutional provisions of Singapore, as just and morally upright, the rational response to an unjust break-up.

Construction of a Multiracialist Nation

The failure of the 1963–65 merger produced an enthusiastic state without a national identity. Moreover, Singapore's citizens were composed of largely immigrant stock and plagued by the baggage of racial disharmony. All these factors were obstacles to the process of developing social cohesiveness. The process of nation-building thus required the construction of identity, which in the case of Singapore had to accommodate ethnic, cultural and linguistic pluralism. The policy of multiracialism was implemented to meet those needs; yet it cannot allow for an unbridled growth of cultural plurality. It is a discourse of race in which the ontology of race is discursively rationalized into the discretely delineated 'CMIO' categories: Chinese, Malays, Indian and Others. The PAP's construction of multiracialism has marginalized the various dialect groups as a strategic means of disciplining the social body in Singapore.

An acceptance of the multiracial policy enhances the legitimacy of the PAP in the eyes of Singaporeans. Its acceptance by the Singaporean Malays is particularly crucial since Singapore is geographically sandwiched between Malaysia and Indonesia, and the rejection of the 'Malaysian Malaysia' concept would have undermined the authority of the PAP. Singaporean Malays' support for the PAP also serves to confirm the objectivity of the policy of multiracialism.

This is illustrated by the different emphases in the presentation of historical texts by *The Straits Times* and by *Berita Harian*. The former emphasizes the difficulties faced by the PAP during the merger phase — racial riots and the 'non-negotiable and racist' Malaysian leadership that Lee Kuan Yew had to deal with. *Berita Harian* highlighted, instead, the Malay PAP leaders and their role in changing the opinions of the Malay community, figures of Singapore's national history that were hitherto ignored.

BH 3: "A Portion of History that Needs to be Known by Many"

The term "needs to be" in the headline immediately bestows an importance and urgency to the text, focusing on the three personalities selected.

The three Malay PAP leaders are Haji Ya'acob Mohamed, Haji Rahmat Kenap and Haji Mohd Ariff Suradi, and their mission is labelled "*Perjuangan Tiga Serangkai*", which can be translated as "Struggle of the Trio". In fact, the term *perjuangan* means more than just a struggle; it also entails the idea of fighting for a cause. In other words, these three leaders are warriors of the PAP for the Malays. They are given such a lofty title so that all policies adopted by the PAP government towards the Malay community will be justifiable. By calling them "Singapore's older politicians" (Segment 7), the reader is led to identify them as being part of Singapore, hence establishing a continuity such that the PAP government is seen to be synonymous with Singapore.

The statements made by these three Malay PAP leaders have one central theme: their wholehearted acceptance of the multiracial policy promoted by the PAP, and its positive consequences for the Malay community as a whole (Segments 7–14). One of them is quoted as declaring: "It is better to choose a party with a multiracial basis. As a *Malay* [emphasis added], I am still fighting for my own race but through the channel of the PAP" (Segment 9). This statement tacitly places the PAP as the champion for the Malay community, as textually evidenced by Segments 13–8.

Photo Caption:
Struggle of the Trio: Haji Rahmat Kenap, Haji Mohd Ariff Suradi and Allahyarham Haji Ya'acob Mohamed, Malay Members of Parliament of the People's Action Party (PAP) who won the hearts of the Malay voters at Geylang Serai, Kampong Kembangan and the Southern Islands, which were once the strongholds of UMNO.

Segment 7
Berita Harian met a few of Singapore's older politicians, who were directly or indirectly involved in the turbulence of the era's politics, to recall those moments of anguish and their experiences.

Segment 8
Their analysis is in general a straightforward one: in Singapore's multiracial society, a party which fights for the rights of one race only is not appropriate.

Segment 9
Haji Buang Omar, 76, former Parliamentary Secretary for the Ministries of Health and Law, the Deputy Prime Minister's Office and Social Welfare between 1962 and 1971, said: "Singapore's society is multiracial. It is better to choose a party with a multiracial basis. As a Malay, I am still fighting for my own race, but through another channel — the PAP."

Segment 10
Former Geylang Serai Member of Parliament (1963–1980), Haji Rahmat Kenap, also opined that the era of the late 1950s and 1960s was a critical one for the Malay community. Communist influences had penetrated the workers' union movements, on top of the "Destroy Malaysia" campaign initiated by Indonesia.

Segment 11
And at that time, many of them, such as Haji Rahmat and Haji Mohd Suradi, were workers' union leaders at their respective workplaces.

Coincidentally, Lee Kuan Yew at that time was a legal advisor to many of the workers' unions.

Segment 12
The opportunity to meet Lee Kuan Yew opened my eyes to what sort of person he was. I did not think then that he was someone who would practise discrimination towards the Malays.

Segment 13
"In fact, he was concerned about the problems of the Malays," said Haji Rahmat, now 73 years old.

Segment 14
According to Haji Rahmat, the struggles of past Malay MPs resulted in Malay children getting free fees up to tertiary education.

Segment 18
Up till now, those former Malay MPs such as Haji Rahmat, believe the PAP still upholds Malays' rights.

"What is owned by Singaporean Malays today is a result of the struggles of past Malay MPs. We opened up the way for the MPs today to fight for the Malays just as we did," repeated Haji Rahmat.

In the aftermath of the controversy over the visit of the Israeli president to Singapore in 1986, which led to a furore between Singapore and Malaysia, and to Muslim organizations in Singapore following the lead of their Malaysian counterparts protesting against the visit (Leifer, cited in Hill and Lian, 1995: 97), this text served to remind the Malay community that the PAP government has been the 'right choice' since the beginning of nationhood. This was crucial because the Prime Minister had publicly questioned the loyalty of the Malays in Singapore. The 'lesson dispensed' was that the Malays in Singapore can be influenced by the concerns of Malays in Malaysia or Indonesia due to ethnic and religious attachments. Thus, multiracialism disciplines Singaporean Malays to identify themselves with the PAP state and not others.

Conclusion: Frames of National History, and an Incomplete Hegemony

In the texts I have examined, images of a racist and aggressive Malaysia versus a non-communalist and victimized Singapore are consistently conjured. Themes such as multiracialism, crisis and suffering are also recurrent. These are ideologically motivated. The emphasis on race is important due to Singapore's positioning in a Malay-dominated region. With its Chinese majority, Singapore raises the suspicions of her neighbours Malaysia and Indonesia, which fear the formation of a 'Third China' in the archipelago. To prevent future interstate conflicts on this matter, the 'Malay race' discourse must be maintained in order to nullify the image of a 'Third China' and promote Singapore as a multiracial society.

The theme of endured suffering reifies the state's existence as it reminds Singaporeans of the injustice inflicted by Malaysia, the precariousness of the young nation and the need thus for Singaporeans to stand together for the survival of the nation. Threats have been identified as both external and internal (Chua, 1995: 48): Internal threats are posed by religious and ethnic tensions in the domestic arena, while cultural differences with neighbouring Malaysia and Indonesia will always be a potential external problem. However, the PAP is quick to utilize any situation of interstate conflict to its advantage. The atmosphere of 'psychosis' in relation to the perceived challenges of external events is purposely kept up by the PAP (Regnier, cited in Hill and Lian: 34) so as to present itself as a 'solver' of difficulties, which in turn enhances its legitimacy.

The consistent invocation of 'threats' generates a "crisis or siege mentality" (Chua, 1995: 19), as evidenced by the title of the National Education Exhibition — "The Singapore Story: Overcoming the Odds". The result is an over-anxious tendency that justifies any pre-emptive measures taken by the state to 'save' the nation. As such, the demands of the state for higher levels of behavioural discipline from the people will be accepted as natural and necessary by the community. When ruling ideas and ideology become common-sense reality, the PAP can be said to have succeeded in maintaining its hegemony with very minimal use of physical coercion. Once a common ideology has been entrenched, the citizens will in turn work to reproduce and perpetuate the party in dominance (Chua, 1995: 43). However, it should be noted that, while the party may have been successful in 'naturalizing' its ideology of multiracialism among Singaporeans, its hegemony is never complete because, judging by past electoral results, there has always been a portion of the population who view the nation differently.

Notes

1. See <http://www.nhb.gov.sg/WWW/HistoryNMilestone.html> [accessed 13 August 2011].
2. Malaysia's dominant ruling party.
3. According to Scholte, globalization is often understood as increasing cross-border exchange or internationalization (increased movement between countries of goods, investments, people, money, messages and ideas) and increasing the opening of borders to international trade, travel, financial transfers and communications. The second definition presumes an integrated planetary system such as a unitary global economy replacing country-based economies. Globalization here is taken to be synonymous with liberalization.
4. For example, the *Eastern Sun* "which was launched in 1966 was closed in 1971 after the Government found evidence of an attempt of subversion by the communists" (Chen, 1991: 307).
5. 1980 figures cited in Chen (1997: 307); more recent figures from <http://www.singstat.gov.sg> [accessed 13 August 2011]. In addition, from 1965–1980, total newspaper circulation in Singapore trebled from 214,030 to 615,612. By 2010, total daily average circulation of the nine main daily papers had increased to 1,241,012 (figures from Singapore Press Holdings, <http://www.sph.com.sg/ourproducts_newspaper_st.shtml> [accessed 13 August 2011]). While Internet use has also soared in the past 20 years and Singaporeans can now easily access an array of international news sources online, these figures indicate that local newspapers continue to serve a leading role as suppliers of information.
6. The newspaper texts used, *The Straits Times* and *Berita Harian*, are drawn from the period June–December 1998, following the publication of two books, *A Moment of Anguish: Singapore In Malaysia and the Politics of Disengagement* by Dr. Albert Lau, and *The Singapore Story: Memoir of Lee Kuan*

Yew, by Lee Kuan Yew, as well as the history exhibition of the National Education Programme.

7. I did not consider the Chinese or Indian press due to my inability to read Mandarin and Tamil.
8. The full original text can be found in the author's original thesis.
9. From 1968, history became a non-examinable subject at certain primary levels and could be dropped completely from the Primary School Leaving Examinations (PSLE) from 1972. From 1975, it became part of a new non-examinable subject called Education for Living (EFL), designed to teach good morals to primary school students. When EFL was abolished in 1979, history and geography were taught under a new subject, Social Studies, introduced from Primary Four onwards. The beginings of a concern for history can be traced to the 1980s.
10. This riot involved a Dutch/Eurasian Christian couple who left their daughter in the custody of a Malay couple in Java when they were interned during the Japanese Occupation of Indonesia. Years later, this Dutch couple traced the girl and her adoptive family to Malaysia and claimed her back. In the meantime she had become very close to her adoptive family and had adopted Islam. They wanted her to denounce her Islamic faith in favour of Christianity. The controversy surrounding the ensuing court case, held in Singapore, erupted into a riot triggered by religious and anti-colonial sensitivities.
11. In the Islamic concept of *talak*, once the term has been used three times with intention, the marriage is nullified and the couple cannot reunite. Reconciliation is only allowed when the second marriage of the wife fails and she wants to reconcile with her first husband.

References

Anderson, Benedict (1983). *Imagined Communities: Reflections on the Origin and Spread of Nationalism*. London: Verso.

Banton, Michael (1967). *Race Relations*. London: Tavistock Publications.

Benjamin, Geoffrey (1976). *The Unseen Presence: A Theory of the Nation-State and Its Mystifications*. Singapore: Department of Sociology, National University of Singapore, Working Paper No. 125.

Carr, E.H. (1973). *What is History*. London: Penguin Books.

Chen Ai Yen (1991). "The Mass Media, 1819–1980", in Ernest Chew and Edwin Lee (eds), *A History of Singapore*. Oxford and New York: Oxford University Press.

Chew, Ernest and Edwin Lee (eds) (1991). *A History of Singapore*. Oxford and New York: Oxford University Press.

Chieh Loy Hui and Wee Liang Tong (1997). "Nation and Imagining", *The History Journal 1997*: 13–7.

Chua Beng Huat (1995). *Culture, Multiculturalism and National Identity in Singapore*, Paper No. 125. Singapore: Department of Sociology, National University of Singapore.

______ (1996). *Communitarian Ideology and Democracy in Singapore*. London and New York: Routledge.

Clutterbuck, Richard (1973). *Riot and Revolution in Singapore and Malaya: 1945–1963*. London: Faber and Faber Limited.

Drysdale, John (1984). *Singapore: Struggle for Success*. Singapore: Times Books International.

Fletcher, Nancy McHenry (1969). *The Separation of Singapore and Malaysia*. New York: Southeast Asia Program, Department of Asian Studies, Cornell University, Ithaca.

Foucault, Michel (1972). *The Archaeology of Knowledge*. London: Tavistock Publications.

Gellner, Ernest (1986). *Nations and Nationalism*. United Kingdom: Basil Blackwell Ltd.

Hill, Michael and Lian Kwen Fee (1995). *The Politics of Nation Building and Citizenship in Singapore*. London and New York: Routledge.

Hobsbawm, Eric and Terence Ranger (1989). *The Invention of Tradition*. Cambridge: Cambridge University Press.

Hong Lysa and Jimmy Yap (1993). "The Past in Singapore's Present", in *Commentary*, vol. 11, no. 4.

Kaye, Harvey J. (1991). *Past: Reflections on the Crisis and the Promise of History*. Minneapolis: University of Minnesota Press.

Lau, Albert (1991). "The National Past and the Writing of the History of Singapore", in Ban Kah Choon, Anne Pakir and Tong Chee Kiong (eds), *Imagining Singapore*. Singapore: Times Academic Press.

______ (1998a). *A Moment of Anguish: Singapore in Malaysia and the Politics of Disengagement*. Singapore: Times Academic Press.

______ (1998b). *"End of Empire: Malaya". Issues and Perspectives*. Paper presented at the 7th Malaysia–Singapore Forum. Singapore: Faculty of Arts and Social Science, National University of Singapore.

Lee Kuan Yew (1961). *The Battle for Merger*. Singapore: Government Print Office.

Levine, Donald N. (1996). "Sociology and the Nation-state in an Era of Shifting Boundaries". *Sociological Inquiry*, vol. 66, no. 3: 253–66.

Marshall, Gordon (ed.) (1994). *The Concise Oxford Dictionary of Sociology*. Oxford and New York: Oxford University Press.

Marx, Karl (1970). *The German Ideology*, edited by C.J. Arthur. London: Lawrence & Wishart.

Miller, Peggy (1994). "Narrative Practices: Their Role in Socialization and Self-Construction", in U. Neisser and R. Fivusch (eds), *The Remembering Self.* Cambridge: Cambridge University Press, pp. 158–79.

Ostrom, Charles Richard (1970). *A Core Interest Analysis of the Formation of Malaysia and Separation of Singapore.* Unpublished PhD dissertation submitted to the Claremont Graduate School.

Scholte, Jan Aart (1997). "Global Capitalism and the State". *International Affairs* 73, 3: 430–1.

Smith, Anthony D. (1996a). "Anthony D. Smith's Opening Statement: Nations and their Pasts". *Nations and Nationalism* 2 (3): 357–63.

——— (1996b). "Memory and Modernity: Reflections on Ernest Gellner's Theory of Nationalism". *Nations and Nationalism* 2 (3): 371–88.

Thompson, John B. (1984). *Studies in the Theory of Ideology.* Cambridge: Polity Press.

Tudor, Henry (1972). *Political Myth.* London: Praeger Publishers.

Tunku Abdul Rahman (1997). *Looking Back: Monday Musings and Memories.* Kuala Lumpur: Pustaka Antara.

Turnbull, C.M. (1977). *A History of Singapore: 1819–1975.* London: Oxford University Press.

Young, Robert (1981). *Untying the Text: A Post-Structuralist Reader.* Boston, London and Henley: Routledge and Kegan Paul.

CHAPTER 6

Remembering, Misremembering and Forgetting: The Struggle over *Serangan Oemoem 1 Maret 1949* in Yogyakarta, Indonesia

Heddy Shri Ahimsa Putra

Introduction

This chapter is about the ways in which Indonesians have tried to keep their memories of war alive, and the controversy over one particular wartime event: the *Serangan Oemoem 1 Maret 1949* or *SO 1 Maret* (General Attack of 1 March, 1949), which took place in Yogyakarta. The incident was part of what is called the Second War of Independence (*Perang Kemerdekaan ke Dua*). The controversy became a national issue because of the involvement of two prominent figures in Indonesian history, the late Sultan Hamengkubuwono IX of Yogyakarta and Soeharto, ex-President of Indonesia.[1]

Indonesians have used various means to keep the memories of the *Serangan Oemoem 1 Maret 1949* alive — monuments, movies, museums, books, comics, rituals and organizations — a commemorative effort I regard as the most systematic, organised and complete in Indonesian history; I do not know of any other historical episode related to the Dutch Occupation that has been so elaborately commemorated. Under the New Order, the local government, participants of the war and people in Yogyakarta seemed to have agreed not to forget this battle that so shaped the Republic of Indonesia. Increasingly elaborate commemorations of the event were held during the 1980s, which received strong support from the central government in Jakarta.

Remembering and collectively commemorating a particular event are not easy processes. How is the event to be remembered — through books, movies and monuments? What should be remembered — the battles, the signing of an agreement, the strategy or the spirit? And who should be remembered and how — as leader, soldier, initiator or architect? All these are questions to which answers should be agreed upon by those who participated in the event and know the details well. Otherwise, the commemoration might fail to achieve its ends.

Any such acts of remembrance contribute to the shaping of current relationships and may be read at one level as a kind of commentary on them. As Fentress and Wickham have put it, "recalled past experience and shared images of the historical past are kinds of memories that have particular importance for the constitution of social groups in the present" (Fentress and Wickham, 1992: xi). Discussing the formative work of Halbwachs (1950) on social memory, these authors built on his proposition that "social groups construct their own images of the world by establishing an agreed version of the past" (Fentress and Wickham, 1992: x). Such agreed accounts of the past can achieve a social effect only if they are communicated to others, and in this process disagreement sometimes occurs concerning the version to be accepted, the things to be remembered and the things to be forgotten. There is thus a politics of remembering and forgetting, and a politics of creating and revising social memory (Benfell, 1999). In recent years, historians have become increasingly sensitive to the relations between their craft and the wider field of social memory (Hutton, 1993). Memories of war often contain difficult political and moral issues, and a number of works have probed into the continuously changing ways in which wars are recollected and publicly commemorated as the events recede while political conditions continue to alter in the present (Fussell, 1975; Benfell, 1999; Winter and Sivan, 1999). Given the diversity of opinion about what actually happened in the past, in addition to the different political interests that may be at stake, agreement is something that cannot be taken for granted. It is in the process of achieving the agreement that contestation and negotiation take place over what can be, should be and will be allowed to be remembered. The controversy over the *Serangan Oemoem 1 Maret 1949* shows how the content of a social memory can be contested.

Social memory, as Fentress and Wickham (1992: xi) maintain, is "often selective, distorted and inaccurate", but it can also be "extremely exact, when people have found it socially relevant from that day to this to remember and recount an event in the way it was originally experienced". What is more important from the anthropological or sociological point of view is not the accuracy of the representation or description of things to be remembered, which is the concern of the actors, the participants and the historians, but distortions most commonly brought about by "a series of external constraints, usually imposed by society" upon remembering (Fentress and Wickham, 1992: xii). It is these constraints surrounding a particular version of social memory that are the chief concern of this paper, and not the question of accuracy per se.

Here, the social context, and the relations between those who have the interest and the power to influence the content of the history, can be seen to account for the changes in the way a particular episode of history is written. The development of the controversy showed how views of this episode in Indonesian history changed as Soeharto's power and the army's popularity declined in the late 1990s. It also revealed the individuals and groups with an interest in this period of history and how they have attempted to revise it. In this case study, I would like to show that stories about the past are not stories that can be easily passed on to the new generations, when the stories themselves are believed to have been invented and when there are contesting versions of the same story.

Serangan Oemoem 1 Maret 1949 and Its Meanings

Serangan Oemoem 1 Maret 1949 — sometimes called *Enam Jam di Yogya* (Six Hours in Yogya) — was a general attack launched by the Indonesian army on Dutch positions in Yogyakarta on the morning of 1 March 1949 (Haryasudirjo, 1997). Although it only had a small impact on Dutch control of the city (the Indonesian army was able to occupy the city for only six hours), the attack was considered a political success since it attracted world attention. As a result, the United Nations urged the Dutch to start negotiations with the government of the Republic of Indonesia. This put Indonesia's representatives in a stronger position in their negotiations with the Dutch, and they were subsequently successful in securing the support of the United Nations.

The negotiations produced six agreements to be implemented by both sides (Indonesia and the Netherlands), one of which was the acknowledgement by the Dutch of the existence of the Republic of Indonesia in Yogyakarta as a state within the United States of Indonesia. This meant that Dutch troops had to be withdrawn from the city of Yogyakarta, the capital city of Indonesia. The implementation of the agreement was arranged and supervised by the Committee of Three Countries (the United States of America, Australia and Belgium). The withdrawal took place on 29 June 1949 and was observed by the late Sultan Hamengkubuwono IX and the late Paku Alam VIII, Vice-Governor of Yogya. On that day, Dutch soldiers left Yogya peacefully and withdrew to Magelang. At 11 am, when Yogya was already emptied of Dutch soldiers, the Indonesian army and freedom fighters entered the city from various directions. This event is known as the Return of Yogya (*Yogya Kembali*) (*Kompas*, 2 March 1997).

For Indonesians, especially the people of Yogyakarta, the return of Yogyakarta to the Republic on 29 June 1949 was an important historical episode that must not be forgotten. It was the outcome of the successful combination of diplomacy and armed struggle that was the *SO 1 Maret 1949*. It is also regarded as the beginning of the end of Dutch colonisation in Indonesia, because from that date on the Dutch gradually withdrew their soldiers from the whole of Indonesia. It is from such a perspective that some Indonesian leaders have viewed the event. Its political significance lies in its success in attracting world attention and the acknowledgement of the government of the Republic of Indonesia (*Angkatan Bersenjata*, 2 March 1997; *Kompas*, 2 March 1997).

Nevertheless, while Soekarno was President, the *SO 1 Maret 1949* was relatively unpopular among Indonesians in the outer islands, nor was it commemorated. It was only when Soeharto came to power in 1969 and Sultan Hamengkubuwono IX became Vice-President that the *SO 1 Maret 1949* started to gain in popularity. This can be explained by the fact that Soeharto and the Sultan were the main protagonists in the attack. It is believed that the Sultan had been the initiator of the attack while Soeharto, then a lieutenant colonel, was the architect and commandant of the attack. Both men were from Yogyakarta and shared the opinion that the *SO 1 Maret* was an important, if not a decisive, event in the history of Indonesian armed struggle against the Dutch.

In the 1980s the popularity of the *SO 1 Maret 1949* increased from year to year. In almost every annual commemoration of the attack, the president prepared a written speech to be read by the vice-governor of Yogyakarta, Paku Alam VIII. The story of the General Attack became more popular among the new generation when the government produced two docudramas entitled *Janur Kuning* (*Yellow Young Coconut Leaves*)[2] and *Serangan Fajar* (*Attack at Dawn*). Schoolchildren, especially those from elementary and junior high schools, were encouraged to see these films, especially *Janur Kuning*. This continued into the 1990s.

Keeping the Memory Alive through Monuments

Annual commemorations of the *SO 1 Maret 1949* began in the 1980s, when the local government of Yogyakarta succeeded in building a 1 March Monument in the centre of the city to immortalise the event (Dinas Sosial, 1993). Since then and up till 1998, the people of Yogya gathered every year to commemorate the Attack, keeping alive the social memory of the event.

In the 1980s the mayor of Yogyakarta proposed an even bigger monument to commemorate the *SO 1 Maret 1949*: the Monumen Yogya Kembali (Monument of the Return of Yogya). The proposal was accepted by the governor of Yogyakarta, Sultan Hamengkubuwono IX. It was the Sultan himself who designated the site where the monument should be constructed — in the village of Jongkang in the northern area of Yogyakarta. This site was chosen because the Dutch soldiers left Yogyakarta taking the northern route. Moreover, the village was situated along the axis of Mount Merapi and the palace, the axis that — according to the Javanese belief system — symbolically and spiritually connects the supernatural guardian of Mount Merapi and the Kings of Mataram, the dynasty of Hamengkubuwono.

As explained by the Sultan, the construction of the monument was a form of veneration, a way to remember and commemorate the heroic soldiers who sacrificed their lives to free Yogyakarta from Dutch occupation and return it to the people of Indonesia. The monument was meant to arouse the spirit of struggle among later generations of Indonesia and enable them to relive the history of Indonesia's struggle against all forms of colonialism or oppression. The Sultan claimed that the return of Yogya in 1949 sounded the death knell for Dutch colonialism, since after this, other provinces were gradually returned to the Republic of Indonesia (*Kompas*, 30 June 1985).

Similar sentiments were expressed elsewhere. A *Kompas* article of 1989 noted that the monument was meant to "remember the struggle of those who had defended the former capital city of Indonesia. The peak of its success was the withdrawal of the Dutch soldiers on 29 June 1949. This event was known as the Return of Yogyakarta and had inspired the construction of the monument" (*Kompas*, 5 July 1989). Again in 1992 it was reported that the construction of the monument was an expression of the "appreciation and the gratitude of Indonesian people today to the soldiers who had sacrificed their lives for the return of the capital city of Indonesia at that time [Yogyakarta] to the Republic Indonesia" (*Kompas*, 5 December 1992).

Of the monument President Soeharto said that it was intended not only to remember or glorify the past but to "immortalize the meaning of that great event, so that it becomes the national tradition of our nation, a nation of freedom fighters" (*Kompas*, 7 July 1989):

> If we today build the monument it is actually an expression of our deep gratitude both to those who had struggled, who had fought, and to God.... We build our future, but our roots are deeply implanted in our long history of struggle. We should always be aware of the continuity of our struggle, so that our younger generations will not live without any clear direction, or without any roots to our past.... The monument of the Return of Yogya is only a point of remembrance in our long history of struggle. We commemorate the past, but it is also a message for the future.

The monument was officially opened by the President on 6 July 1989. The date was also symbolic. There were three possible dates to choose from: 29 June, 6 July and 10 July. 29 June was the day Dutch soldiers left Yogyakarta. This date was felt to be unsuitable because it might be interpreted as a commemoration of the withdrawal of Dutch troops and not the return of Yogya itself (although this was actually two sides of the same coin). 6 July was the date of President Soekarno's and Vice-President Hatta's return from exile to Yogyakarta, while 10 July marked the return of the Commander-in-Chief of the army, General Soedirman and Syafruddin Prawiranegara to Yogyakarta.[3] 6 July was finally accepted as the date for the official opening of the Return of Yogya Monument. It was the day Soekarno and Hatta returned to Yogyakarta and were warmly greeted by the people lining the road from the airport to the city of Yogyakarta to catch a glimpse of their leaders (*Kompas*, 5 July 1989). The return of the leaders to Yogyakarta symbolised the resumption of Yogyakarta's function as the capital city. That was a very "clear sign that the Republic of Indonesia never disappeared, and that the Indonesian army never surrendered to the Dutch", said one of the committee members.

The monument was built in the shape of a cone with its tip cut off. It is reminiscent of the *gunungan*, the symbol of a mountain, sacred in Javanese-Hindu cosmology. The complex consists of two main parts: the main building and the courtyard. In the courtyard is the plaza, the playground, the wall called *rana*, and a pool encircling the monument. The plaza is used for ceremonies, public gatherings and public activities. It is separated from the rest of the building by a wall 3 metres high and 60 metres long stretching from east to west.[4]

On the outside of this wall is inscribed the legend *Gapura Papat Ambuka Jagad* (Four Gates Opening the World [to us]).[5] This is the *candrasengkala*, a Javanese way of stating the date of an event through a meaningful sentence. The phrase can be interpreted to mean 9491, which is to be read in reverse as 1949. On the inside, inscribed in gold paint, are the names of the 408 soldiers who died in the General Attack of 1 March 1949 and other guerilla wars before and after the attack in *Wehrkreise III* (Battle Area III), as Yogyakarta was designated, from the start of the Dutch invasion on 19 December 1948 to their surrender on 29 June 1949.

Amidst the names of the heroes is inscribed the famous poem by Chairil Anwar, the pioneer of modern Indonesia poetry, entitled "*Antara Krawang dan Bekasi*" (Between Krawang and Bekasi).

> Kami cuma tulang-tulang berserakan
> Tapi adalah kepunyaanmu
> Kaulah lagi yang tentukan nilai tulang-tulang
> Berserakan
>
> Ataukah jiwa kami melayang untuk Kemerdekaan,
> Kemenangan dan harapan atau tidak untuk apa-apa
> Kami tidak tahu, Kami tidak bisa lagi berkata
> Kaulah sekarang yang berkata.
>
> We are only scattered bones
> But they belong to you
> You are the one who will have to decide
> What our scattered bones are worth

Whether we died for the cause of Freedom
And victory and hope, or whether it was all for nothing
We don't know, we can no longer speak
Now it is left to you to speak.

The main building, the monument, is covered with small white ceramic tiles. It has three floors. On the first floor, which is about 4.5 square metres, are a museum, a library, the main hall, a souvenir shop, a VIP room and a small meeting room. The museum conserves artefacts, or their replicas, related not only to the General Attack but also other important episodes in the Indonesian struggle for Independence. Thus we find here, for instance, the replicas of three Indonesian Navy ships which were used in the war for Independence.

On the second floor are dioramas showing 10 scenes of important episodes in the history of the return of Yogya and 40 reliefs showing scenes of the Indonesian Independence struggle. The ten dioramas show, among other things: the invasion of Yogyakarta by the Dutch, the consolidation of the army, the planning of the attack, the departure of Commander-in-Chief General Soedirman to the countryside to conduct guerilla attacks, the Roem-Royen negotiations, the departure of the Dutch soldiers from Yogya and the celebration of Independence Day on 17 August 1949.

The entire third floor is named *Garbha Graha*, meaning a place for meditation. It is a place to reflect upon the exhibits that the visitors have seen in the museum. Here visitors find an Indonesian flag hanging from a pole in the centre of a round room with a cone-shaped ceiling. The room is about 29 metres in diameter and 14 metres high. On the wall opposite the entrance is inscribed a short poem by Soeharto.[6] On the right and left sides are reliefs of hands, symbolising the diplomatic struggle and the armed struggle for Independence. Visitors are expected to spend a moment to reflect upon the struggle of the Indonesian heroes for the independence of Indonesia.

Keeping the Memory Alive through Rituals

The collective remembrance ceremony of the *SO 1 Maret 1949* is held annually at the plaza of the 1 March Monument in the centre of Yogyakarta. According to newspaper reports, this ceremony started in 1985, perhaps on the initiative of some influential bureaucrat.[7] 1985 was also the year the competition to design the Monument of the Return of Yogya was held and the winner announced (*Kompas*, 16 January 1985).

In 1985, the ceremony was held on the night of 28 February. It was opened by Brigadier-General Sarjono, a veteran who had taken part in the attack of 1949. He read out the inscription on the monument and ignited the torch symbolising the spirit of 1 March and the struggle for Independence. A speech had been prepared for the occasion by President Soeharto, the architect of the attack, which was read by Paku Alam VIII, Vice-Governor of Yogyakarta. Before that, the speech of Sultan Hamengkubuwono IX, Governor of Yogyakarta, was read by GPH Mangkubumi.[8] Thereafter some people went home while others maintained an all-night vigil until dawn. The ritual was said to be both *tirakatan* and *syukuran*. *Tirakatan* means staying awake the whole night until dawn, while *syukuran* means praying to God to express gratitude for His blessings.

In 1986 the commemoration was a little different. This time an event was also held in Jakarta, where many of the ex-participants of the 1 March attack, including its commandant (Soeharto), were living in prosperity (many had since become high-ranking bureaucrats). The ceremony was held in the Mataram Pavilion of Taman Mini Indonesia Indah (Miniature Garden of Beautiful Indonesia), attended by about 100 ex-participants of the attack. Soeharto gave an improvised speech touching on his personal experience as commandant, how he consolidated the army and the guerillas in and around Yogyakarta, the reason behind the attack, and so forth. The commemoration was referred to as both *syukuran* (thanksgiving) and *silaturahmi* (a restrengthening of social relations) (*Kompas*, 22 March 1986). The secretary-generals of the Ministry of Manpower, Sutopo Yuwono, and of the Ministry of Information, Abdul Kadir, veterans of the 1 March attack, were also present.

In 1987, the commemoration was even more organised. It was held simultaneously in Yogyakarta and Jakarta, made possible with the establishment of the Organisation of Battle Area III Yogyakarta, officially founded by the President on 28 October 1986. The commemoration in Jakarta included activities such as a tennis championship, a week of movies about the independence struggle, a blood donation drive and other social and cultural activities. The peak of the commemoration was a night of *syukuran* on 28 February, which was attended by veterans and their families, as well as members of the Organisation of Battle

Area III. In Yogyakarta the commemoration included a re-enactment of the attack staged by student regiments from universities in Yogyakarta, members of the army, veterans, and some 20 members of the second generation of Battle Area III from Jakarta (*Kompas*, 21 February 1987). The night before the re-enactment, a commemoration was held at the plaza of the 1 March Monument, during which Vice-Governor of Yogyakarta, Paku Alam VIII, gave a speech. He emphasised that the *SO 1 Maret* was not just a military action but a combination of military action and diplomacy (*Kompas*, 2 March 1987). The audience also encircled the monument wearing yellow young coconut leaves around their necks. This modestly staged commemoration was meant "to keep alive and to continue the spirit and values of the struggle for Independence" (the Mayor, quoted in *Kompas*, 2 March 1987).

A similar commemoration was held in 1988. It started with a night of vigil (*tirakatan*) at the plaza of the monument. The next morning the re-enactment, led by veteran Brigadier-General Sardjono, was carried out in all areas within the city of Yogyakarta, involving about 1,700 participants (*Kompas*, 2 March 1988).

A very similar commemoration ceremony was held in Yogyakarta for the fortieth anniversary in 1989. The *tirakatan* was held at the plaza, opened by the reading of President Soeharto's speech, written by Paku Alam VIII. The night before, a *sarasehan* — an informal forum for sharing ideas and experiences — was held at Tegalrejo Monument, on the west side of Yogyakarta. The forum was attended by members of the Organisation of Battle Area III and its younger generation (*generasi penerus*). On the same day, ex-members of the student soldiers' Brigade III-17 held a commemoration in one of the villages where Indonesian troops had camped and had been helped by the villagers during the attack. The next morning, the re-enactment of the attack was again staged by ex-freedom fighters and youth. That year, another event relating to the commemoration of the *SO 1 Maret 1949* was held in Yogyakarta. This was the official opening of the Monument of the Return of Yogya. It was a great success for it became a reunion for hundreds of ex-freedom fighters, members of the army and veterans (*Kompas*, 7 July 1989).

In addition to these annual rites of commemoration, the government-produced docudrama *Janur Kuning* (*Yellow Young Coconut Leaves*) also helps to keep the *SO 1 Maret* alive within the social memory of the people. It portrays the history of the General Attack as Soeharto wished it to be remembered.

Up until 1997, the commemoration of the *SO 1 Maret* and the building of the Monument had gone very well. The film, history books and commemorative rituals had passed without much scrutiny by the people, although the controversy over who had actually initiated the attack had started as early as 1985. However, at that time Soeharto had been too strong to challenge. But with the economic crisis of 1997, Soeharto was forced to step down, and rumours, gossip and criticism swirled around him and his family. The political situation deteriorated rapidly, and within a short time Soeharto had become a very unpopular figure. Many of his former close friends and allies tried to avoid anything that might link them to Soeharto or his children.

The controversy over the initiation of the *SO 1 Maret*, which seemed to have been settled since 1989, the year Sultan Hamengkubuwono IX passed away, now reemerged and entered a new phase. Those who had not dared initially to speak about the controversy now joined in. The Sultan's supporters came to include a number of prominent historians and bureaucrats, as well as some veterans (Moedjanto, 1999; Suhartono, 1999; Suwarno, 1999, 2000; *Merdeka*, 1 March 1998; *Kompas*, 9 October 1998; *Kompas*, 1 March 2000). In the meantime, Soeharto's supporters were experiencing considerable difficulty in their efforts to defend the latter's version of events (Haryasudirdja, 2000).

The Controversy

Although Soeharto and Sultan Hamengkubuwono IX had been close allies in the early years of the New Order, they later drifted further and further apart as the Sultan declined to serve a second term as vice-president. However, on the surface, in a typically Javanese way, they publicly maintained good relations until the Sultan passed away in 1989.

Before 1985, not much attention was paid to the *SO 1 Maret* — even today, only a small group of people in Yogyakarta really care about this historical event and its place in Indonesian history — but in 1985 a controversy emerged over who actually initiated the attack. It was the late Purwokusumo, the mayor of Yogyakarta, who raised the question when he was interviewed by a journalist from *Suara Merdeka (Voice of Independence)*, the daily newspaper in Semarang, Central Java

(Atmaksumah, 1999). The question was then taken up by the President's assistant.

People knew that the attack was led by Soeharto, but they did not know much about who had suggested the attack, nor did they think it important to know. In certain circles it was known that Sultan Hamengkubuwono IX was the initiator of the attack, for the Sultan sometimes told his close friends the history of the incident (Atmakusumah, 1999). By his own account, it was he who first had the idea. Thus when Soeharto began to claim that he himself was the initiator, people started to wonder which version of the events was true and who had actually planned the attack. The controversy became interesting not only for historians but also for the public because its outcome would eventually expose 'the liar'. Would it be Soeharto or the Sultan? Honesty, pride and reputation were at stake in this controversy. Nevertheless, the Sultan preferred to keep a low profile. He did not want to have a debate but he knew that Soeharto was lying.

At that time Soeharto's version of the *SO 1 Maret* was circulated widely and came to be accepted as the true version because he was in power. During his presidency the *SO 1 Maret* was immortalised in various forms: the building of the Monument of the Return of Yogya (*Kompas*, 2 September 1986; 26 April 1988; 27 January 1989); the production of the film *Janur Kuning*, and the publication of his autobiography as well as a book on the history of the attack by SESKOAD (Kompas, 7 March 1989).[9] Moreover, it was Soeharto who usually gave the keynote speeches at commemorations of the *SO 1 Maret*, and he would invariably tell the same stories about the history of the event from his perspective.

Soeharto saw the *SO 1 Maret* as part of the overall strategy of the army to drive the Dutch away from Indonesia. The first attack on Yogyakarta (which had been seized by the Dutch on 11 December 1948) took place on 30 December 1948. Soeharto claimed that if this attack had not been carried out, there might not have been any other subsequent attacks and the history of Indonesia would have been different (*Kompas*, 31 December 1994). Like other Indonesian military leaders and people in Yogyakarta at that time, Soeharto had been very disappointed when the Dutch managed to seize the city of Yogyakarta and capture the political leaders Soekarno and Hatta. The people lost their faith in the Indonesian army. What concerned Soeharto at that time was how to regain the people's support and renew their confidence that they could defeat the Dutch, and how to show that the Indonesian army still existed and remained organised (*Kompas*, 1 March 1989). The only way, he thought, was to launch guerilla attacks on various Dutch positions in Yogyakarta.

At that time Soeharto was only a lieutenant-colonel. The Commander-in-Chief was General Soedirman, who was sick and had been taken to the countryside by his soldiers. From his hiding place Soedirman gave commands to his subordinates, one of whom was Soeharto, on how to launch the attacks. For one week Soeharto consolidated the army in Yogyakarta, establishing four war fronts (north, south, east and west) and organising the army on each front. On 30 December 1948 the first attack was launched to show that the Indonesian army was still alive and active. This was followed by other guerilla attacks on the nights of 9 and 16 January 1949, and another on the night of 4 February.

In his book, *Soeharto: Pikiran, Ucapan dan Tindakan* (*Soeharto: My Thoughts, Words and Deeds*) (1991), Soeharto said that one day while listening to the radio with Purwadi, a liaison officer, he learned about the debate that was to take place in the United Nations about the Dutch position in Indonesia. Soeharto also learned that the Dutch had told the world about the success of their *politieele actie* (police action). They had succeeded in occupying Yogyakarta, the capital city of Indonesia. It was also said that the Indonesian National Army (TNI) no longer existed, and that the extremists — they meant the guerillas — were disorganised. Soeharto was furious. He had led four night attacks on Yogyakarta, but they seemed to have had little influence on the Dutch position in Indonesia and how the world saw it. The night attacks had gone unreported. Thus he concluded that the strategy would have to be changed.

He then planned an all-out daylight attack on Yogyakarta. On the morning of 1 March 1949, when the siren was sounded at six in the morning to mark the end of the curfew, the Indonesian army and freedom fighters attacked the city from four directions. For six hours Yogyakarta was occupied by Indonesian freedom fighters. Then they had to return to the countryside as more Dutch soldiers came from Magelang to recapture the city. This is a rough version of Soeharto's account of *SO 1 Maret 1949*.

The Sultan did not have much to say about the attack, for as a ruler of the Mataram Kingdom he did not participate in it himself.

But at that time he was also the Minister of Defence and Security of the Republic of Indonesia, and he had his own story about the idea for a general attack, and how the attack might be launched on the city and its timing. It was said that when the Sultan met his close friends, he did not hesitate to tell them his own account of the *SO 1 Maret*, but when asked to tell the story openly to the public, as a counter to Soeharto's version, he refused. He tried to avoid arousing any conflict on the subject (Atmakusumah, 1999).

Long before the controversy was taken up by the mass media, he told the editor of his book *Takhta Untuk Rakyat* (*Ruling for the People*) (1982) about the situation in Yogyakarta before the attack took place. He said that social conditions in Yogyakarta at that time were uncertain and the people's morale was low. He sensed this and was worried that if things were to continue in this way, the situation might deteriorate and the people's support for the government of the Republic of Indonesia would weaken. He decided that a shock therapy was needed to arouse the people and awaken their fighting spirit. He pondered over the best way to provide such a shock therapy.

When he learned from the radio that the problem of Indonesia and the Dutch would be discussed at the United Nations at the end of February, his concern was how he could send news to the world that the Republic of Indonesia still existed, and that the Dutch did not really control the situation in Indonesia as they had boasted. An idea came to him but time was running out as it was already mid-February. So he sent a messenger to Commander-in-Chief Soedirman in his hiding place, to ask for his permission and agreement to carry out his plan. General Soedirman gave his permission and suggested that the Sultan contact Lieutenant-Colonel Soeharto, the army commandant of the Yogyakarta area.

The Sultan managed to send a message to Soeharto asking him to come to the palace to meet him late at night. This secret meeting took place on 13 February in the house of GBPH Prabuningrat, his younger brother, in the complex of his palace.[10] At this meeting where no-one else was present, he sought Soeharto's agreement to prepare a general attack on the city within two weeks. That was the only meeting between the Sultan and Soeharto with regard to the plan. Thereafter contacts were made through messengers (*Kompas*, 2 March 1997; 1 March 1999).

Herein lies the controversy over who was the originator of the plan. According to the Sultan, it was his idea to launch a sudden attack on Yogyakarta, but Soeharto claimed otherwise. The debate is pointless since there was no other person present at the crucial meeting who could corroborate either party's account and put an end to the controversy. The only witnesses were Prabuningrat (the Sultan's brother), an *abdi dalem* (palace guard) and an assistant of Soeharto at that time, Marsoedi, who were present when Soeharto was brought in to meet the Sultan but who were not privy to the discussion (*Kompas*, 2 March 1997). What transpired at the meeting remains a secret, and Soeharto never disclosed anything to anyone. From whom came the idea of launching a general attack on the city? No-one knew, except Sultan Hamengkubuwono IX and Soeharto.

Indeed Soeharto never even mentioned this meeting. This made some people who knew about the meeting surprised, and others furious. It also led them to conclude that Soeharto was trying to give the impression that the attack was his own initiative. The Sultan's younger brother, Prabuningrat, and Marsoedi, Soeharto's assistant, were particularly upset for Soeharto's version had deleted and changed some important parts of the history of the event. They could not understand how Soeharto could have so easily forgotten such an important meeting.

Not once in his improvised speeches at events commemorating the *SO 1 Maret* did Soeharto ever mention his meeting with the Sultan in the palace, emphasising instead the political significance of the attack and his own role in its organisation (*Kompas*, 2 March 1986; 1 March 1989; 31 April 1994; 20 March 1995). The story of the attack became his personal story, which no-one dared to challenge. The story of *SO 1 Maret* became a means for his own self-glorification. Soeharto was undeniably the 'leading man' of the battle — even the Commander-in-Chief, General Soedirman, accepted this (*Kompas*, 9 March 2000) — but Soeharto downplayed the role of others who had also made significant contributions to the success of the 1 March attack, specifically Sultan Hamengkubuwono IX.

While some people had reservations about Soeharto's story, many others who did not know much about the controversy accepted his version of the events. Some historians felt this was dangerous. Soeharto's version concealed certain important historical facts, and this could have a negative impact on the teaching of history, and indeed on the standing of history as a scientific enterprise (*Kompas*, 9 October 1998).

Who Cared about the Controversy?

It was historians and those interested in history who really paid serious attention to this controversy (*Kompas*, 9 October 1998; 24 June 1999). Historians are expected to settle such disputes about the past but unfortunately, historians are not gods. In this case they needed more informants in order to get to the bottom of the story, but there were none except for Soeharto's former assistant, Marsoedi. Some historians were of the opinion that if the question were not resolved, people might grow skeptical about the role of historians in general (*Kompas*, 9 October 1998). If historians could not settle the matter 'scientifically', they feared, then history as a 'scientific endeavour' would be seen as having nothing significant to contribute to society. Such skeptical views on the role of history and historians might endanger the future of the discipline, they felt.

Aside from historians, there was little real concern with the controversy. Reactions could be divided into three categories. First, there were those who thought that the issue was unimportant since it did not affect their daily life. Many Indonesians did not even know that a controversy existed. For them the issue was really a local one (that is, confined to Yogya) and a contest between two parties — Soeharto's circle and those who supported the Sultan's story. The second group comprised those who were mildly interested in the controversy for the ramifications it had for Indonesian history. They agreed that the writing of Indonesian history should be based on empirical facts or what really happened in the past. Many of those who fall into this category are educated people, veterans of the attack, or those with an interest in Indonesian history. They followed the controversy and were curious about its results but did not join in the debate. The third group comprised a small handful of people who were really involved in the controversy. They were divided into two camps: the group that defended Soeharto's version, mostly military men and veterans, and the opposing side who believed in the Sultan's version. The two parties agreed that the leader of the attack was Soeharto, but there was disagreement on the initiator.

On the Sultan's side were some prominent Indonesian historians, most of whom were civilians (Suwarno, 1999, 2000; Moedjanto, 1999; Suhartono, 2000). Their interest was more in revealing 'the truth of the matter'. While they accepted the fact that Soeharto was the leader and conductor of the attack, they questioned why Soeharto did not say that he had met the Sultan before the general attack, claiming instead that he only met him after? Did he not remember that his assistant Marsoedi and the Sultan's younger brother had helped him to prepare to meet the Sultan? How could he have forgotten such an important moment, yet recall in great detail how he prepared for the attack? Did he not consider the meeting important? Why should he hide those facts? Why has he not mentioned this meeting in his numerous accounts of the event in public? These questions were never put to Soeharto, either directly or indirectly, so they remain unanswered. Thus we can see that although the controversy seemed to be about who had initiated the attack, it had shifted to why Soeharto had kept silent about his meeting with the Sultan.

For those who supported the Sultan's story, his version seemed more plausible, since the Sultan was then the Minister of Defence and Security of the Republic of Indonesia, while Soeharto was only a lieutenant-colonel. It would more make sense if Soeharto had been the executor of the Sultan's idea in the field, for the Sultan's position did not allow him to be the executor. If this interpretation is accepted, the emergence of Soeharto's version can be understood from two perspectives. First, it is unlikely that Soeharto had really forgotten about this meeting. How could he forget it, even the fact that he had to change his clothes before meeting the Sultan, while he could recount in great detail his strategy to launch the attack? His assistant still remembered it vividly. We may conclude that Soeharto concealed that important part of *SO 1 Maret*'s history. Why should he hide it? We can infer that Soeharto wanted to be remembered as the person who had launched the idea of the attack, and not only as the executor of the Sultan's order or idea. The fact that he was the architect of the attack did not seem to satisfy him. If he could be remembered as both the initiator and the architect, and the attack recalled as a political success, then Indonesians might conclude that he had played a very important role in the process of defeating the Dutch politically because, without that attack, there would not have been any significant change in the relations between the Netherlands and Indonesia. Thanks to the attack, the bargaining position of Indonesia's representative in their negotiations with the Dutch was strengthened. The fact that the Indonesian military could launch such an attack in daylight, and had managed to seize the city of Yogya for several hours, was proof that the Indonesian government and military were still a force to be reckoned with.

From a military point of view, however, Soeharto may have downplayed the meeting because he judged it unimportant. Soeharto and the Sultan only met once, and their meeting lasted for only a few hours. There was no information on what the Sultan and Soeharto had discussed. As it did not have a bearing on military strategy, Soeharto might have felt that this meeting was forgettable. If that is the case, I would agree with Moedjanto (1999), a historian at Sanata Dharma University, that accounts of the war for Indonesian Independence have been much too centred on the military. Such an interpretation gives the impression that the Indonesian military was chiefly responsible for freeing the country, while in fact it was the civilians who had played a more important role. Without the support of the people, the military would not have succeeded in carrying out their plans.

The End of the Controversy?

Today historians and some influential intellectuals in Indonesia are of the opinion that Soeharto lied, and that he has concealed some important episodes of the history of *SO 1 Maret*. Their main concern is no longer who initiated the attack but why Soeharto did not tell the public that he had met the Sultan beforehand? Soeharto never answered this question; indeed we do not know if he was ever asked. However, had he affirmed that he did meet the Sultan, this would certainly have weakened his claim that he was the initiatior of the attack. This seems to be the interpretation favoured by some Indonesian historians.

In 1999 historians began to challenge Soeharto's version of the history of the *SO 1 Maret (Kompas*, 1 January 1999). A seminar on this topic was held in Yogyakarta and on the morning of 28 February 2000, an interactive dialogue was aired by the Radio of the Republic of Indonesia Studio II. Three historians were involved in the dialogue, the main conclusion of which was that the Sultan, and not Soeharto, was the initiator of the *SO 1 Maret*. Criticism was also levelled at the army, which was judged to have been insufficiently objective in writing about this controversial episode (*Kompas*, 1 March 2000).

The army's version can be found in the book published by SESKOAD. The book mentions that both Sultan Hamengkubuwono IX and Soeharto had listened to the radio, from which they learned the news about the debate that was to be held in the United Nations on the relations between Indonesia and the Netherlands. This gave both the Sultan and Soeharto the idea to launch the general attack. However, it skirted the question of who precisely came up with the idea. Thus the military's version was a compromise designed to put an end to the controversy, but as Anhar Gonggong, historian and bureaucrat in the Ministry of Culture and Education (now Ministry of National Education) charged, finding a compromise should not have been the aim (*Kompas*, 1 March 2000).

In the meantime, the new government seemed to have become aware of the dispute over the *SO 1 Maret* from the newspapers and felt the need to resolve it. Thus it was decided that the government would re-open the discussion on some controversial episodes in Indonesian history and would try to rewrite them so that they would look "more objective" and not as "politicized" as the versions under the New Order. The State Secretary said that the government would "straighten" some episodes in Indonesian history, which had been "twisted" by Soeharto's regime (*Kompas*, 24 June 1999; 1 March 2000). Concerning the 1 March attack, the government had obtained new documents that strongly support the Sultan's version. The head of the National Archives, Mukhlis Paeni, declared during a press conference that the initiator of the 1 March attack was Sultan Hamengkubuwono IX, and not Soeharto. His statement was based on a recorded interview conducted by the BBC with the Sultan when, as Vice-President, he had visited England in 1984 (Direktorat Sejarah, 1999; *Kompas*, 1 March 2000; 10 April 2000). The new government's version of some contentious episodes in Indonesian history was published in 2000 in the form of a National History Supplement (*Suplemen Sejarah Nasional*).[11]

Conclusion

I have tried to show in this chapter how some Indonesians attempted to construct their social memory of an important episode in Indonesian history, the *SO 1 Maret 1949*. The development of its commemoration was in some way related to those who were in power at the time. The *SO 1 Maret* was never considered important while Soekarno was in power. Under Soekarno's regime, the date worth commemorating was 1 June, the birth of Pancasila or the Five Principles of the State.

When Soeharto took power the commemoration of the birth of Pancasila ceased. There were even efforts to write a new history, in which Soekarno would no longer appear as the creator of Pancasila. The New Order emphasised instead 1 October, the date Soeharto and his army took control of the situation, then wrested power from Soekarno in a systematic way. With the stabilisation of the economic and political situation, Soeharto became a more popular president and desired to make himself more and more powerful. Some of his close aides nominated him as *Bapak Pembangunan* (Father of Development). In 1985, at the peak of his power, he issued his own version of the *SO 1 Maret*, which as we have seen was questionable to some historians and many people in Yogyakarta. However, they remained silent about Soeharto's account, neither accepting it nor openly denying it. The Sultan himself did not challenge Soeharto's version and did his best to avoid an open controversy. He allowed Soeharto to tell his version of events to the people of Indonesia unchallenged.

Today the Indonesian political map has changed significantly. Once Soeharto was no longer in power, the threat for those who dared to challenge him quickly diminished. Thus it was their moment to put forward different versions of some controversial episodes in Indonesian history. Social memories about the *SO 1 Maret* may yet change under the new political situation — even after this chapter was written, I received a manuscript of yet another account of the event from Batara Hutagalung (unpublished).

What is interesting about the controversy is that the government, and almost everyone who knew and cared about it, seem to have paid attention only to written versions of the episode. No-one has paid any attention — as far as I know — to how it has been represented in other media, such as the dioramas within the Monument of the Return of Yogya or the old film. No-one has questioned if a new version ought to be presented on film or video. Indeed if a new version is not spread and socialised as systematically as the old one, it might not be possible to revise the social memory of the people on this contentious episode in Indonesian history.

Over the past decade, the effort to spread a new version of the history of *SO 1 Maret* continued vigorously for some time (*Kompas*, 10 April 2000), before gradually losing impetus, though space does not permit me to write at length of these developments. Not long after the initial debate, there was a strong will in some circles to make changes to the existing historical narrative about the *SO 1 Maret*. The new government gave its support to this initiative, and seminars were held at which various suggestions for a revised account were put forward. However, further research would be needed in order to know how successfully any new version has since been disseminated to the public. Some other efforts to revise school textbooks, particularly with regard to the narrative of the events of 1965–66, have been stymied by the hostile reactions from those who feel threatened by such changes. The rewriting of Indonesian history thus promises to be a slow and continuing process.

From 1999, some significant changes were introduced to the annual ritual of commemoration, but this was discontinued in subsequent years. Shortly after Soeharto's fall, a 'counter-monument' was built inside the Yogya Kraton, on the western side, not far from the entrance to the Kraton courtyard, to commemorate the Sultan's contribution to the event. In Javanese, such a monument is called *tetenger* ('a sign'). A new ritual was performed at its inauguration, but it never became established as an annual public ritual, as some would have wished. The attempt to create an entirely new ritual was unsuccessful, due partly to a lack of commitment from both central and local governments, as well as from those who had particular interests in the 'truth' of the event. The effort was hampered by a lack of funds, the absence of any obvious concrete benefit to be gained from conducting such a ritual, and the declining number of surviving veterans who had been personally involved in the events. Since Reformasi, Indonesia has seen several changes of government, and in the context of continuing rapid social and political transformation, such a ritual quickly loses its national relevance. These developments at least tell us something about the views and attitudes of ordinary Indonesians towards a piece of their national history, whose relevance to their daily lives may not be obvious to them. But to Indonesian historians concerned for the integrity of the nation's memory, and of their own discipline, it is hardly trivial. In the aftermath of Soeharto's fall, they committed themselves to the task of *meluruskan sejarah* or 'straightening history', a history whose narrative had in more than one place been 'bent' by a regime which had no qualms about using history as a means to legitimise its own hold on power. In contesting that official narrative, what was at stake was not just a concern for accuracy, or the duty of historians to discover as much as possible 'what really happened', but also a deeper moral principle.

Notes

1. I am greatly indebted to Roxana Waterson for reading and editing my draft, polishing my English and making valuable suggestions. I would also like to thank Prof. Suhartono and Prof. Kiichi Fujiwara for lending me articles and papers related to this topic; and Destha T Raharjana for her secretarial assistance.
2. This was the badge worn by Indonesian soldiers and guerillas during the attack, so that people in Yogyakarta could distinguish them from the Dutch soldiers and thus give them support.
3. Syafruddin Prawiranegara was at that time the Minister for Foreign Affairs, as well as acting Prime Minister and President of the Emergency Government (*Pemerintah Darurat*) of the Republic of Indonesia based in Padang, Sumatra. After the Dutch occupied Yogya, President Soekarno and his Cabinet members were arrested and sent into exile (1948–49). When the Dutch withdrew from Yogya, Soekarno, Hatta and Syafruddin were able to return.
4. This description is based on my own observations as well as the description given by Sri Utami *et al.* (2000) in their museum guidebook.
5. The words are intended to convey a mystical meaning: the world, or cosmos, formerly closed to the self, by means of the gates, becomes opened so that the self can enter.
6. The text of the poem is as follows:

   Rakyat dan ABRI selalu manunggal
   Perjuangan dan Cita-cita pantang gagal
   Negara Pancasila tetap jaya dan kekal
   Berkat Ridho Tuhan Yang Maha Tunggal.

   The people and the Army will always stand united
   Their struggle and ideals must never fail
   The nation of Pancasila will be eternally victorious
   By the blessing of the One Almighty God.

   One may detect a Javanese flavour in the use of words like *manunggal*, as well as a certain militarist tone.
7. See References for a full list of newspaper reports consulted.
8. GPH stands for *Gusti Pangeran Haryo*, the title of one of the officials within the Yogya Kraton.
9. SESKOAD: Sekolah Staff Komando Angkatan Darat (Army Staff College).
10. GBPH: *Gusti Bendara Pangeran Haryo*, the title held by the Sultan's brother.
11. See also Anon. (2000).

References

Anon. (2000). *Peresmian Tetenger Pelurusan SO 1 Maret 1949.* Yogyakarta (publisher unknown).

Atmakusumah (1999). "Dua Versi Serangan Umum: Dari Hamengku Buwono IX dan Soeharto." *Kompas*, 1 March 1999, p. 4.

Benfell, S. (1999). "A Past Worth Forgetting: Politics and Institutionalization of War Memories in Japan". Paper for the Annual Meeting of the American Political Science Association, 2–5 September, 1999.

Dinas Sosial (1993). *Tempat-Tempat Bersejarah Perjuangan Bangsa di Propinsi Daerah Istimewa Yogyakarta*. Yogyakarta: Pemda DIY.

Direktorat Sejarah dan Nilai Tradisional dan MSI (1999). *Bahan Pengajaran Sejarah*. Jakarta: Departemen Pendidikan Nasional.

Fentress, J. and C.Wickham (1992). *Social Memory*. Oxford: Blackwell.

Fussell, P. (1975). *The Great War and Modern Memory*. Oxford: Oxford University Press.

Halbwachs, M. (1950 [1925]). *The Collective Memory*. With an introduction by Mary Douglas. New York: Harper-Colophon Books.

Hamengkubuwono IX (1982). *Takhta Untuk Rakyat*. Yogyakarta: Gramedia.

Haryasudirdja, P.K. (1997). *Perang Kemerdekaan di Yogyakarta dan Sekitarnya*. Yogyakarta: Balai Kajian Sejarah dan Nilai Tradisional.

______ (2000). *Peranan Wehrkreise III Pada Masa Perang Kemerdekaan Ke-Dua (1948–1949) di Daerah Istimewa Yogyakarta dan Sekitarnya*. Yogyakarta: Balai Kajian Sejarah dan Nilai Tradisional.

Hutagalung, B. "Fakta Baru Mengenai Serangan Umum 1 Maret 1949 Atas Yogyakarta". Unpublished paper.

Hutton, P.H. (1993). *History as an Art of Memory*. Hanover: University Press of New England.

Moedjanto, G. (1999). "Sekitar Serangan Umum 1 Maret 1949". Conference paper, Universitas Janabadra, Yogyakarta.

Priosupadmo, S. (1988). "Peristiwa 29 Juni 1949". *Kompas*, 5 June 1988, p. 2.

Soeharto (1991). *Soeharto: Pikiran, Ucapan and Tindakan* [Soeharto: My Thoughts, Words and Deeds, An Autobiography]. Jakarta: Citra Lamtoro Gung Persada.

Sri Utami, Benny Sugito and Yudi Pranowo (1999). *Buku Petunjuk Koleksi Monumen Yogya Kembali*. Yogyakarta: Badan Pengelola Monumen Yogya Kembali.

Suhartono (1999). "Serangan Umum 1 Maret 1949: Antara Negarawan dan Militer". Conference paper, Universitas Janabadra, Yogyakarta.

Suwarno, P.J. (1999). "Sejarah Serangan Umum 1 Maret 1949". *Kompas*, 2 March 1999, p. 4.

______ (2000). *Prakarsa dan Pelaksana Serangan Umum 1 Maret 1949*. Yogyakarta: Balai Kajian Sejarah dan Nilai Tradisional.

Winter, J. and E. Sivan (1999). "Setting the Framework," in J. Winter and E. Sivan (eds), *War and Remembrance in the Twentieth Century*. Cambridge: Cambridge University Press, pp. 6–39.

Newspaper Articles

Angkatan Bersenjata, 2 March 1992. "Tajuk Rencana: Serangan Umum 1 Maret 1949".

Kompas, 16 January 1985. "Kelompok Janur Kuning Menangkan Rancangan Monumen "Yogya Kembali".

———, 1 February 1985. "Redaksi Yth.: Monumen Yogya Kembali".

———, 30 June 1985. "Batu Pertama Monumen Yogya Diletakkan Hamengku Buwono IX".

———, 2 March 1986. "Serangan Umum 1 Maret 1949: Peristiwa Heroik yang Tidak Berdiri Sendiri".

———, 13 May 1986. "Monumen "Yogya Kembali" Belum Menentu".

———, 8 August 1986. "Penjualan Kaset Lagu untuk Dana Monumen Yogya Kembali".

———, 2 September 1986. "Bertahap, Pembangunan Monumen Yogya Kembali".

———, 29 October 1986. "Yayasan SU 1 Maret 1949 Disahkan".

———, 20 December 1986. "Pembangunan Monumen "Yogya Kembali" Dimulai".

———, 21 February 1987. "Rangkaian Acara Memperingati Serangan Umum Yogyakarta".

———, 28 February 1987. "Mengenang SO 1 Maret: Desa Bibis Mencatat Partisipasi Rakyat".

———, 2 March 1987. "Paku Alam VIII: SO 1 Maret Bukan Cuma Perjuangan Militer".

———, 27 June 1987. "Peringatan Yogya Kembali".

———, 2 March 1988. "Peringatan SO 1 Maret".

———, 25 April 1988. "Monumen Yogya Kembali: Jangan Paksakan Pembangunannya".

———, 26 April 1988. "Monumen Yogya Kembali Terus Dikerjakan".

———, 27 January 1989. "Monumen Yogya Kembali Diresmikan Tahun Ini", p. 6.

———, 1 March 1989. "Presiden Soeharto: Perjuangan Masa Lalu Bukan Keberhasilan Tanpa Kekurangan", p. 12.

———, 7 March 1989. "Tim Seskoad Selesaikan Buku "Serangan Umum 1 Maret 1949", p. 1.

———, 21 June 1989. "Sulit Mencari Benda Asli untuk Monumen Yogya Kembali", p. 11.

———, 5 July 1989. "Monumen Yogya Kembali Perkaya Yogyakarta sebagai Kota Budaya", p. 6.

———, 6 July 1989. "Monumen Yogya Kembali Butuh Rp.300 Juta/Tahun", p. 6.

———, 7 July 1989. "Presiden Heningkan Cipta di Monumen Yogya Kembali", p. 1.

______, 20 December 1989. "Serangan Umum 1 Maret Punya Hasil Positif", p. 12.

______, 15 June 1991. "Daerah Sekilas", p. 14.

______, 18 October 1992. "Tikus Ancam Benda Bersejarah di Monumen Yogya Kembali", p. 13.

______, 5 December 1992. "Garbha Graha Monumen Yogya Kembali Berubah Fungsi", p. 14.

______, 23 February 1993. "Serangan Oemoem 1 Maret, Pengakuan Politik Kedaulatan RI", p. 12.

______, 26 July 1993. "Daerah Sekilas", p. 13.

______, 3 March 1994. "Serangan Umum 1 Maret 1949 Diperingati di Yogyakarta", p. 17.

______, 10 October 1994. "Sumitro Soal Serangan Umum 1 Maret '49", p. 13.

______, 31 December 1994. "Presiden Soeharto Mengenai Serangan Umum 1 Maret: Pernah Terjadi Salah Paham Dengan Hamengkubuwono IX".

______, 2 March 1995. "Presiden Soeharto: Negara Kebangsaan Yang Rapuh Ikatannya Selalu Tertinggal Dalam Persaingan", p. 18.

______, 19 March 1995. "Pak Harto: Nekat, Tapi Penuh Perhitungan...", p. 1.

______, 20 March 1995. "Serangan 1 Maret Dalam Kesaksian Letkol Soeharto", p. 1.

______, 24 June 1995. "Presiden Akan Canangkan Hari Keluarga Nasional", p. 3.

______, 29 June 1995. "Harganas Memilih Monumen Yogya Kembali", p. 14.

______, 2 March 1997. "Serangan Oemoem 1 Maret: Bagian Dari Romantika Sejarah Bangsa", p. 1.

______, 9 October 1998. "Pendidikan Sejarah Tidak Boleh Selewengkan dan Gelapkan Fakta", p. 10.

______, 1 March 1999. "Serangan Oemoem 1 Maret 1949: Perseteruan Pemaknaan Sejarah Itu", p. 1.

______, 2 March 1999. "Peringatan SU 1 Maret 1999 Jadi Ajang Protes Perlunya Pelurusan Sejarah", p. 6.

______, 24 June 1999. "Orde Baru Lakukan Banyak Rekayasa Penulisan Sejarah", p. 9.

______, 1 March 2000. "Soeharto Bukan Penggagas Serangan Oemoem 1 Maret 1949", p. 19.

______, 9 March 2000. "A.H.Nasution: Banyak Tuntutan Masyarakat Tidak Tunjukkan Esensi Reformasi", p. 6.

______, 11 March 2000. "Menurut Dokumen BBC London: Hamengkubuwono IX Penggagas Serangan Oemoem", p. 9.

______, 10 April 2000. "Belum Semua Guru Dapat Suplemen Sejarah", p. 9.

______, 13 April 2000. "Suplemen Pelajaran Sejarah: Tarik Ulur Kebenaran dan Kekuasaan", p. 7.

Merdeka, 29 February 1992. "Serangan Umum 1 Maret Bukan Peristiwa Berdiri Sendiri".

———, 1 March 1998. "Menggugat Inspirator Serangan 1 Maret: Itu Inisiatif Sultan IX, Bukan Soeharto".

Pelita, 29 February 1992. "Semangat Pelaku SU 1 Maret Tak Pernah Luntur".

Republika, 30 September 1998. "Sultan Hamengkubuwono IX Pernah Luruskan SO 1 Maret 1949".

Suara Karya, 1 March 1992. "Mengenang Serangan Oemoem 1 Maret 1949 di Yogyakarta".

PART III

Traumatic Memories: Interpenetrations of Collective and Personal Experience

CHAPTER 7

War and Violence, History and Memory: The Philippine Experience of the Second World War

Ricardo T. José

The subject of the Second World War and the Japanese Occupation still evokes intense emotions in the Philippines today, over 60 years after the events. Issues such as collaboration with the Japanese, Japanese war responsibility, America's failure to defend the Philippines and the apparently excessive use of force in the liberation campaigns, the truthfulness of war heroics, non-payment of Philippine claims for rehabilitation, or reparations for damage and loss of life, and non-recognition of Filipino veterans who fought side by side with US soldiers, all tend to make war memories a sensitive topic. In many cases, polemics and stereotypes dominate in spite of factual evidence.

Stormy up to now, the controversy has been made even more dramatic with the bringing into the open of previously suppressed accounts of wartime experiences (such as of the Comfort Women and of forced labour). The government, on the other hand, has tended to belittle or even ignore the more sensitive issues, while selecting specific anniversaries for celebration. Few historians and research institutes have given serious thought or attention to the war and the Japanese Occupation, choosing to focus instead on the 1896 and 1898 revolutions and the Philippine-American war. But the Second World War and the Japanese Occupation are ripe with lessons, stories and experiences that should be better understood, for the past to be viewed in full perspective.

An Ambiguous Legacy

Perspective, however, is not easily achieved. Wars, by their nature, do not lend themselves to dispassionate analysis and examination, except perhaps in the works of military historians. The pain, suffering and sense of loss are too moving to peruse with a cold eye. Apart from the destruction and dislocation caused by war, the legacy of war can best be described as an ambiguous legacy, to borrow a phrase used by David Joel Steinberg (1972).

The renowned historian Harry Benda, for example, has called the war in Asia a watershed in Asian history. This was accepted for many years, especially given the difference between the relatively more stable and orderly prewar world, and the chaos of the postwar one. Later studies, however, tended to show that, particularly in the Philippines, there were no long-term transformations, especially in the social and political fields. On the contrary, there was a remarkable continuity in pre- and postwar Philippine society, especially in the disparity between the landed elites and the oppressed peasants; and between political rivals and economic leaders, both local and regional (Benda, 1972; Silverstein, 1966; McCoy, 1980; Lacar, 1984).

What then are the legacies of the war? War memories seem to be determined more by one's present perceptions of the war, rather than by delving into past facts. Today, when one speaks of the war and the Japanese Occupation of the Philippines, subjects likely to crop up are the Comfort Women, reparations from Japan, veterans' benefits from the United States and the injustice Filipino veterans suffered under the Americans.

This is very different from the situation 60 years ago. Then the pain was still keenly felt and books and articles were written about the atrocities that took place, often with a focus on the courage and patriotism of Filipinos. One book entitled *The Crucible* demonstrates how the war and the Japanese Occupation were a test of the Filipino people, one which they passed with flying colours. The Americans, especially General MacArthur, were seen as heroes and liberators, and the Japanese were the 'bad guys'.

In the late 1940s through to the 1960s, many works with political overtones were published, usually timed to appear before or during local or national elections. Attacks became vicious, sometimes refuted by equally vicious counter-attacks. Meanwhile, studies, articles and books on the guerrilla movement also surfaced regularly to dramatize Filipino courage and love of freedom; a few, in fact, were used to launch the political campaigns of some candidates. The guerrilla resistance movement was seen in conjunction with the anti-Spanish revolts and the anti-American struggle at the turn of the nineteenth–twentieth century, and so served to feed nationalistic emotions. Such studies conveniently assumed that any collaboration with the Japanese had been an exception or aberration, and that the majority of Filipinos chose to resist and fight the Japanese.

But as time wore on and the Cold War deepened, disappointment with the United States set in, and the simplicity of the immediate postwar analysis came under fire. As the Americans came to be perceived as supporters of the unpopular Marcos government, writings on American neo-imperialism came into vogue, sparking off a reinterpretation of the war years. The Americans were seen less as the 'good guys' and as being more concerned with their own interests than in the ideals of democracy and freedom, which were battle cries during the war.[1]

Instead, scholars and intellectuals began to consider the war as one between the United States and Japan, into which the Philippines had been plunged simply because it was a US colony in 1941. The Americans were no longer seen as allies, whose blood flowed with Filipino blood in a joint war, but came to be judged as selfish imperialists, not too different from those of imperial Japan. The word 'liberation' was enclosed in quotation marks, if used at all, in these revisionist works (Constantino and Constantino, 1978).

Who then were the real heroes? The guerrillas who fought the Japanese? But which guerrillas — those who remained loyal to the Philippine Commonwealth government in exile and the United States, or those who, like the left-leaning Hukbalahaps, had their own social agenda for the postwar Philippines? Or were the politicians who served as a buffer between the Japanese and the people more patriotic? What about the people who chose to wait for the war to end, simply making ends meet for the duration? Or those who chose to side with the Japanese, truly believing in Japan's promise of redemption and an Asian world? These questions still spark lively debate in academic conferences in the Philippines and elsewhere, as well as in classrooms, but definite answers continue to elude.

What was the war fought for? Immediately after the war, the Four Freedoms and the Atlantic Charter were virtually memorized by Filipino students and veterans as an explanation of the war. The Four Freedoms — Freedom to Worship, Freedom of Speech and Press, Freedom from Want, Freedom from Fear — had been one of the war's battle cries, appearing in numerous pro-American and pro-guerrilla publications. The Atlantic Charter guaranteed a peaceful, democratic world based on self-determination, freedom of trade and movement, and international cooperation — all of which were grand ideals that motivated the guerrilla resistance movement and promised a better postwar world.

In other Asian countries, the war was not as clear-cut a historical phenomenon as in the Philippines. In Indonesia and Vietnam, for example, the Japanese Occupation formed part of the struggle for independence, and the end of one war was simply the start of another, the war for independence. In Japan, the war takes on different meanings depending on the writers or the groups. Those on the left use it to criticize militarism and imperialism; those on the right argue that Japan fought a holy war, one to liberate Asia, and one that was forced on Japan by the United States and Britain. Both groups, however, are agreed on commemorating Hiroshima and the end of the war, in which context the Japanese see themselves as victims rather than aggressors of the war.

Commemorations

The Philippines, like many other countries, has had a tradition of commemorating key events, many of which relate to the Second World War. Every year on 9 April, veterans flock to Mount Samat in Bataan, where heavy fighting took place towards the end of the campaign, and whose capture by the Japanese led to the subsequent surrender of Filipino-American forces in April 1942. At Bataan, Filipinos of all ages and walks of life had fought to protect their country from foreign invaders; of those who had fought in the country's defence, more were to die in the subsequent Bataan Death March and as prisoners-of-war.

The annual commemoration of the Fall of Bataan was originally meant to honour all Filipinos who fought and died in Bataan; a massive cross, under which was an impressive altar, was erected on the occasion of the twenty-fifth anniversary of the fall. As the years went by, however, cynics and skeptics doubted the worth of 'celebrating' a defeat. It was at times played down and at one point, it ceased to become an official holiday. The government has since restored it as a public holiday, commemorating not only the fall of Bataan but also the rest of the

Second World War heroes. The week in which April 9 falls has also become Veterans' Week, when various presentations and programmes are held in addition to the ceremonies on Mount Samat. Japanese who want their young people to know what happened sometimes even re-enact the Death March, which followed the surrender of Bataan.

On a happier note (for Filipinos) are celebrations of their liberation from the Japanese. The American landings at Leyte on 20 October 1944 are reenacted every year, with combined Philippine and American ships, aircraft and soldiers. The highlight of the reenactment is the landing of MacArthur, whose role is played by an American who bears a resemblance to the heroic general. The entry of the American forces into the University of Santo Tomas in Manila, liberating thousands of Allied internees held there by the Japanese, is another annual event. Various towns in the Philippines also celebrate the day the Americans returned and ended the Japanese Occupation. But these commemorations have tended to highlight the spectacle and colour of the events, rather than any true meaning. During the fiftieth anniversary celebrations in 1994, the reenactment of the arrival of the Americans backfired — the person playing MacArthur slipped and fell in the surf off Leyte. US critics saw this as symbolic of American clumsiness in handling foreign affairs; for others it showed how the superpower could be humbled. Consequently the Americans bore the brunt of this humbling accident.

Such commemorations reduced the impact of the war to mere spectacle. Only occasionally did some groups try to make the commemoration more meaningful: Memorare Manila 1945, an association of survivors and relatives of survivors of the Battle of Manila, sponsored a special mass and the playing of Mozart's Requiem for the victims. Over 100,000 civilians died in the one-month battle, but never had the dead been remembered appropriately; always it was the American return that was dramatized. Memorare Manila has also sponsored the establishment of memorials around Manila to remind people of the painful events and the non-combatant lives lost, so many of which have been deliberately forgotten or have never been taught about in schools.

The commemorations have had their political uses: the US and the Philippine armed forces have always cooperated in these reenactments, which serve as a show of force and unity. Yet, stripped of a political use, these events were soon forgotten. The fiftieth anniversary of the start of the war in 1991, for example, was hardly observed; neither was the fiftieth anniversary of Bataan and Corregidor, which was dismissed in the wake of a presidential election. And no one remembered the fiftieth anniversary of the Japanese proclamation of independence of the Philippines either. (As part of its war plans, the Japanese government declared the Philippines independent on 14 October 1943, and set up an ostensibly sovereign government under President Jose P. Laurel.) 14 October has never been commemorated as a special day in the Philippines.

The Philippine government in the mid-1970s and early 1980s attempted to put the pain of the war behind it and launched what was called the Reunion for Peace. Veterans from Japan, the United States, Australia and other countries that had fought in the Philippines during the war were invited for sentimental visits to the old battlefields. The reunion of former warriors made for good press releases, but the tension was present: some Filipinos shook hands with the Japanese veterans but others kept their distance. Some Americans refused to have lunch under the same roof with the Japanese. I was trying to interview as many of them as I could, from all sides. An American veteran asked me why I was trying to interview the Japanese. "To hear their side," I said. His reply: "Oh, the Japanese? They have no side!" The Reunion for Peace program may have paved the way for genuine reconciliation, but beyond the reunions of the veterans, no lasting works were produced for the succeeding generations.

While the reunions of Americans and Filipinos brought back memories and rekindled friendships, the return of the Japanese brought mixed reactions. Some friendships were established, but the Japanese who came to the Philippines had a bigger agenda; many came for the rituals of recovering the bones of the war dead and conducting the requisite religious ceremonies for their repose. The Japanese erected many memorials for their war dead, some simple markers but others more elaborate affairs with Shinto shrines.

Some Filipinos welcomed this move as a more balanced view of the war; a group of Filipinos even organized the Kamikaze Memorial Society in the 1970s to keep alive the memory of the patriotic Japanese Kamikaze pilots. The Kamikaze concept had formally started in the Philippines on the eve of the American return, and the house in which the Japanese admiral first suggested the tactic was located and given a historical marker. The first Kamikaze airfield was also located and a shrine erected. The shrine was buried under *lahar* (mud lava) when

Mount Pinatubo erupted in 1989, but it was reconstructed in 2000 with Japanese assistance.[2]

The active inclusion of Japan in the war commemorations and the establishment of their own markers could not have happened in the 1960s because of the strong anti-Japanese sentiment of the time. From the 1970s onward, however, it was possible not only because of the government's open attitude towards Japan, but also due to the increasing role of Japan in the Philippine economy — a role which the Philippine government could not do without. Thus, despite criticism from other sectors of Philippine society that the Japanese were finally succeeding in establishing the Greater East Asia Co-Prosperity Sphere, the official response was not to offend the Japanese.

As part of the move to open up towards Japan, the government under Ferdinand Marcos — himself a Second World War veteran — undertook a joint project with the Japanese to build a Japanese Memorial Garden in Caliraya, Batangas. This completed the major memorials to the Second World War military dead. The Americans had the Manila American Cemetery and Memorial, approved by the Philippine government in 1948 and completed in 1960, and the Filipinos had the Libingan ng mga Bayani (Heroes' Cemetery). The civilians, however, did not have any comparable cemetery or memorial until those put up by Memorare Manila — and these were private endeavours not supported by the government.

Apart from historical commemorations, friendly visits by returning veterans were perceived from other perspectives. In 1998, Hiroo Onoda, Japan's last Second World War straggler to give up, returned to Lubang Island on a sentimental visit. This visit, his first since his surrender in 1974, was given much publicity and dramatized the fact that the war was over and that the Philippines and Japan were on friendly terms. Local officials of Lubang welcomed the visit because it might bring in tourism and Japanese investment; they admitted to this openly in TV interviews. But there were other reactions — protestors who demanded that he account for the property and lives he destroyed before he surrendered.

Another visit with a political agenda was the visit of General Douglas MacArthur to the Philippines in 1961. MacArthur is reported to have been hesitant to visit the Philippines after his departure in 1946. At the time that he left for Japan as Supreme Commander for the Allied Powers, much of the Philippines was in ruin and the Filipinos were struggling to pick up the pieces. MacArthur was unsure about the reception he would get, but was egged on by the Philippine government (which invited him) and the US government (which provided the means), as both felt it was a good way to restore and strengthen Philippine-American ties. The visit turned out to be a success for the Americans and the Filipinos, bringing back memories of a wartime alliance (James, 1985: 677–8; Manchester, 1978: 696–8).

Hence, visits and commemorations bring back war memories and reinforce images and stereotypes. Historical markers and monuments at Second World War sites do the same. There are big war memorials at Mount Samat in Bataan; in Corregidor, an island fort at the mouth of Manila Bay where the sprawling Pacific War Memorial can be found; in Red Beach, at Tacloban, Leyte, where larger-than-life statues of MacArthur, President Sergio Osmeña and others of the landing party stand; in Kiangan, where General Tomoyuki Yamashita surrendered to the Americans in September 1945; and in Iloilo on the island of Panay, to commemorate the guerrilla resistance movement. Various other towns have war relics (usually Japanese artillery pieces or machine guns) on display in the town plaza, and a list of townsmen who served or who died during the war. Some of these were put up by the local government, others by local veterans' associations. The National Historical Commission of the Philippines, a government body that attempts to preserve historical buildings and sites, has put up several markers on buildings and sites where military camps once existed, or where battles were fought.

Markers are not only put up by Filipinos or the Philippine government, however. Americans have put up their own markers in Bataan and the island fortress of Corregidor, and in places where officers were killed or where battles were fought. Since the 1970s, the Japanese have also put up their monuments and markers, usually to commemorate a particular battle or unit, and sometimes an individual. The Japanese markers are sometimes written entirely in Japanese, although many also have English and Tagalog translations. At least one, showing silent opposition to the Americans, is only in Japanese and Tagalog. The English/Tagalog translation of some of the markers, however, does not correspond to the actual Japanese text. There are instances where the English and Tagalog speak of remembering the dead, whether they be Japanese, Filipino or American; the Japanese text, however, only memorializes the Japanese in Shinto or Buddhist terms.

Associations

Various organizations throughout the Philippines commemorate the war or aspects of it. The most prominent are the veterans' organizations, usually by unit or region; the Veterans' Federation of the Philippines is an umbrella organization which continues to fight for the recognition of unrecognized veterans, and seeks the increase of veterans' benefits. The Federation, as well as the unit or regional associations under it, participates in the various commemorations of the war, and organizes reunions and parties for Christmas and other key dates. Veterans' organizations used to have political clout when many officials in government were veterans themselves, but as the veterans have aged and retired, they have lost much of their power. The national congress, as a sign of respect and recognition, has a veteran as sectoral representative. The government body that takes care of official veterans' affairs, pensions and other benefits is the Philippine Veterans' Affairs Office, which until recently had a reputation for corruption.

As the veterans aged, their children saw fit to continue the tradition — not so much to set the historical record straight, but to keep the camaraderie and serve as a support organization. A few of the veterans were keen on researching and writing their histories, resulting in a number of books, some commissioned by the veterans' organizations.

Apart from the veterans' associations are civilian associations. Memorare Manila 1945 is the only association of civilians who suffered and survived the Battle of Manila; it is dedicated to preserving the memory of that battle and the dead.

There are local historical associations that, while documenting and writing histories of provinces and towns, also cover the war and Japanese Occupation. Of particular note is a local historical association in Tarlac Province that has built memorials in various towns relating to Second World War operations and battles. It is also unique in that it tries to solicit information from all sides — Filipino, American and Japanese. In the 1970s, another local association, the Kamikaze Memorial Society, was established in Pampanga Province as an attempt to go beyond Philippine boundaries and understand the Japanese viewpoint. Nationalist historians, however, criticized it as glorifying Japan rather than the Philippines.

Then there are the cause-oriented associations, which seek redress of grievances or justice. Among these are the groups that campaign for the Comfort Women and another that lobbies for payment of claims by Filipinos forced to work by the Japanese. For both the Comfort Women and the forced labour compensation, one would wonder why it took so long to raise these issues. While rape and killings were addressed during the postwar war crimes trials in Manila, the issue of forced prostitution, as in the case of the Comfort Women, was not investigated. One reason was that many of the women, still traumatized by their experience and made outcasts by their families and friends, were afraid to talk about their experiences. A second reason would be the problem of social disorder in the immediate postwar period in the Philippines: towns and villages where Comfort Women had been held, or mass rape conducted, could not be reached because of the collapse of peace and order. The forced labour issue was not raised during the war crimes trials, and again because of domestic conditions and the immediate necessity of survival, had to be relegated to the background or shelved. Both issues were raised in the late 1980s and the 1990s because conditions had become more open, and Japan had risen to a new position as an economic power. To both the Japanese and Philippine governments, however, these issues are seen more as thorns in their side or aberrant issues; they would prefer to give precedence to friendly relations and the promotion of economic activities. Besides, to both governments, the issue of war reparations had ended with the San Francisco Peace Treaty, signed in 1951, and the Reparations Agreement, ratified in 1956. However, the Reparations Agreement was a purely government-to-government deal and did not address any of the private claims. Because the private claims were not addressed, the cause-oriented groups fight for justice; failing to find support from their respective governments, they have filed class suits in Japan and the United States.

There are groups of Nikkeijin, or Filipinos of Japanese descent, who try to locate parents or relatives in Japan who will support the (mostly) poor Nikkeijin. In the years immediately after the war, almost all Filipinos of Japanese descent were so ashamed of their line that they changed their names or disowned their Japanese blood. With the recovery of Japan and her rise as an economic power, however, these Filipinos began to come out into the open, tell their stories and describe how they were separated from their parents. In addition, from the 1950s until the early 1970s, there were groups seeking the redemption of Japanese Occupation currency (called 'Mickey Mouse money' because it had no value and was not real, just like the famous cartoon character) or payment for losses caused by the Japanese.

All these groups range in political colour from right of centre, through centrist, to those on the left; some of the groups, particularly those seeking redress and reparations, may even be radically left-wing, and use war issues either to embarrass the government, press for modifications of foreign policy, or embarrass Japan. Some work in a Filipino environment, while others have connections with Japanese or American non-governmental organizations. They indicate the extent to which popular memory, and ordinary people's concerns, are likely to be ignored or pushed aside by the official government and military organizations. They thus remain unfinished business — unfinished, but not forgotten, since many of these groups have been tenacious in pressing for settlement of their claims, even in the face of repeated failures.

Mythmaking and Counter-mythmaking

Of the many books, articles and textbooks about the war, interpretations vary as to the importance of the war and the actions of the Japanese. Some still mention the Tanaka Memorial (an alleged Japanese master plan for the conquest of Asia which was later shown to be a hoax), while others actually believe that Japan's war was to liberate Asia from Western colonialism (Yu-Jose, 1995). Others tend to be too impressionistic, with little significant data that is new. But the sources certainly exist, from documentary evidence, photographs to interviewees. A big stumbling block is the inability to read Japanese, and hence gain insights into the Japanese perspective.

There has been no organized oral history project such as Singapore has had, although there have been moves to document war memories on a smaller, local scale. The National Historical Institute made a bold start in 1981, by holding a conference on the guerrilla resistance movement, inviting key guerrilla leaders to share their experiences. This conference was held annually for another two years, but was overtaken by the anti-government mood spurred by the assassination of Benigno S. Aquino in 1983. In 1992, the Cultural Center of the Philippines sponsored a conference and exhibit on culture during the Japanese Occupation. But these initiatives have not been followed by more systematic projects to document war memories.

In writing war history, or in remembering it, many myths have been created, and are believed without question. For example, it is widely believed that the defence of Filipinos and Americans at Bataan and Corregidor disrupted Japan's war timetable and saved Australia from invasion. This is good for building national pride and finding meaning in the defeat in Bataan, but it does not hold up under close historical examination. It is still also a common misconception that the invading Japanese forces outnumbered the Filipino-American forces by at least two to one — which again sounds good as a means to rationalize the defeat in 1941–42, but which is not supported by the facts.

On the other hand, as a result of the anti-American sentiment that arose in the late 1950s and 1960s, it is believed by some that the Americans deliberately destroyed Manila, especially the Spanish portions of the city, in order to eradicate the last vestiges of Spanish culture in the Philippines and replace it with American culture. Again, this does not stand up to close scrutiny.

Other myths which tend to cloud the real impact of the war and its lessons are the result of stories told and retold. One such myth is that the perpetrators of atrocities were mainly Koreans and Taiwanese, and not Japanese. According to this belief, Koreans and Taiwanese were sent to the Philippines in large numbers as Occupation troops. Since the Koreans and the Taiwanese had been mistreated by the Japanese, they vented their frustrations on the Filipinos during the war. This, however, has not been confirmed by further research, which shows, on the contrary, that most of the Japanese Occupation troops were, indeed, Japanese. The Koreans and Taiwanese were basically labour troops, prison guards or members of the Kempeitai (Japan's military police). As labour troops, there was little chance for them to commit atrocities. As prison guards, they did ill-treat prisoners-of-war, but this under the supervision of Japanese officers. As Kempeitai officers or men, they severely punished their prisoners, but again together with Japanese and under Japanese officers.[3]

Another story associated with the war is the legend of Yamashita's gold. According to this tale, General Yamashita, the Tiger of Malaya, brought with him to the Philippines tons of gold and precious stones, which he had looted from Southeast Asia. Since he was unable to ship the loot to Japan, it remained buried in the Philippines. As a result, hordes of treasure hunters have searched for the gold in vain since the end of the war. Whenever I give a lecture on the war and the Japanese Occupation, whether to students or to a public forum, there inevitably arise questions on the Comfort Women and Yamashita's gold — an indication of what issues continue to occupy the popular imagination with regard to the war.

In studying and resolving problems relating to the war, the impediments created by present-day *realpolitik* have to be faced. Japan is the number one aid donor to the Philippines and its second major trading partner. The government has, in the last two decades, tried to play down controversies relating to the war. It has not stood by the Comfort Women in their struggle for recognition and compensation but has supported the holding of an annual Philippine-Japan Festival. The Philippine-Japan Festival had to be altered because of war memories, though: when it was first held, it was designated a "Philippine-Japan Friendship Month" and was held in February. February, however, was the bloodiest month of the war, in which the atrocities of the Battle of Manila in 1945, and various massacres in nearby provinces, had been committed. In response to popular objections and repeated criticism by World War II survivors, it was thus renamed the 'Philippine-Japan Festival', and in 2006, the Japanese Embassy agreed to shift the Festival to July. This was the month in which, 50 years earlier, the Reparations Agreement and the Peace Treaty were formally ratified. This fiftieth anniversary of the 1956 ratification event may thus have provided some useful extra degree of encouragement to the painfully slow, yet continuing, work of reconciliation.

The Need for Joint Research

Landmark events in joint research have helped us work across national boundaries to transcend the limitations of earlier histories written from the perspective of a single country. On the fiftieth anniversary of the start of the war, a conference was organized in Japan along the lines of an earlier conference held in 1969. The 1969 conference had focused on US-Japan relations and Pearl Harbor, and examined the collapse of Japanese-American relations from different sectors. The 1991 conference brought in participants from other countries in Asia, thus broadening the field. On the fiftieth anniversary of the end of the Second World War, joint conferences on the Japanese Occupation of Southeast Asia were sponsored. First, a conference was held in Japan, in Japanese, involving scholars working with the different countries. This was followed by a conference in Singapore on the Japanese Occupation of Southeast Asia in Singapore. Similarities in experiences, as well as regional differences, were discovered. Equally important, there was a realization of the necessity to establish stronger links between Asian scholars through joint research, and not just develop links between country specialists of particular countries.

Only now is joint Japanese-Southeast Asian research on the war developing. The Toyota Foundation has sponsored serious research on Japanese-occupied Southeast Asia. The first study group formed concentrated on Indonesia and included Japanese and Indonesian scholars. Following completion of the Indonesian research forum, Toyota next funded a research group on the Philippines. The Forum for the Survey of Records Concerning the Japanese Occupation of the Philippines was the first concerted attempt at joint research, involving several Japanese scholars and one Filipino. It has already published the results of its work: several volumes on primary, unpublished documents in Japanese; transcripts of interviews; and finally, a volume of serious studies on aspects of the Japanese Occupation. This book has since been translated into English and thus furthers the move towards joint research and a more dispassionate treatment of the war years (Ikehata and Jose, 1999). A second volume in both languages followed (Ikehata and Yu-Jose, 2003). Subsequently, the Toyota Foundation funded a research group on Malaya and Singapore (Akashi and Yoshimura, 2008). This research has unearthed a great deal of new material, in the form of both documents and interviews, much of it in Japanese. Its publication in English is significant in making these source materials more accessible to English-speaking scholars; however, the idea of joint research seems to have receded in this latter project, since no Malaysians or Singaporeans participated in it. It is unclear whether an ongoing project on Burma has included any Burmese scholars.

As we move further into the new millennium, a deeper understanding of the war is needed. This understanding must break national barriers and move into joint research, leading to comparative, and truly cooperative, studies. The results of such studies should not, however, be limited to a narrow group of scholars; they must be disseminated to as large a number of people as possible, so as to deepen our understandings of the wartime experience. Although there will still be the question of injustice, war guilt and political manoeuvering, war memories should and will be clarified by basic and joint research. Although any final proof of 'facts' may well prove impossible, some stereotypes may be altered or at least understood and seen in context. Any attempt at joint research will probably produce more controversy. Points of view will always be diverse even among scholars and historians, and popular memory will persist, whatever the latest academic findings. But recognizing the diversity of views and trying to understand them rather than trying to enforce one version of history is a hallmark of a democratic society. Historians may say what they will, and may argue with each other, but war memories will continue along with — and perhaps in spite of — the work of historians. Perhaps a stronger and more dynamic link can be established whereby academics can, in joint international research, work to shed more light on popular memories, while at the same time reaching a deeper understanding of them.

Notes

1. Among the earliest works to question American motives and actions in the collaboration question was Hernando Abaya's *Betrayal in the Philippines* (1946). This was reprinted in Manila in 1970.
2. The re-establishment of the shrine was marked by strong protests in the newspapers as being un-Filipino and denigrating Filipino sufferings during the war.
3. There was one Taiwanese division which fought in the Philippines, but it spent only two months on Philippine soil, after which it was pulled out to fight in Java. There was one Korean division in the Philippines, but it arrived in October 1944 and went direct to Leyte where it was decimated.

References

Abaya, Hernando (1946). *Betrayal in the Philippines*. New York: Wynn, 1946, Manila reprint 1970.

Akashi, Yoji and Yoshimura Mako (eds) (2008). *New Perspectives on the Japanese Occupation in Malaya and Singapore, 1941–1945*. Singapore: NUS Press.

Benda, Harry J. (1972). *Continuity and Change in Southeast Asia*. New Haven: Yale University Southeast Asian Studies.

Constantino, Renato and Letizia Constantino (1978). *The Philippines: The Continuing Past*. Quezon City: Foundation for Nationalist Studies.

Ikehata Setsuho and Lydia Yu-Jose (eds) (2003). *Philippines-Japan Relations*. Quezon City: Ateneo de Manila University Press.

Ikehata, Setsuho and Ricardo Trota José (1999). *The Philippines under Japan: Occupation Policy and Reaction*. Quezon City: Ateneo de Manila University Press.

James, D. Clayton (1985). *The Years of MacArthur: Triumph and Disaster 1945–1964*. Boston: Houghton Mifflin.

Lacar, Luis Q. (ed.) (1984) *Proceedings of the Fifth National Conference on Local History: Continuities and Discontinuities: The Japanese Occupation*. Iligan City: Mindanao State University.

Manchester, William (1978). *American Caesar: Douglas MacArthur 1880–1964*. Boston: Little, Brown.

McCoy, Alfred W. (ed.) (1980). *Southeast Asia under Japanese Occupation*. New Haven: Yale University Southeast Asian Studies.

Silverstein, Josef (ed.) (1966). *Southeast Asia in World War II: Four Essays*. New Haven: Yale University Southeast Asian Studies.

Steinberg, David Joel (1972). "An Ambiguous Legacy: Years at War in the Philippines". *Pacific Affairs*, Summer: 165–90.

Yu-Jose, Lydia N. (1995). "The Treatment of the Japanese Occupation in Philippine Textbooks". Unpublished paper.

CHAPTER 8

The Past in the Present: Memories of the 1964 'Racial Riots' in Singapore

Adeline Low Hwee Cheng

Introduction: Processes of Social Memory and the Riots of 1964

The 1964 racial riots are seen as the worst in Singapore's history because of the relatively large number of casualties involved: 22 people killed and 454 injured, according to official statistics. This chapter aims to examine the riots and their impact today from the perspective of collective memories. The riots constitute an event that has been constructed and reconstructed over time. This reconstruction can be observed through a comparison of official memory with popular collective memories obtained through personal narratives. These memories will be analysed in terms of ethnicity and generations. Memories of each ethnic group are compared to determine differences in their discourse about the riots and the impact on their attitudes, thoughts and feelings on multiracialism and inter-ethnic relations in Singapore today. Personal memories become social when they are shared or transmitted across generations. Individuals in the older generation have directly experienced the riots, while the younger generation learnt of them indirectly through education or from the older generation. This study aims to determine to what extent memories of the riots are passed on from generation to generation and whether the attitudes and opinions of the older generation have any impact on the young. The implications of these memories on present-day politics are also examined. Although the riots occurred more than 40 years ago, they have not been forgotten. The past still lives in the present because it serves a purpose.

Halbwachs (1980, 1992 [1925]) postulates that memories are collective because there are social frameworks for memory (1992: 38). Individual memories exist only because they are linked to the memories of others within a social group to which one belongs. The group keeps the memory alive for the individual and in turn, individual memories support the collective memory of the group, because group memory is realized and manifested in individual memory. Therefore, there is a dialectic between individual and collective memory. Wachtel (1990: 6) adds that our personal memories are actually a network of memories corresponding to various social groups, for example, the family, ethnic group and social class. As we are members of numerous social groups, each of which has distinctive memories of its past, we will have as many collective memories as we are members of these groups and institutions. It is also because of these overlapping groups that memories may differ and become contested. Halbwachs distinguishes between historical memory and autobiographical memory. Historical memory consists of events remembered indirectly through education or from reading written records. This is further reinforced through commemoration, "traditions" (Hobsbawm and Ranger, 1983) and rituals. It is when the present generation participates in those commemorative events that the past is recreated within. These commemorative events hold society together within a common historical past and identity. Autobiographical memory, on the other hand, is the individual's personally acquired memory of an experience. But the interests we have in the present affect memory, thus there is an active process of selection. Therefore memory is not fixed at a particular moment in time, nor is it constant; rather it is retrospective and fluid. Halbwachs (1980: 67) also discusses the "living bond between generations" where the generation before "leave their stamp" on the next generation, effecting a "historical continuity" (Connerton, 1989: 37).

The process of transmission between generations has been best elaborated by Mannheim (1952). In his formulation, contemporaries become socially significant only when they are involved and participate in the same historical and social circumstances. The common social location of these individuals forms the unity of a generation, based firstly on the biological rhythm in human existence and on social interaction between human beings, without which there would not be a social structure or historical continuity, but only the process of birth, ageing and death. These common experiences integrate the group but also limit their "range of potential experience", pointing them to a certain definite range of "possible modes of thought, experience, feeling and action" (Mannheim, 1952: 368). They are participants in a "common destiny" and in the "characteristic social and intellectual currents of their society and period" (Mannheim, 1952: 378). Social location is also based on the social interaction of members within the same generation, to effect historical continuity through intergenerational transmission. This is a vital and potentially radical factor, since the new generation may interpret the assimilated information in terms of their own social location and potentially develop new ideas, thoughts and behaviour.

In analysing the relations between family and institutional sources of information about the past, it is useful to consider Foucault's concept of the "discursive formation". To identify a discursive formation, one has to analyse the dispersion of statements. It is discourse that allows the formation of a discursive object. Foucault considers three elements which define the object: how the object was formed, the "authorities of delimitation" and the "grids of specification", referring to the ways in which the object can be "divided, contrasted, related, regrouped and classified" (Foucault, 1972: 42). Foucault also considers the type of statements made in the formation of "enunciative modalities", which refers to the position of the subject, as "defined by the situation that it is possible for him to occupy in relation to the various domains or groups of objects" (Foucault, 1972: 52). Because there is no total subjectivity, one needs to be embedded in a discursive field where subject positions can be taken up in order to make a statement. This formulation parallels Halbwachs' conceptualization of collective memory, because in order to evoke memories one has to be embedded within the social frameworks of a group and participate in its frame of reference. Since memories must be spoken of in order to be collective, we can say that memories in themselves are composed of discursive statements embedded in a discursive field. Within this field, power relations will come into play. The discourse of a controlling elite, for example, can shape the memory of an event for its own interests and purposes.

In this study, I interviewed 33 people, taking into account stratification variables such as ethnic group and gender. They were selected from a network of acquaintances, friends and relatives of the key informants. They were from the 3 major ethnic groups in Singapore[1] and comprised 15 Chinese, 11 Malay and 7 Indian informants, of whom 17 were men and 16 were women. The informants' education, religion and other variables were also noted during interviews. For purposes of analysis, I divided the interviewees into two categories, the older generation (23 respondents, aged 43–83), and the younger generation (10 respondents, aged 16–25). All the interviews were held in my informants' homes where it was most convenient for them and where they felt most at ease. Interpreters were enlisted to help with interviewing the Malay informants. In addition to interviews, data was also obtained from a resource file on riots compiled by the National Archives of Singapore containing oral history recordings of interviews with two ethnic groups, Malays and Indians. Significantly, no interviews in this file had been conducted with Chinese individuals.

Through oral history, we are able to elicit memory that would otherwise be silenced. Written historical records are usually records of the deeds of the elite within society. Silenced memory could be used to compare with official, historically recorded versions of the past. Oral history of subordinate groups will also produce another type of history — personal histories — in which different emphases and details of the past produce a different narrative. Oral history widens the field of investigation and "implies a questioning of official historiography which tends to give pride of place to the dominant actors of history"; it provides a "counter-history 'from the bottom up'" (Wachtel, 1990: 1). Thus the oral archives' recordings, and my own interviews, attempt to give voice to the 'common people' through the reconstruction of their memories. Other materials, such as National Education (NE) videos, students' NE folders, National Museum exhibits and old recordings of television documentaries such as *Diary of A Nation*, were also studied in an attempt to obtain a comprehensive picture of both national and popular memories.

Most interviewees expressly wished to remain anonymous since they felt that issues of race and religion were sensitive. As such, I have changed the names of my informants. My compliance to their requests enables them to control the circumstances in which their views enter "the discourse with others in their social worlds" (Minichiello, Aroni, Timewell and Loris, 1990: 125). Borland (1991: 64) adds that researchers should be sensitive to the issue of "interpretive authority".

Thus in the interviews, there is a constant exchange of ideas as each seeks to understand the other, creating a collaborative relationship between interviewer and informants. In order not to "ventriloquize a discourse" in endeavours to reconstruct the collective memory of particular groups (Debouzy, 1990: 71), I avoided the "academization" of my informants' memories by going into the field with an open mind and exploring the reasons behind their actions and statements, in an effort to understand their own viewpoints.

Frames of Remembrance: Official Memory

A nation is a collective group whose members' individual memories are tied up with the rest of the community. However, on this level, the articulation of what is to be remembered belongs to the political leaders and intellectual elites who bring their personal memories and interpretations to bear heavily on the social memories of Singaporeans. Thus within Singapore, the dominant discourse on the riots provides the official or "national" memory (Fentress and Wickham, 1992: 127). Memories can therefore be reconstructed or manipulated, or used as a tool against internal or external opponents. In Singapore, "national" memory is seldom openly contested by social groups. It is transmitted through educational institutions and the media and used to entrench institutional interests and ideology. National memory articulated through dominant discourses is imposed from the ruling elite down to the general population through private or public means. These conceptions of the past are linear and chronological, leading eventually to a legitimate present situation. The dominant memory can become hegemonic and totalizing, such that alternative memories are regarded as irrelevant, inaccurate and at times even illegitimate. This subjugation of alternative memories depends on the level of tolerance of the national culture and the degree to which it can be challenged. Individuals or social groups can support or challenge public representations of the past because these will either "guarantee their identity or deny its significance" (Tonkin, 1992: 10). In Singapore, the dominant memory of the riots serves to define the identity of a multiracial society.

Television documentaries have been one important means for constructing national memories of Singapore's recent history. The Television Corporation of Singapore (TCS) and Times Learning Systems produced *Days to Remember* in 1997. It features "significant milestones in the history of Singapore" organized into five themes: National Transitions, Building of A Nation, Industry and Economy, Housing and Education, and Reaching the People. The events are placed chronologically in a timeline beginning with the Japanese surrender in 1945, to the first presidential election in 1993. The 1964 riots are positioned under the theme of "National Transitions", in the context of the separation from Malaysia. The discourse on the separation begins with the political tension arising from the merger with Malaysia and the rationale behind it. Merger in 1963 was seen as "best for survival both economically and politically" and "many welcomed it". However, there were difficulties as "Singapore did not quite fit into the Malaysian political role" as Singapore was predominantly Chinese and the government believed in meritocracy. For Malaysians, the central government "endorsed the principle of Malay predominance". Conflict surfaced in the 1963 Singapore general election when the United Malays National Organization (UMNO) leader and Malaysian Prime Minister (PM) Tungku Abdul Rahman attempted to rally the Malays in Singapore. The People's Action Party (PAP) saw this as an intrusion into Singapore domestic politics. For their part, UMNO saw the PAP as attempting to change the existing political structure in their fight for a non-communal Malaysia, and launched an attack against them.[2] Things came to a head on 21 July 1964, when a scuffle broke out during the Prophet Muhammad's Birthday procession, escalating into riots between Chinese and Malays. Then the PAP set up the Malaysian Solidarity Convention in May 1965, bringing together major opposition parties to contend for a "democratic Malaysian Malaysia". This was seen by UMNO as a Chinese takeover of Malaysia. "To defuse political tension and avoid a full-scale racial clash, Tungku Abdul Rahman decided that Singapore had to leave Malaysia." Thus the separation is considered as inevitable. These narrated events, accompanied by music and moving pictures, are placed under several themes in chronological order, making the events seem causally linked, beginning with "Political Discords", such that "Tensions Rise", escalating in the "Riots", and further heightened in "Conflicting Ideals" that finally led to the "Separation from Malaysia". This extremely simplified three-minute audiovisual representation focuses solely on political events. The riots are represented as the turning point that caused the separation from Malaysia. The riots, placed in a discourse on the "Separation from Malaysia", are in turn embedded in the discourse on "National Transitions" and a process of "Nation Building".[3]

One United People — Struggle for Independence and Nationhood was produced for national television in 1997, in preparation for National Day. It was put together by TCS together with Mindef Public Affairs, National Heritage Board and Singapore Tourism Board. This programme contained the same narrative structure as the previous production but with a different presentation, consisting of interviews with nine individuals who had experienced the riots. The statements made by these interviewees were placed consecutively within the main narrative to form a coherent narrative structure. The majority of the interviewees were former political leaders and intellectuals, consisting of two former Cabinet Ministers, a lawyer, the Singapore Development Board Chairman, and a few others. In these remembrances, Singapore's separation and independence was portrayed as an important historic moment. The narrative, however, consisted mostly of statements made by the two former Cabinet Ministers. Former Cabinet Minister Othman Wok emphasized that the riots were planned: "People in KL (Kuala Lumpur) knew at 2 p.m. that the riots were going to take place in Singapore even before it happened". Few statements from the other interviewees were included. Thus, in building up a national memory, discursive space is limited for those who are perceived to be outside the authority structure. In this production, there was a greater emphasis on the economic situation in Singapore after merger and on the riots themselves. The narrative structure is the same except for a shift in emphasis, and the same images were used. Here, the main focus was the trials and tribulations of building up Singapore and of "overcoming our constraints and developing challenges" to "forge our identity and ideals". It was fitting that the finale of this production was also different. It included statements made by the various interviewees proudly proclaiming the meaning of being a Singaporean: "Being Singaporean has nothing to do with race", "I'm Singaporean, not Indian", and "My birthplace, my home".

The riots are also on permanent public display at the National Museum of Singapore in an exhibition entitled *From Colony to Nation*, organized by the National Heritage Board and Singapore History Museum. The exhibition traces Singapore's history chronologically, beginning with the end of Second World War and the Japanese Surrender, and ending with the Presidents of Singapore. The exhibition is divided into three sections: "Colony in Chaos", "Tides of Transition" and "Nation-Building". The 1964 riots are placed in the second section.

In each of these discourses, the narrative structure of the riots in national memory has remained the same. The selection and ordering of events creates a moral order. Chronology can therefore be used by historians in order to construct a timeline to connect and compare the sequence of events. This in turn can direct thought, since the narrative structure suggests that events are causally connected. The riots are presented as an outcome of political tension over racial issues raised by politicians, and the racial divisions existing within the population. This then becomes a factor in the separation from Malaysia. The moral drawn is that we need interracial harmony, or rioting and chaos will be the inevitable end. This moral story is used by the political elite to discipline the population. In the official memory, the narrators lend their authority to the account, and the moral precedent legitimates the ideology supported by the teller.

Frames of Remembrance: Popular Collective Memories

The Precipitating Event

The riots started during the Prophet Muhammad's Birthday procession along Geylang Serai. My informants were all taken by surprise. Mdm Siti was caught in the procession itself:

> The procession started from City Hall towards Jamiyah.[4] There were thousands of people. It's one of the biggest religious festivals. All the Malays are down there, everywhere. When we reach around Lorong 3 Geylang, gangsters start throwing stones, bottles from shophouses, so a group of youngsters in the procession rush up to retaliate. Then people started attacking here and there, throwing things and fighting, so I took my kids and run *lah*. A lot of people ran into the houses along the streets. I ran into a Hindu lady's house, couldn't go home what. The Hindu lady let anyone come in and give us food and drink. Then we stopped a bus and climbed up, the bus were all Telok Kurau (her kampong) people.[5] When we reach Joo Chiat, this group of Chinese stop the bus you know. Wanted the people to get down. They block the place, won't let the bus move. We shouted "move on, move on" so the bus driver just move through very fast didn't stop *lah*, didn't allow it to stop. From the bus we saw the Chinese take out *parang* (machetes). Bus driver Indian fella. If he was Chinese, he would most probably stop the bus and let the Chinese kill us Malays but he just drove. If he hit anybody, die right, also never mind. Hit and run, hit and run.

> He just ram through them. So everybody run *lah*. I saw and we were crying from fear. You can see these people rolling on the ground. We saw, we all scared. It was like live documentary. If the bus stop all will die. Then a group of Malays stop the bus. They climbed the bus, pulled the men down, wanted all the men to fight. Girls can go *lah*. But I quickly pushed my son under my sarong. Ask him to hide. When I reached the kampong, the people thought we had died.

Others were stranded because the curfew had already begun and they did not feel safe to go home. Mr Goh, who lived at the outskirts of Geylang Serai, recalled:

> On the way home, we met some Chinese, they told us the riots start already, if you want to go home you must have at least a pistol to carry. We were scared. We stayed at my friend's house and we heard a lot of police cars screaming up and down. On the way home, next day, we saw along Geylang Road, some houses and shops burnt, signs of looting, signs of destruction *lah*.

Most informants heard about the riots and the imposition of the island-wide curfew indirectly through secondary sources such as television and radio broadcasts, newspapers, friends and others who came back from the procession itself.

After the initial outbreak of fighting during the Prophet Muhammad's Birthday procession, there were other acts of violence. These were localized to the adjoining areas of Geylang Serai. Sporadic fighting did occur in other small areas but it was minor. For those living within and around Geylang, it was especially terrifying for the next few days, particularly at night when the rioters were active:

> They attacked that night. All kampong Malay living in the front and the back. 15, 20 people can see at the window. Pass our house. Carrying knives, metal rods, bars. (Mr Tan)

> At night very frightening, I heard a lot of shouting, screaming for help, but I don't know whether it was Malay or Chinese. (Mr Goh)

> The Malay kampong faced the Chinese kampong. The two sides were fighting like kids playing *masak* (cooking): ping pang pong! Glass pieces flying around everywhere. I went to hide, scared *lah*, then the police came and all of them ran away. I also saw the Malays, each one

> hold one kris. Other people from other kampongs also come and join the fight. It is never ending. When the police come everybody run back into the house but once they are gone, they come out and start all the nonsense *lah*. (Mr Cheong)

However, just as many of my informants did not experience any fighting or rioting at all because they lived in calm areas and carried on their lives as normal. For them the rioting seemed far removed from their everyday life:

> Queenstown nothing much, Strathmore Avenue areas, very quiet, we don't have racial riots. We have Chinese, Malay living peacefully together. Not frightened at all. No problem. We chit-chatted with our neighbours, our family members, older people. Same things we do every day. My mother go to market, go past all the Chinese areas what. Life is normal for us. (Mr Buang)

> My place got no fight or killing. The riots are outside the village, not inside. Only certain places got fight, not whole of Singapore. (Mr Farid)

> Our Kampong Batak is peaceful. Nobody disturb. (Mr Lim)

> Not the whole Singapore fighting. Just small groupings of people. Whole country normal. (Mr Aziz)

Thus the area of residence was an important factor in whether my informants experienced the violence, fear and shock. Of the 23 informants who lived through this period, 16 were unaffected by the riots because their residences were calm and peaceful. The only fear was that outsiders would enter their kampong and pick a fight with them. Thus, contrary to official discourse, which claimed widespread fighting, the popular discourse showed otherwise. Violent clashes only occurred in areas near the precipitating event.

Cause of the Riots: Malay Informants

The Malays as a collective ethnic group believed that the riots were not racial to begin with. Contrary to the official memory, it began as a religious riot because it occurred during one of the biggest religious festivals in the Muslim calendar.

> It was traditional for Muslim organizations to march singing slogans in praise of God towards Jamiyah. It was a joyful occasion. The birth of Prophet Muhammad brings deliverance and joy to Muslims, from the age of darkness to the age of light. That's why the Muslim community celebrate the birth of Muhammad. (Mr Hassan)

Most of the Malay informants took a collective religious perspective when speaking about the riots, viewing this memory through the social framework of their religious group. Thus the Malay informants, both those who had been in the procession and those who learned about it later, concluded that it was an attack and an insult on their religion, Islam:

> It is not just racial but religious. It was a religious procession. When somebody throw a bottle, they thought that they were cursing our religion so they retaliate. (Mr Farid)

> This involves a Muslim religious matter already. The procession is a religious function you know. We feel very deeply for this. When they come and disturb our religion we fight back. (Mr Awang)

Many Malay informants also observed that the Muslim procession was a mix of a majority of Malays and Indians and perhaps some Chinese and thus could not have been racially motivated. Collectively they expressed a sense of loss, since the procession was subsequently banned because of the riots.

All the Malay informants also believed that it was the Chinese who first began the attack on the procession. Besides the fact that the riots occurred during a Muslim religious festival, Malays are also associated with Islam, and Chinese with other religions.

> Chinese *lah*. The notorious Chinese in Lorong 23 throw bottles at us. (Mdm Siti)

> It seems some Chinese use the pork to throw. That's the way it started. The Chinese during the procession slaughtered the Malay *lah*, so we retaliate after that. (Mr Buang)

> The Chinese attack the Malay, that's the cause of it all. (Mdm Zulaaka)

Although they believed it was the Chinese who initiated the riots, some thought it was specifically the Chinese gangsters from secret societies

(SS), taking advantage of the chaotic situation, to initiate fights with rival SS members, leading to skirmishes between Chinese and Malay youth gangs in certain parts of the island. Many believed that the local community was not involved.

> Most of them gangster youngsters who did this *lah*, Malay and Chinese youths clash. Not exactly the Malays and Chinese fight. Neighbours within the kampongs don't fight with each other. Sometimes there are fights and everybody take for granted that it is race. (Mr Farid)

Informants who read widely or held civil service jobs believed that the riots could be politically motivated due to the internal politics between the two opposing parties, PAP and UMNO, and the ongoing Indonesian Confrontation. Mr Buang, a civil servant, believed it was "mainly motivated by political parties", but was unsure which party was the instigator:

> They say during the procession the Chinese throw pork oil. Will any decent Chinese do such thing? No! So some political party pay the gangsters to do it. I think PAP was in power already at that time. Then we have Barisan Socialis. Could be one of them or some independent parties. Because you see, one country got two PM, cannot be. Lee Kuan Yew Prime Minister, Tengku Abdul Rahman also Prime Minister. Malaysia want to go control everything in Singapore, so that's the problem.

Others thought Indonesian agents instigated the riots and shifted the blame onto the Chinese. This was the opinion of Mr Awang, a former police officer, who obtained his information from newspapers he read during and after the riots, and from discussions with his colleagues:

> Actually the Indonesian agents want to cause trouble between the Chinese and Malay, make trouble in Singapore. This caused the separation.

> Actually who throw nobody knows but after investigation found out it is Indonesian agent who start this. But they put the blame on Chinese you know. (Mdm Siti)

The riots did leave the Malay informants initially angry at the Chinese. In some kampong, this affected relationships and interactions with one another. However, these feelings did not last long when they realized that there could be other causes of the riots:

> Sure angry *lah*, how can the Chinese fellow throw stones, kill these fellow, do these things. But after that nothing *lah*, relationship the same. (Mr Farid)

Mr Awang, who saw himself as part of the collective group of Malays in Singapore, expressed this anger in a collective mode rather than an individual one:

> Everybody you know. Majority of Malays all angry, but 1964 was a small misunderstanding between Malay and Chinese. Most of the villages in Singapore were living peacefully together.

The official discourse claims that UMNO Secretary General, Syed Jafaar Albar, instigated the riots, but none of the Malay informants mentioned him at all. All of them believed that the first person who threw the offending object was a Chinese. Many reasons for the riots were put forward. Some believed that the riots occurred spontaneously with no political motive:

> It happened at the split of the moment. (Mdm Zulaaka)

Informants who read widely or who held government occupations, and were in touch with the political scene of that time, tended to attribute the cause of the riots to the political situation. These informants were also mostly males. During the 1960s, men had more chances to pursue an education while for women, education was not as highly valued. Thus the women tended to be less widely read. Besides ethnicity, then, we can see that occupation and gender also play a part in shaping informants' memories of the riots.

Interestingly, in discussing the 1964 riots, the Malay informants would be reminded of the 1950 Maria Hertogh or Nadra riots.[6] There is an overlapping of memories as the Malays shuttle back and forth between both riots to compare their feelings and thoughts. Contrary to selective official memory, which views the 1964 racial riots as Singapore's worst riots, the Malay informants remember the Nadra riots as bigger. The Nadra riots were recalled as a significant occasion on which they had stood and fought for their religion. Religion is of greater importance in the Malay construction of identity than is typical for other groups. Islam evokes such deep feelings in the community that all of them felt involved:

> 1964 not so big fight; 1950, the Nadra riots was bigger fight. It was totally religious purpose for fighting and if we fight, we fight for religion. It is about Islam and Christian. 1964 riots more racial than religious. (Mr Farid)

> '64 riots is a misunderstanding only. Nadra case is more a dissatisfaction. We were ready to fight. '64 riots had no planning, no motive, nothing. Suddenly fight, but Nadra riots was planned already, between the British and Malays. (Mr Awang)

As we have seen, the Nadra riots were not emphasized in the official discourse examined thus far, perhaps because, having a religious rather than a racial colouring, they are perceived to be less useful in a narrative devoted to emphasizing the importance of ethnic harmony.

Cause of the Riots: Chinese Informants

In contrast, all my Chinese informants, especially those who witnessed frightening episodes, believed that the Malays were responsible for starting the riots. This was especially evident in the case of an elderly couple living on the outskirts of Geylang Serai:

> The Malays all prepared already, want to fight with the Chinese. Because the Malay they pray, wear black then carry *kris*. They march on Prophet Muhammad's Birthday from Geylang and start attacking the Chinese. (Mr Tan)

> The Malay say Chinese attack the Malay. Actually the Malay attack the Chinese. It's a cover-up. Then they march and prepared to attack Chinese, don't know why. (Mrs Tan)

The fear they felt had a great impact on them. Till this day they feel unable to trust or have a close friendship with Malays. Even though they have Malay friends and there is no longer any anger, these friends are "not so close, you go your way, I go mine" (Mr Tan). Moreover, they did not hear or believe any show of kindness or helpfulness between the two races during the riots. They emphasized rhetorically, "No *lah*, Chinese and Malay are enemies, how to help each other?"

Another two of my informants accepted the official discourse that the riots were instigated by Malay extremists. Both had a college education and obtained this information from press reports published throughout the years. Mr Lim is a director of a multinational corporation, while Mr Goh is a civil servant.

> From press reports later, we knew there was some instigation by some Muslim extremist. It was more or less planned. That's what we read. But it wasn't reported immediately. Only reported, I believe, years later. (Mr Lim)

And he attributed the riots to the political situation facing Singapore:

> It was politically sensitive because Singapore was mainly Chinese and Malaysia mainly Malay. This is what we read in the papers. Lee Kuan Yew wanted a Malaysian Malaysia so anyone who is good can excel. Whereas Malaysia had Bumiputra rules *lah*, where they give the indigenous Malays privileges, so definitely they don't want a Malaysian Malaysia, because that means being Malay doesn't matter so there's a conflict. It becomes very sensitive and if somebody instigates, a riot will start. The political situation was definitely a major factor that trigger this feud you see. (Mr Lim)

> We read papers *lah* that those at the rally broke away and then start hitting Chinese. Actually this was instigated by some political figure from Malaysia, I think Syed Alfar Jabaar? (Mr Goh)

Mr Goh uses the same political discourse as Mr Lim to explain the reason for the instigation of the riots. Their memories replicate the national memory.

Informants who witnessed the violence and who were very affected by their experience of frightening episodes felt anger towards the Malays, thereby affecting their relationships within the kampong. Some like Mr and Mrs Tan moved out of Geylang Serai immediately after the riots. Many also expressed that there was less trust between neighbours. On the contrary, informants living in close-knit kampong, and who had built up good relationships with their neighbours of other ethnic groups, continued to maintain the same closeness:

> As far as neighbours are concerned, no problems because those we knew were not rioting. The relationship is the same in terms of being cordial. Those Malays we knew, we still remain friends *lah*, those we

> don't suspect. But with acquaintances, we suspect *lah*. (Mr Lim, who lived near Geylang Serai)
>
> Initially after the riots of course got feeling of uneasiness *lah*, you know, but as time goes by, things become quite normal again. (Mrs Goh)
>
> When we opened the coffee-shop again both of us were not embarrassed *lah*. We were still on good terms with each other. It was only a misunderstanding between the races, what. We have to make money, do business. Nobody has time to think about fighting or animosity or that you are a Malay and I am a Chinese. We have to cooperate. (Mr Cheong, a coffee-shop owner who has a Malay tenant)

Generally the feelings of the Chinese community are summed up succinctly by Mr Lim, who takes a collective perspective when discussing how the Chinese community felt at that time:

> Anger? Yes, because the Chinese community felt that we were the ones being attacked during the procession. We were angry that we were beaten, killed for nothing.

However, because of his belief that it was instigated by Malay radicals, he qualifies his statement:

> But if you think of how it happened, a few instigators, then you think the guilty party is those few who started it, you see. So you shouldn't feel angry at the whole Malay race. It's some extremists. You get angry at why the majority of the Malays believe these extremists.

Cause of the Riots: Indian Informants

The Indian informants, on the other hand, seem marginal to the riots. They had very vague memories and were unable to recollect much. Most of them stayed in areas that did not experience any violence or fighting, but they did remember that they felt apprehensive because of the tensions and the inconvenience caused by the curfew:

> Actually I cannot remember much *lah*. What I can remember is suddenly there is a radio announcement that you cannot go out. I don't know why the fight started or the cause of it. Our area was very quiet. But scared *lah*. I didn't see anything, I can't imagine because all I remember is quiet. (Mdm Faridah)

> We were not frightened of anything. Not at all, actually I didn't bother, I didn't really want to know. (Mrs Prabalakshmi)

The only information they got about the riots in other parts of the island was through the television, radio, friends, and the mobile vans that toured the kampong to inform people to keep indoors. The riots in turn did not affect their lives nor their relationships with the other ethnic groups. There was also no long-lasting impact on them.

> We had a close relationship with our neighbours, all on friendly terms with one another. (Mdm Latifah)

> The relationship between the kampong people was very deep because they lived there for a long time, so there was no problem. (Mr Kumar)

Moreover, some only formed opinions about the cause of the riots a few years later, sometimes through education:

> A few years later when I started working, I heard that the Malays and the Chinese were killing each other, this lorry driver who gave us transport, mentioned that he killed a Malay. (Mdm Prabalakshmi)

> At the university I took a module on Singapore relations and what happened in Singapore. Now I know for a fact that the communists were very unhappy with the merger with Malaysia, and the riots could be sparked off by communist-inspired elements, just to destabilize Singapore. (Mr Kumar)

There are differences between the memories of the three ethnic groups. The Malay and Chinese informants were directly concerned since their ethnic communities were seen to be antagonistic towards each other. Many viewed the riots from a personal and ethnic perspective, with some switching to the collective level to discuss feelings of anger through the ethnic group's frame of reference. The memories are further shifted to the institutional level when political issues are discussed (for example, the cause of the riots), widening the context of interpretation and offering a different perspective. Education and occupation play a role in constructing the narratives. The better-educated, well-read informants and those in the government service were more influenced by the official discourse, believing that the riots were politically inspired. However, the cause of the riots is a contested arena. Contrary to official memory, which specifically names a Malay extremist, Syed Jafaar Albar, as instigator of the riots, popular memory proffers a range of other reasons. The Indian community had a nebulous memory of the riots. Most of them spoke as individuals and rarely as a collective Indian community. As the riots had in no great way affected their lives, it was an episode about which they have not fully developed their opinions and judgements.

Helping One Another

Within the dominant memory, mutual antagonism, fear and hatred prevailed between ethnic groups. The spectre of the racial riots is used often in the state's discourse to justify and legitimate ideology and policies. In order for it to be effective, memories have to evoke scenes of violence and fighting. However, within popular memory, helpfulness and cooperation is a recurring theme. In ethnically mixed settlements, the riots served to gel the two races together to protect their own kampong. My informants recollect many instances of people living in harmony. The fact that this theme runs so consistently throughout the popular discourse testifies that this was a common phenomenon during the riots:

> In some kampongs there is a good understanding between the Malays and Chinese. They prevented their own races from coming to kill their fellow neighbours, say, the Chinese. (Mr Buang) [Mr Lim and Mr Farid recalled similar experiences.]
>
> Some of the Chinese bought food for the Malays because the Malays were too afraid to go out. (Mdm Zulaaka)
>
> My Malay neighbours tell us, "Don't worry, don't worry, we will help you in any way, you all want to come over or not, safer." Malay house so outsiders wouldn't come in so we Chinese will be safe there *lah*. (Mrs Lim)
>
> Everyone in the kampong cooperated, whether Malays, Chinese or Indian. We formed a vigil *lah*, in case any outsiders come into the kampong. We will collect money from everyone to buy food, drinks, coffee to last us through the night. (Mr Mak)

Competing and Completing Memories

Halbwachs (1980: 86) observes that there is only one national memory but several collective memories, because national history is written by historians who are supposed to be objective and impartial. A historian supposedly does not write through the social framework of any particular social group. Instead, he relocates them into another narrative structure, external to the group, providing an "unfolding sequence of transformations". Thus, "History may be portrayed as the universal memory of the human race. But there is no universal memory. All collective memory is supported by a group that is limited in space and time."

Hence, the official memory of the riots portrays a one-sided picture of chaos, violence and fighting between the Malays and the Chinese over the entire island, while popular memory shows otherwise. The fighting and rioting were confined to areas adjoining Geylang Serai. Many of the informants pointed out that sporadic incidents did occur in other parts of the island but these were only small skirmishes and many other parts were unaffected. In contrast to official memory, which represents the two races living in fear of one another, many informants relate living harmoniously and helping one another.

Within the official discourse, Malay extremism is the sole cause of the riots. This is debatable among my informants, who propose a variety of other possible causes. As a collective group, the informants also remember trying to protect their kampong from rioters from other kampongs, and the uneasiness they all felt as they went about their daily affairs after the riots. Furthermore, the Malay informants view the riots from both racial and religious perspectives. As a consequence, they position their memories differently, judging the events of 1964 in relation to those of 1950, which alters their meaning significantly. They also believe that the Chinese initiated the riots. Conversely, the Chinese informants believe that the riots were initiated by the Malays, and they view the events from a racial perspective. The memories of Indian informants, by contrast, were vague. Those informants who are government servants, more highly educated or more widely read, presented a similar narrative structure to the official discourse. The national memory has become incorporated into their personal memory.

Intergenerational Transmission, Collective Memory and the State

In modern societies, intergenerational transmission is superseded by the state through formal education, which has become a major intermediary between the older and the younger generation in transmitting memories. It is an instrument of the state, used by the authorities to instil national ideology and consciousness in the younger citizens. Memories of the 1964 riots are transmitted through both family and formal education. Therefore, both national and popular memory compete for a place in the historical memory of the young.

Through discursive practices, the 1964 riots have evolved as a discursive object. Since their occurrence, they have been discussed by ordinary people, the media and the state. The riots as a discursive object is embedded in a discourse of multiracialism. It is invoked by the government, both to raise racial awareness and to justify social policies. The representations of the riots as racial can be associated with the process of state- and nation-building, within which "political rhetoric" depends on the past as a "legitimation device" for political action (Fentress and Wickham, 1992: 132). Once this rhetorical discourse is in place, it affects present actions and conditions future activity as well. The past is a "resource to deploy, to support a case or assert a claim" (Tonkin, 1992: 1). Institutionally, the riots are used by the state to justify constitutional arrangements and laws. As former PM Lee Kuan Yew stated in the Parliamentary debates a year after the 1964 riots:

> The people of migrant stock here who are a majority learnt of terrors and the follies and the bitterness which is generated when one group tries to assert its dominance over the other on the basis of one race, one language and one religion ... so it is that into the Constitution of the Republic of Singapore will be built safeguards, so far as the human mind can devise means whereby the conglomerate of numbers, or likeness, as a result of the affinities of race, language or culture, shall never work to the detriment of those who, by accident of history, find themselves in minority groups in Singapore ... we have vested interest in multi-racialism and a secular State, for the antithesis of multi-racialism and the antithesis of secularism holds perils of enormous magnitude. (14/12/1965)

This led to the Constitutional statutes proclaiming that there would be no discrimination based on race, religion or place of origin, guaranteeing minority rights and specifically the rights of the Malays as Singapore's indigenous population. The event of the riots is also framed in racial and religious terms to legitimize the Maintenance of Religious Harmony Act:

> Twenty to thirty years ago, Singapore did not have religious harmony. The country was beset by racial and religious riots. And even though religious harmony exists today, there are problems. Therefore it is better to have such legislation now while relations between different religious groups are still good, rather than later when trouble may break out and each religious group is suspicious of the other.
>
> WHAT DO THE RACIAL/RELIGIOUS RIOTS OF THE 1960S HAVE TO DO WITH RELIGIOUS HARMONY TODAY?
>
> The 1964 racial riots in Singapore and the 1969 racial riots in Malaysia, which spilled over into Singapore, are still fresh in the minds of many Singaporeans. In addition, the Maria Hertogh custody case in 1950 also resulted in communal riots in Singapore. Although these events took place more than twenty years ago, we must ensure that they do not happen again because racial and religious harmony is absolutely essential for our survival as a nation. We should not forget that racial and religious harmony is very fragile. (Ministry of Information and the Arts, 1992: 2–3)

In this context, by contrast with the earlier instances analysed, we see issues of race and religion, and the riots of 1950 and 1964, being linked. In January 1997, when both the Chinese Lunar New Year and Hari Raya Puasa fell consecutively within the same week, Deputy PM Tony Tan took the opportunity to emphasize that "racial and religious harmony are the most precious assets which Singapore has" and "we do not want to go back to the tense period of the 1960s" where racial tensions were prevalent (*The Straits Times*, 19 February 1997). The government has also used the riots to justify social policies. In 1989, the government was concerned that certain minority groups were forming concentrations in certain estates. The Minister for National Development explained that these "enclaves will become seedbeds for communal agitation" (*The Straits Times*, 7 January 1989). The spectre of the riots was used to rationalize the policy of ethnic quotas for each estate in this discourse on race relations. There is a prevalent belief that spatial segregation would lead to racial conflicts similar to the 1964 riots (Hill and Lian, 1995: 116). Framed in such a manner, the riots are decontextualized and over-simplified. The existence of ethnic enclaves need not lead automatically to antagonism and riots.

Within this institutional formation, the press has the freedom to publish relevant materials. However, it is "subordinated to the overriding needs of the integrity of Singapore, and to the primacy of purpose of an elected Government" (Lee Kuan Yew quoted in *The Straits Times*, 22 May 1987). The press has also used the riots to examine issues of acceptance, tolerance and interracial mixing in the community. *The Straits Times* ran an article, "Three Tragic Reminders", about the Maria Hertogh riots in 1950, the 1964 riots and the 13 May riots in 1969 which spread from Malaysia to Singapore, to remind Singaporeans that "racial tensions can lead to very ugly ends" (*The Straits Times*, 4 June 1987). This article was written in the wake of debates on the loyalty of Malay Singaporeans, to show how volatile religious and ethnic loyalties are.[7]

My informants of both generations have in turn appropriated the official discourse, as reflected in their statements. They accepted as truth the definition of the riots as racial, and appeared unaware of how the riots are used as part of the multiracial discourse to reinforce nation-building. Within the multiracial discourse, race is seen to be a powerful primordial sentiment requiring laws and policies to maintain interracial harmony. Mr Kumar explains succinctly:

> Racial sentiment is very powerful, once something bad is said about your race, you cannot help but feel a need to justify. You can't help it but identify. *It is only natural.* That's why racial bigotry and prejudice cannot be taken for granted. We must be careful.

To the informants the socially constructed concept of race is translated into an inherent biological disposition. Race becomes an innate quality within persons and not a question of perception:

> If I see a group of Malays, "Oh, Malay group" will come into my mind because they are attracting attention. They're very loud as a group. (Melissa)

The multiracial discourse allows racial stereotyping. It accepts that there are natural qualities about each race that "cannot be helped" (Mr Kumar), thus "we have to learn to respect and be aware of racial differences" (Norlina). Similarly, Mr Hassan believes that the riots "opened up our eyes. We begin to realize that people are sharply divided because of racial differences." It is because the ideology of multiracialism has been so naturalized as a matter of fact that the use of the riots in a multiracial discourse is accepted in the same manner:

"This is an important lesson for Singapore, to study the cause and effect of the riots and not make the same mistake" (Mr Goh). The riots are transmitted in this manner as knowledge to the younger generation by their parents, the media and the state, and seen as a lesson in racial tolerance: "I learn about the racial riots, that we must have harmony between races to live peacefully" (Karen). The possibility that political disagreements between UMNO and PAP, and their struggle for leadership, could have been a factor in the cause of the riots, is rarely mentioned. Although the older generation, having been through the riots, have their personal memories — which at times contradict national memories — this contradiction is confined to the private arena due to the state's hegemonic control over the public sphere. Their statements reflect this dilemma. On the one hand, they emphasized that: "Riots will never happen again" (Mrs Prabalakshmi); "Life is so secure now, who wants to cause trouble and destroy all we have today?" (Mr Cheong); or "Today people more educated, how to happen again?" (Mr Farid). On the other hand, being embedded within the multiracial discourse, they contradictorily state that racial harmony and tolerance is important because: "Racial issues so sensitive, someone want to take advantage can easily spark it off" (Mr Awang); "We must be sensitive" (Mr Cheong); or "We will face riots days again" (Mr Goh). Contrastingly, the younger generation's distance from the event, and lack of personal memory, makes it easier for discursive action to take place.

In the mid-1990s, recall of the 1964 riots was turned to a new purpose. PM Goh Chok Tong, in his 1996 National Day (ND) rally speech, pointed out that the younger generation was losing touch with the past. Important historical events were not "a vital part of their collective memory", he said, emphasizing that this ignorance is detrimental since "they will not know what dangers lie just off the highway", and they might "trip up over sensitive issues of race, language and religion". Consequently they will "slacken" and "Singapore will fail". The values necessary for "building a nation" in the twenty-first century should therefore be transmitted "from generation to generation". To achieve this, PM Goh proposed a new programme of National Education (NE) to develop national cohesiveness by building up the national collective memory and to foster a sense of identity, pride and self-respect as Singaporeans. Just a month later, he announced the immediate implementation of NE in all schools. Interestingly, as we have seen, the 1964 riots are the only riots to be included in the NE materials.

When the second generation was asked which events in Singapore's history they considered important, none included the 1964 riots. Of all the second-generation informants, only one Indian boy had not heard of the riots prior to the interview. All my other informants' parents had told them of the riots. However, most of their historical memory is formed through additional information through the latest educational programme (National Education), from books, or through television programmes. Most were also unable to furnish further details of the events that unfolded prior to or after the riots. None could discuss political or economic issues in 1964, or could give a well-defined account of what had happened in the riots. The collective memory of the second-generation informants is vague compared to the richness of the first generation's memory.

Most of the first-generation informants thought that the transmission of their autobiographical memory is important. As there are no more riots to experience today, "it is an eye-opener" (Mr Buang) and "a part of history, a turning point" (Mr Hassan) that needs to be told so that "the younger generation will not take for granted racial harmony, and be more racially tolerant" (Mrs Goh). However, many also felt that their children are rather unconcerned about the past: "My eldest son doesn't have much interest in such things. His impression is not very deep" (Mr Cheong). Some felt that even though they do tell their children of it, "they don't experience it, so they don't really know how people felt at that time" (Mr Buang), and others suggest that "Life is so different now, theirs is the Orchard Road type of fight, to them, it's for fun" (Mrs Lim).

According to Portelli (1981: 162), "there are times for telling stories" depending on which stage of life the tellers are in and on the circumstances. Thus though the older generation may be willing to pass on their memories and convey their thoughts to their children, the younger generation may not be as open nor willing to listen. Mannheim postulates that it is only knowledge personally acquired from real situations that "really 'sticks' and it alone has the real binding power" (Mannheim, 1952: 371). The younger generation does not possess personal memories. Thus their frame of reference for viewing race relations would be shaped more definitely by the media, education and books. Moreover, the older generation has formed a framework of attitudes and opinions influenced by this experience, through which new experiences can be explained. The younger generation, however, is still forming their framework, which is mostly learned at school.

For them, a historical memory of the riots is built up through various activities such as viewing video clips, field trips to the National Museum and lectures, organized to help them better understand the riots. However, although students have gone through these activities, how much is retained in their memory is debatable. One of my informants commented that "it was all very boring. Some of us skip the lectures *lah*" (Karen). Jamil was not at all interested: "I didn't pay attention, so I can't remember what they said." For Peter, "I forgot already ah, can't remember what it is all about." However, the discourse only requires the riots to be remembered factually as race riots and as a natural consequence of interracial disharmony. The images that students have retained, either from the media or their exposure to the NE programme, are suitably lurid:

> It's not out of the question that riots will come again. (Norlina)
>
> Anarchy, chaos everywhere, homeless people, burning house. (Melissa)
>
> If a riot occurs, the government will step in with their tanks. (Anita)

These extreme images are a contrast to the older generation's popular memories of the riots being localized and peaceful relations prevailing. Thus the NE programme serves to further disperse statements on the 1964 riots and make them more effective and powerful tools for justifying and legitimating state initiatives.

Conclusion

The evidence presented shows how the past is subject to multiple interpretations. Even within the dominant official discourse, interpretive emphasis can be shifted according to the context in which events are evoked or recalled, but in popular memory the multiplicity of understandings is, as we might expect, far more marked. There are tensions between the official perspective and those of ordinary people who lived through the events, but also between the memories of different groups or collectivities within the population. Ethnic group memories differ as informants interpret and reconstruct the riots from an ethnic perspective, supporting Halbwachs' notion that memories are constructed and localized within social groups. The fact that Malay informants recalled the events of 1964 in connection with the Nadra riots of 1950, and judged the latter to be more important, shows how the meaning of an event for a particular group can be altered according to its positioning in relation to other events.

The unruly plurality of popular memories contrasts with the enforced coherence of official memory, which tends to be highly selective in its choice of what it judges to be the most important events. The state regularly calls upon the riots to justify and legitimize laws and policies, and tries to shape the younger generation's memories of the riots through the National Education programme. Thus, recall of the riots is now put to use to justify the need for a Singaporean national identity, and as a means of extending the discourse of 'being Singaporean'. Personal memories of the riots are also transmitted intergenerationally from the older generation of informants to a younger but uninterested generation, with uncertain results. The younger generation is building up a historical memory and has no personal memory of its own to counter the official memory. Consequently, young people would be most open to the state's discourse.

Those in authority have the power to reconstruct the memories of the past, disseminating them to the people through the media and educational institutions. They can thus shape the people's memories for their own ideological, political and disciplinary purposes. Popular memories, on the other hand, flourish outside of such constraints. By exploring them, we may never succeed in uncovering some more definitive version of "what really happened". But we can at least achieve a keener awareness of the plurality of possible and competing interpretations of the past, an insight that has the effect of problematizing the tidy linearity of official versions. Portelli reminds us that people's acts of retelling the past are in themselves events, and recalls for us the words of Walter Benjamin who declared that "an event lived is finished and bound within experience, but an event remembered is boundless, because it is the key to all that happened before and after it" (Portelli, 1981: 175). Although the riots can be reconstructed and made use of by the state, so long as others remember the event, the memory lives on and it will also be constantly subjected to interpretation in the hermeneutic spiral of interpretations, to which this chapter is one contribution.

Notes

1. I am using the state's categorization of racial groups for the purpose of my study. Although there are many racial subsets within each racial group, this form of categorization is widely accepted and it has become a cultural reality for many Singaporeans. The Chinese make up approximately 74 per cent of the total population, the Malays approximately 13 per cent, the Indians approximately 9 per cent and 'Others' approximately 3 per cent in the 2010 census statistics. 'Others' is a residual category and not an ethnic group, created from a bureaucratic need to place those who do not belong to the other racial groups and who are considered statistically insignificant by the state.
2. It is significant that there is no mention of the PAP's participation in the Malaysian elections, which was a factor leading to UMNO launching an attack on the PAP. This emphasizes the selectiveness of memories for presentation.
3. *Days to Remember* was actually a condensed version of an earlier Singapore Broadcasting Corporation (SBC) series, *Diary of a Nation*, broadcast over eight or nine months in 1988. In that series, too, the riots were framed in the context of the separation from Malaysia. There is considerable overlap in materials between the two programmes — narrative statements, music and photos were selectively chosen from *Diary of a Nation* to form a shorter and more simplified narrative in *Days to Remember*. Two events left out were the portrayal of Syed Jafaar Albar, then Secretary General of UMNO, as the instigator of the riots, and a narrative of the economic problems facing Singapore after the merger.
4. Jamiyah is the Muslim Missionary Society of Singapore, which was supposed to be the end point of the procession; the procession did not reach its destination.
5. At that time there were still many kampong ('villages' or squatter settlements) within the urban fabric of Singapore. Some of these were mainly populated by members of a single ethnic group, while others were mixed. The fighting eventually spread into some of these settlements.
6. The Maria Hertogh or Nadra riots that occurred on 11–13 December 1950 were the result of a lawsuit over a 13-year-old, Maria Bertha Hertogh. Her Dutch/Eurasian Catholic parents had left her in the care of a Malay Muslim couple in Java during the Japanese Occupation. Her adoptive parents brought her up as a Muslim. Some years after the war, her Dutch parents managed to trace her and wanted her back. Her adoptive Muslim parents, by then living in Malaysia, refused since they had become very attached to her, and going back meant she would have to convert to Catholicism. The case was brought to court in Singapore, and the judge

ordered the child to be returned to her natural parents. The Malays felt that their religion had been insulted and this led to a riot against the British colonial government.

7. Two episodes sparked off the debates. The first was the visit by the Israeli President in 1986, which led to a protest from the Malays. A forum of Muslim and Malay organizations in January 1987 called for greater government sensitivity to the Malays in Singapore. The debate on Malay identity was then brought up. The second incident was the arrest in June 1987 of four Malays under the Internal Security Act for spreading rumours that there would be clashes on 13 May, the anniversary of one of the racial riots in Singapore.

References

Borland, Katherine (1991). "'That's not What I said': Interpretive Conflict in Oral Narrative Research", in S. Gluck and D. Patai (eds), *Women's Words: The Feminist Practice of Oral History*. New York: Routledge.

Chua Beng Huat (1995). *Communitarian Ideology and Democracy in Singapore*. London and New York: Routledge.

Connerton, Peter (1989). *How Societies Remember*. Cambridge: Cambridge University Press.

Debouzy, Marianne (1990). "In Search of Working-Class Memory: Some Questions and a Tentative Assessment", in Marie-Noelle Bourguet, Lucette Valensi and Nathan Wachtel (eds), *Between Memory and History*. France: Harwood Academic Publishers.

Fentress, James and Chris Wickham (1991). *Social Memory*. Great Britain: Blackwell Publishers.

Foucault, Michel (1972). *The Archaeology of Knowledge*. Translated from French by A.M. Sheridan Smith. London: Tavistock Publications.

Goh Chok Tong (1996). *Prime Minister National Day Rally 1996*. Singapore: Ministry of Information and the Arts, Singapore.

______ (1997). *Prime Minister National Day Rally 1997*. Singapore: Ministry of Information and the Arts.

Halbwachs, Maurice (1980). *The Collective Memory*. New York: Harper and Row Publishers.

______ (1992 [1925]). "The Social Frameworks of Memory", in *On Collective Memory*, edited, translated and introduced by Lewis Coser. Chicago: University of Chicago Press.

Hill, Michael and Lian Kwen Fee (1995). *The Politics of Nation Building and Citizenship in Singapore*. London and New York: Routledge.

Hobsbawm, Eric and Terence Ranger (eds) (1983). *The Invention of Tradition*. Cambridge: Cambridge University Press.

Mannheim, Karl (1952). "The Problem of Generations", in Paul Kecskemeti (ed.), *Essays in the Sociology of Knowledge*. London: Routledge and Kegan Paul.

Minichiello, Victor, Rosalie Aroni, Eric Timewell and Alexander Loris (1990). *In-depth Interviewing, Researching People*. Sydney: Longman Cheshire.

National Archives of Singapore, Oral History Department. "The 1964 Riots". Compiled materials in File Copy. National Education materials obtained from teaching staff in secondary schools and junior colleges.

Portelli, Alessandro (1981). "'The Time of My Life': Functions of Time in Oral History". *International Journal of Oral History* **2** (**3**): 162–80.

The Straits Times. Singapore: Various editions.

Tonkin, Elizabeth (1992). *Narrating Our Pasts*. Cambridge: Cambridge University Press.

Wachtel, Nathan (1990). "Introduction", in Marie-Noelle Bourget, Lucette Valensi and Nathan Wachtel (eds), *Between Memory and History*. New York: Harwood Academic Publishers.

CHAPTER 9

Memories at the Margins: Chinese-Educated Intellectuals in Singapore*

Kwok Kian-Woon and Kelvin Chia

The Chinese-Educated in Singapore

With the 'Chinese' comprising more than three quarters of the resident population since the 1920s, there is a tendency to refer to 'the Chinese community' as one large, indeed the largest, component in the demographic make-up of Singapore society. References to the Chinese community or 'Chinese society' in Singapore imply a single ethnic group, whose members putatively share common cultural characteristics or a common 'Chineseness' (Kwok, 1995, 1998b; Tu, 1994). In the Chinese language (in this case Mandarin), terms used to refer to the Chinese (*huaren*, Hua people) as a social group (*huaren shequn* or *huashe*) or an ethnic group (*huaren zuqun* or *huazu*) also connote some form of racial unity, a common ancestral culture and a shared ethnic consciousness. In the case of Singapore, such connotations are given added weight by the state's official model of multiracialism, which divides the population under the categories of 'Chinese', 'Malay', 'Indian' and 'Others', with each race having its own 'culture' and 'mother tongue' (Benjamin, 1976; Lai, 1995; PuruShotam, 1998; Chua, 2003). Mandarin is officially regarded as the mother tongue of the Chinese as a race, in spite of the common use of Chinese dialects or other languages at home.

* *The views expressed are those of the authors and do not reflect the position of the institutions they are associated with.*

Apart from dialect group differences, the idea of a single 'Chinese community' glosses over the historical bifurcation between two broad sectors: the 'Chinese-educated' (*huaxiaosheng*) and the 'English-educated' (*yingxiaosheng*). As these terms imply, the basis for differentiation is the dominant language in which successive cohorts of students were schooled in an educational system based on the British colonial model of four language streams — English, Chinese, Malay and Tamil (Chelliah, 1947). In their policy of benign neglect and divide-and-rule, the colonial authorities permitted ethnic communities to set up schools teaching in vernacular languages, while promoting English education principally for the purpose of recruiting locals into the lower ranks of the civil service. Christian groups also established English-medium schools as part of their missionary work. With self-government in 1959, the People's Action Party (PAP) government, in line with its ideology of multiracialism, allowed the separate streams to coexist.

The historical formation of the 'Chinese-educated' as a major sector of the larger Chinese community in Singapore is a complex one (Borthwick, 1988, 1990; Kwok, 1998a). It is useful, however, to highlight its main threads here. During the colonial era, Chinese-medium schools were established by clan associations or *huiguan* (for example, the Hokkien Huay Kuan or, in Mandarin, *Fujian Huiguan*) with funding from philanthropists and business people (Cheng, 1985, 1990). In the immediate postwar years, Chinese-medium schools and their student intake clearly outnumbered their English-medium counterparts, but the latter were beginning to increase at a faster rate. By 1955 the Chinese stream comprised 277 schools and about 94,000 students. The English stream counted 239 schools, but student enrollment had surpassed those in the Chinese stream by more than 2,500 students. Subsequently, Singapore witnessed the steady decline of Chinese education with the consolidation of PAP rule in the immediate post-Independence decades (Yong, 1992: 93; Trocki, 2006: 149–50).

The heyday of Chinese education in Singapore saw the establishment of Nanyang University (*Nanyang Daxue*, popularly called Nantah) — the first Chinese-language university outside of the People's Republic of China and Taiwan — in the mid-1950s. The idea was proposed by Tan Lark Sye, chairman of the Hokkien Huay Kuan, in early 1953. Hitherto, Chinese high school graduates who wished to pursue tertiary education had to enroll in universities in China or Taiwan. Schooled mainly in Chinese, they were not eligible for admission to the University of Malaya (the local English-medium university, later called Singapore University). Nantah was a community project endowed with symbolic significance from the very beginning. Fundraising efforts for the building of a campus, on 500 acres of land in Jurong donated by the Huay Kuan, involved the mass participation of diverse sectors of the Chinese population in Singapore and Malaya. The outpouring of community support, cutting across clan and class lines, became the stuff of legend, inscribed in popular memories that recollect the efforts of trishaw riders, boatmen, taxi and lorry drivers, hawkers and cabaret dancers in donating their day's earnings to the Nantah building fund (Kee and Choi, 2000: 43–54; see also Yao, 2008: 174). With such support, the campus was built from scratch within a few years. Following the groundbreaking ceremony officiated by Tan Lark Sye on 26 July 1953, after the construction of the first road on the campus site, the pace of building allowed the first cohort of 584 students to begin classes in March 1956. More than a hundred thousand Nantah supporters attended the official opening ceremony in March 1958, an event that has been remembered for, among other things, the unprecedented massive traffic congestion on Jurong Road and the thousands of participants who walked more than ten miles to reach the campus (Kee and Choi, 2000: 25; Yao, 2008: 170–1).

By the 1950s a growing divide between the 'Chinese-educated' and the 'English-educated' became obvious. These are relational terms in the sense that they were — and, in many cases, still are — used as terms of identification among graduates of the two language streams, positioning one vis-à-vis the other either consciously or in a taken-for-granted manner. The social differentiation between these two major sectors of the educated Chinese population could be seen in not only the dominant language used in everyday and intellectual discourse but also in cultural knowledge, political orientation and occupational status. The Chinese-educated were exposed to the waves of modernism in mainland China, influenced by the legacy of the May Fourth movement of 1919 and affected by the civil strife leading to the establishment of the People's Republic in 1949. Moreover, graduates from Chinese schools did not easily find jobs in an economy that privileged the English-speaking, a legacy of the colonial era. In the process of decolonization, vast numbers of Chinese school students were involved in the political activism of the day, the student unions joining with trade unions that represented the Chinese masses. To be sure, the

Chinese-educated youth and adults of this period were not uniformly leftist or solely China-oriented in political orientation. There was an internal divide between supporters of the Kuomingtang (KMT) and those of the Communists in China. Left or right, however, many of them had joined the anti-Japanese movement when Japanese forces invaded China in 1937 and were singled out for persecution during the Japanese Occupation in Malaya and Singapore. Both KMT and Communist supporters joined the underground resistance movement, although the latter hardly figure in contemporary national remembrance (see, for example, Foong, 1997).

Although Chinese nationalism was an influential force since the early decades of the twentieth century (Lee, 1987), many among the Chinese-speaking were also sufficiently localised as to conceive of a *Malayan* nationalism in tandem with the politically aware among other ethnic groups. In the literary sphere, since the 1920s, there had already developed a body of works later gathered under the rubric of *mahua wenxue* or Malayan Chinese Literature (Fang, 1977; Tang, 1988; Wang, 1964; Yeo and Leung, 1985; Yeo, 1993). Such works were set in the local environment, demonstrating varying degrees of familiarity and identification with local peoples and practices. The process of 'Malayanization' that could be discerned in the Chinese literary world had its parallel in the political sphere, especially among leftist anti-colonialists who found common ground with their counterparts from different ethnic backgrounds, who were also developing a wider Malayan identity, especially in the wake of decolonization. A significant number of the Chinese-educated strove to communicate with Malays, as evidenced by the publication of Chinese-Malay dictionaries in the 1950s and 1960s and the subsequent development of Malay Studies at Nanyang University.

Among the 'Malayans', too, were the English-educated PAP members who sought the help of the Chinese-educated and the Malay-educated in working towards independence. In particular, in the context of Southeast Asia in the late 1950s, Lee Kuan Yew emphasized that Nanyang University should ultimately be a Malayan University catering to all Malayans rather than being regarded as a Chinese or Chinese-language university. In 1964, following merger with Malaysia, he stressed that Nantah should play the role of a Malaysian university (Hong and Huang, 2008: 120–1). In early 1965, an independent curriculum review committee was set up. It was chaired by Wang Gungwu, who was widely recognized in subsequent decades as a historian of the Chinese diaspora. Its report was submitted to the University in mid-May and released to the public a month after Singapore's separation from Malaysia. In concluding his insightful analysis of the Wang Gungwu Report, which elicited extraordinarily strident student protests against the perceived threat of 'anglicization' and, in turn, equally strong police action against the protesters and their alleged communist subversion, Huang Jianli (Hong and Huang, 2008: 134–5) concluded:

> Premised on the notions of 'Being Malayan' and multilingual learning, the WGW [Wang Gungwu] Report was hopeful that the [language] divide would be narrowed and the two Chinese sub-communities could form a unified whole and, in partnership with other ethnic groups, would march together purposefully towards development and modernity. However, it had proven instead to be a wedge, exposing the different notions of what being 'Malayan' meant and been regarded by its detractors as a political ploy aimed at denying the space for Chinese-ethnicised education to contribute towards the nation-building enterprise.

By the second half of the 1950s, the strong presence of the Chinese-educated in leftist politics tended to contribute to their being stereotyped as 'communist' or 'pro-communist' (and pro-China or pro-Chinese Communist Party at that). At the same time, the predominantly English-educated PAP leadership, while collaborating with key Chinese-educated leaders and gaining legitimacy as representing the interests of the masses, sought to distinguish itself as 'non-communist' or 'democratic-socialist' and as the vanguard of a new 'multiracial' nationalism (Bloodworth, 1986; Drysdale, 1994; Willmott, 1989). Led by Lee Kuan Yew, the PAP cultivated a core of loyal Chinese-educated cadres, some of whom went on to assume key government positions in the early post-Independence decades (Sai and Huang, 1999). But the political landscape could not be simply reduced to a divide between pro-China communists and non-communist PAP activists. The ideological pull from the mainland was palpably felt by large sectors of the Chinese-speaking, especially in the light of the mainland Chinese people's tumultuous road to the crowning moment of 1949. Not all, however, drew inspiration or direction from this in their local concerns, although evidently there were sympathies and activities tied to the struggles of the Malayan Communist Party at a time when the island and the peninsula were still regarded by many as a single territory. In the process of assuming hegemony, the PAP leadership came down hard on those identified as communists or pro-communists, disbanding the 'united front' organizations and detaining leaders and members under the Internal Security Act (Lee, 1977).

In this connection, the case of Lim Chin Siong (1933–96) may be highlighted. Lim was the most important Chinese-educated founder member of the PAP who ended his public political life following his incarceration (1963–69) for being a 'communist'. In an interview late in his life, after decades of silence, Lim rejected the label and spoke of his role as an anti-colonialist (Chew, 1996: 118; Wee, 1999: 174; Harper, 2001: 44). Officially, however, the label 'communist', as it were, followed him to his grave. It was officially reaffirmed just days after his death on 5 February 1996. In a letter to Lim's wife, published in *The Straits Times* (9 February 1996), Lee Kuan Yew paid tribute to his political rival: "The only way we, the non-communists, could counter his attacks was to match his determination, tenacity and stamina." Lee, however, concluded: "My wife and I send our condolences to you and your two sons. We hope they will live up to the promise that their father showed and would have achieved had he been on the non-communist side." In this line of interpretation, Lim Chin Siong died an unfulfilled man, owing to his having chosen to be on the communist side.

As much as the term 'Chinese-educated' implied commitments to leftist radicalism, it also carried connotations of ethnic chauvinism. In the view of the state, ethnic chauvinism, like political radicalism, constituted a threat, especially in what is perceived as a fragile multiracial society. Again, the case of Lim Chin Siong may be used as an example. As pointed out by Zahari (2001: 168–9) in his political memoir, up to the early 1960s, Lim "was also accused of being a Chinese chauvinist by his political opponents.... [T]o be associated with Chin Siong was to invite the labels "communist", "pro-communist", "fellow-traveller", "chauvinist", "anti-national" ...." Yet, upon his death, Lim was eulogized by the eminent Malaysian poet, Usman Awang, in the following terms: "Lim Chin Siong's good deeds towards the Malays and the Malay language were very great and significant. Lim Chin Siong and his

Chinese-educated friends in Singapore had passed a resolution to make Malay the lingua franca, the National Language and the language of communication (for the multi-ethnic nation of Malaya). At that time, even the Malays themselves, particularly elite government officials, had no confidence in the Malay language" (Zahari, 2001: 172). In this assessment, Lim "and his Chinese-educated friends" were hardly Chinese chauvinists — they contributed significantly to the larger project of Malayan nationalism.

In sum, the 'Chinese-educated' as a social collectivity and as a social construction was forged out of both the development of Chinese education and the politics of decolonization. In the process, the Manichean divide of non-communist/multiracialist versus communist/chauvinist tended to privilege the English-educated as a harbinger of modernization and to demonize the Chinese-educated as a danger or obstacle to progress. To the extent that there was a discernible political divide between the English-educated and Chinese-educated, it may be more useful to consider each group as propounding a vision and version of modernity, with their protagonists finding like-minded compatriots across educational backgrounds. In C.J. Wee's analysis (1999: 186): "The confrontation between Lim Chin Siong and the leftists and Lee Kuan Yew and the other moderate socialists was … a clash of two related modes of left-oriented progress, of what it means to be a 'modern' society during the era of decolonization." T.N. Harper (2001: 46–7) offers a complementary interpretation: "At the heart of Lim Chin Siong's conflict with the PAP lay competing ideas of freedom…. Lim spoke for a local radical tradition that pitted the popular will against colonial power. The positions he adopted after 1956 were underpinned by an understanding of freedom that asserted that if one was subject to any form of government that allowed for the exercise of prerogative or discretionary power outside of the law, one would be living in an unfree state."

Put simply, the more radical version of modernity — and vision of freedom — lost out on the road to independence in 1965. This set the stage for the political marginalization of the Chinese-educated in the post-Independence era. Such marginalization, along with the generally weaker social and economic position of the Chinese-educated vis-à-vis the English-educated, became even more pronounced as the new era saw the demise of the Chinese school system.

Chinese Education during the Post-Independence Decades

With Independence, the Ministry of Education took steps to develop a national system, with a common curriculum across the streams (Gopinathan, 1991, 1998). In the process, English became institutionalized as the language of commerce, science and technology — in a word, modernization. It was also promoted as a 'neutral' language for promoting interethnic communication, replacing the Malay language which was widely spoken among older-generation non-Malays. The so-called mother tongues were to be studied as second languages, functioning as languages of transmission of ethnic traditions (Pendley, 1983; PuruShotam, 1998). Chinese-stream schools, which had strong rates of enrollment up to the late 1950s, declined in numbers over the decades. Between 1959 and 1978, the proportion of pupils enrolled in Chinese primary schools fell from 46 per cent to 11 per cent of the total primary student population (Goh *et al.*, 1979). Increasing numbers of parents saw that economic improvement could be better secured by sending their children to English-medium schools. Nanyang University graduates, too, could not compete with their English-educated counterparts in the job market, making its degree less economically valuable and socially prestigious. By the late 1970s, a number of major educational changes took place. Nanyang University first merged with Singapore University in a 'Joint Campus Scheme' so that its students could be offered the same curriculum, with English as the medium of instruction for all subjects except for Chinese Studies. By 1980, the two universities formed the National University of Singapore (NUS), and a new institution of higher learning, the Nanyang Technological Institute, was constituted and given support to develop with the expansion of facilities on the Jurong campus. The institute was reconstituted as a university, the Nanyang Technological University (NTU), in 1991. But in effect the 1980 merger marked the closing down of the university: what it represented in the eyes of its graduates and the larger Chinese-educated — and still larger Chinese-speaking but less-educated — sectors of the population no longer had any concrete institutional expression.

The mother tongues were vigorously promoted as vehicles for the transmission of 'traditional values', along with the annual state-sponsored Speak Mandarin Campaign inaugurated in 1979. By this time, it was officially realized that the vast majority of Chinese pupils came from dialect-speaking backgrounds and were in effect learning two new languages at school (Goh *et al.*, 1979). In the early 1980s, English became the main medium of education, the first school language and the language of instruction for key subjects such as Mathematics and Science. In practice, bilingual education had come to mean that the role of Mandarin as a language of instruction was significantly reduced. In response to the dwindling enrollment in Chinese schools, however, the Ministry of Education identified and apportioned more resources to a small number of well-known Chinese schools such that they could also offer Chinese as another first school language. In this way, it rationalized, the 'best' of the 'traditional Chinese school environment' could be retained in what was called the Special Assistance Plan (SAP) schools. All this, it must be remarked, came after the vestiges of cultural and political modernism — especially the leftist inclinations — associated with Chinese education had been neutralized over the decades. With the SAP schools 'preserved', the remnants of the pre-existing Chinese school system dissolved. Many Chinese-language teachers, now considered excessive in numbers, were retrained or 'converted' so that they could teach in the English medium. This transition engendered great pains and added to the experience of having been marginalized throughout the years (Sai, 1997).

In the following decade, 'Confucian ethics' was officially promoted in political discourse and in the school curriculum (Tu, 1984; Davis, 1993; Kuo, 1996; Kwok, 1999). By the early 1990s, however, this was expanded into the discourse of 'Shared values' and 'Asian values', a discourse that no longer confined itself to the Chinese population — a more politically correct course given the PAP leadership's avowed commitment to the idea of multiracialism (Clammer, 1993). In any case, these developments dovetailed with the new political and academic discourses at the international level concerning the rise of East Asia, with Japan in the lead, followed by the newly industrializing economies of Taiwan, South Korea and Singapore — all touted as 'Confucianist' societies (Berger, 1986; Berger and Hsiao, 1988; Hofheinz and Calder, 1982; Kahn, 1979; Kotkin, 1992; MacFarquhar, 1980; Redding, 1990; Tu, 1991, 1996). And with Deng Xiaoping's open-door policies and China's rise on the global economic and political stage, Mandarin was now promoted in Singapore as not only a language for cultural transmission but also an economically useful language.

'Chinese-Educated Intellectuals': Towards a Sociological Description

Against the larger historical canvas, what is the situation of the Chinese-educated in contemporary Singapore? Drawing from different sources, including selected in-depth interview data from a larger research project on social pluralism in Singapore, we shall confine our discussion to 'Chinese-educated intellectuals' (*huawen jiaoyu zhishifenzhi*), sometimes abbreviated as 'Chinese-language intellectuals' (*huawen zhishifenzhi*) — terms which reemerged in public discourse in the late 1990s. Parenthetically, the phrase 'Chinese intellectuals' is more often used in the English-language press, clearly in a sense that does not include English-educated Chinese. Indeed, the lack of a self-reference among English-educated Singaporeans of Chinese descent to themselves as intellectuals is telling. This may reflect either the paucity of independent English-language intellectual discourse, or the lack of a need to self-consciously position oneself as an English-educated person, given that English has been the dominant language of political discourse in the post-Independence era. The self-positioning among the Chinese-educated, however, is pronounced. The modern Chinese term for 'intellectuals' literally means 'knowledge elements'. At times, the term 'intellectuals' is used rather broadly to refer simply to the more highly educated or literate among the Chinese-speaking. More specifically, it refers to the Chinese-educated who respond publicly (for example, in newspapers and public forums) to community developments, especially to the changes in the education system (Li Yuanjin, 1994). In its most profound usage, however, the term is self-consciously invested with normative assumptions about the special roles or mission that should be undertaken by a special group of people, including being at the 'centre of modernity' (Ke, 1999; Li Yuanjin, 1999). Moreover, a distinction has been made between different generations of Chinese intellectuals (Chua, 1999; Oon, 2000).

In any case, the 'intellectuals' in question are qualified by the larger rubric of 'Chinese-educated', which implies that some years of schooling in the Chinese language and the use of Chinese in intellectual discourse are basic characteristics. But it does not necessarily follow that all members of this grouping were educated up to tertiary level or at Nanyang University, or that they are basically monolingual in Chinese and at home only in Chinese culture. Indeed, many among the older generation did not have the opportunity to attend university. Many were self-taught by building up on their literacy and by reading voraciously, including Chinese translations of Western materials, hence also acquiring a cosmopolitan outlook. Most among the younger generation, however, are bilingual in English and Chinese as a result of changes in the school curriculum since the 1980s. Through family upbringing and peer influence, however, they have grown up in or function comfortably in a Chinese-speaking milieu and are exposed to a Chinese-language universe of intellectual discourse. This also makes them more cognizant of developments in other parts of the Chinese-speaking world, especially the intellectual discourses in Taiwan, Hong Kong and China.

In terms of professional background, Chinese-educated intellectuals have found careers in education, media and business. They have not been uniformly 'disadvantaged' by their Chinese-educated background, although access to the commercial and government sectors among the older generations was hampered by their lack of facility in English. With varying degrees of difficulty, many eventually found — or were 'forced' to find — their own niches in a society in which English has been the dominant working language. The examples that are readily cited are of Chinese-educated persons, including Nantah graduates who, in having less access to conventional civil service jobs, had to fend for themselves and built what are now generally called small and medium enterprises (for example, traditional family businesses in services, manufacturing, import and export), developing in the process entrepreneurial skills, which in turn helped them expand their niche markets. With China's opening up in the 1980s and 1990s, many in this sector of business people were also well placed to move into larger investment arenas and venture partnerships in the mainland.

In light of the variety of persons who can be classified under the category, it might be useful to think about a continuum of ideal types among the Chinese-educated. On the 'purer' end of the spectrum are the older generations who have had long years of exposure to Chinese education. At the apex, this includes Nantah graduates, although the cohorts of the 1970s before Nantah's demise are still a generation apart from the earliest graduates and those of the 1960s during the height of student activism. In any case, many tend to carry with them certain commitments to the legacy of Chinese education as part of their autobiographical past and socio-cultural formation (in the Chinese sense of *xiuyang*, akin to the German sense of *Bildung*). This orientation, however, does not necessarily entail a commitment to progressive or leftist ideology. Just as it can include something of the spirit and substance of the critical anti-traditionalism of the May Fourth movement, it can include an automatic embrace of what ambiguously comes under the rubric of 'Chinese culture' in a larger social environment that is seen to be inhospitable to its growth. In many cases, they also carry with them sentiments and memories associated with having been marginalized in a society that is seen to have privileged the English-educated in terms of political power, economic position and social prestige (Liu, 1994). In other words, they see themselves as, paradoxically and unjustifiably, a minority within the majority Chinese population.

On the 'diluted' end of the spectrum are the younger generations in their twenties, thirties or forties. These have had a more mixed education in terms of exposure to both English-language and Chinese-language universes of discourse. Strictly speaking, the term 'Chinese-educated' cannot be generally applied to those in their twenties or early thirties because, as indicated, they received far greater exposure to the English language in school following the educational changes of the 1980s. Indeed, it has been observed that some among the older and more purely Chinese-educated parents have made it a point to send their children to schools which are more English-oriented, especially with the view that command of the English language would enhance social mobility. In some cases, these children have more in common with the children of the English-educated. But, evidently, others — including, from the 1990s onwards, English-educated parents — have seen to it that their children have a strong immersion in the Chinese language either as a matter of cultural transmission or because of the growing economic significance of China. In these cases, parents attach importance to placing their children in SAP schools, which supposedly still retain elements of the 'traditional' Chinese school environment and maintain high standards of Chinese-language instruction. In light of the above, the term 'Chinese-educated' can still be applied to younger Chinese who routinely, although not exclusively, read, speak and write in the language.

The Experience of Marginalization

It is illuminating to detail some of the experiences and views of individuals who fall into the broad category of the older Chinese-educated, allowing them to speak for themselves and offering a more complex sense of their individual and collective situation. For the purpose of this paper, we highlight three key informants, all Nantah-educated and in their early 50s when they were interviewed in 1999. For the sake of anonymity, we refer to them as Mr. A, a lecturer at a tertiary institution (interviewed in English), Ms. B, a published writer and Mr. C, a clan association leader (both interviewed in Chinese). To begin with, Mr. A points to the paradoxical situation in which the Chinese-educated sector of the predominant Chinese population, fluent in its own language and possessing its own culture, was unable to make headway under the economic conditions of Singapore:

> They become more frustrated as they compare [Singapore] with Japan, Taiwan and Hong Kong. Now look at these societies, predominantly Japanese-speaking or Chinese-speaking or Cantonese-speaking, they can still make the best of it. So [as to] the [official] justification, they cannot see a very strong reason for saying that you must [can only] survive with the English language.

Thus the very idea that Singapore's economic development has to be predicated on the wide use of the English language — and concomitant decline of the Chinese language — is questioned. In any case, there is a strong perception that the Singapore polity is shaped by the English-educated. As Ms. B puts it:

> ... this only happens in Singapore. Malaysia and Indonesia are different. This is a predominantly Chinese society, but those at the centre of power are all English-educated .... The fact is that those in control are basically English-educated. So the English-speaking community has a loud voice, so loud that its influence is much greater than the non-English-speaking minorities .... Those who are in the minority ... have a very weak voice.

When asked about her status as a 'Chinese-educated', Ms. B offered a long answer, which fleshes out some of the qualifications that I have earlier teased out concerning the term 'Chinese-educated':

> Personally, for my age and background, I'm not an 'old-generation Chinese-educated' (*laopai huaxiaosheng*) .... People always think that Chinese-educated are all left-inclined. I did not go through the social movements in the 50s and 60s .... Some activities were related to

> politics then. Looking back today, those were not really political activities, but just youth movements. Unfortunately, they were seen as related to politics. I was never really involved. And my thinking would have been considered rightist-inclined by the leftists of that time. There is actually no such thing as left or right, it's just youthful passion towards society.... We talked about Western philosophies, and that was different from what the China-oriented Chinese-educated were like. So in the 70s when the line was still very clear, many felt that I was not like a Chinese-educated. I did not fit in the image of a Chinese-educated. Later when [some among] the Chinese-educated were influenced by the Cultural Revolution, I was uneasy about that. There were actually many Chinese-educated like me. Do not have a stereotypical image of the Chinese-educated.... When we talk about Chinese community, we always have that stereotypical image. And the sad thing is that now that I'm getting older, I'm being seen in that image as well. When I was young, I sang Beatles [songs], and all the English songs. I was more cosmopolitan.... I didn't know any of those leftist songs, not *Dongfang Hong* [The East is Red]. So I have familiarity with Western thought, [but] I'm also concerned with Chinese culture and [the] community...

The stereotype that the 'Chinese-educated' are uniformly ideologically leftist and monocultural, rather than politically and culturally diverse, is something that Ms. B is keen to contest. This contestation on her part should be seen against the backdrop of harsh official action against those identified as leftists, who in Ms. B's eyes were idealistic and concerned about the larger society. However, the memory of official repression in the form of detention without trial is clearly retained:

> Thinking back, now I remember that it was a time when there were many so-called political detainees who went on TV to confess. They signed confessional letters, and went on TV to confess, and it appeared that they would be released after that. A lot of such things. And I just accepted it. After we watched them [on TV], we did not have any doubts. Because at that time, they said that you have to confess that you had contacts with the communists, and after you confessed, they would release you. Thinking back, those people [the detainees] always said that they took part in study groups and that those 'study groups' were fringe groups of the Malayan Communist Party. They got involved in so-called subversive activities because of this. Of course today I'll not look at things this way. At that time, I was in my 20s, and

> after seeing all these, I would relate to my own experience. When I was in secondary school, I went to a study group, but of course back then I didn't know that it was called a 'study group'. When I was in middle school, I went to the house of a fellow female student; she was helping us with Mathematics and English because I was weaker in these subjects. After that we would sing, *Liu Sanjie* [a popular Mainland-recreated folk song about a young woman's heroic resistance to feudal oppression] and things as such. I did not feel that there was anything wrong. I went only once. After that somehow I didn't continue. To be honest, when I saw all these so-called ex-communists going on TV, I was glad that I did not continue taking part in the study groups, if not I might be involved. Actually, thinking back, there were a lot of people who were not Malayan Communists. They might have taken part in some activities, they might not have known of the motives behind. It's just the passion of youth, their concern for society, that they took part in all that. But at that time [of the arrests and TV confessions], I thought, luckily, I didn't join in.

The state, however, had dealt harshly not only with communists and their sympathizers among the Chinese-educated. There was also constant official caution against 'Chinese chauvinism'. In spite of the neutralization of Chinese-based political activism, the label served as a form of surveillance that could render expressions of concern for the decline of Chinese education and of the status of the Chinese language in Singapore politically suspect. Hence the perception that political capital could be made out of issues related to Chinese education and language, as highlighted by Ms. B:

> ... I believe you've heard frequently that in Singapore, the Chinese language is always a convenient and useful political tool. I agree fully with this, and I have very strong feelings [about this]. A useful and very convenient tool when you use it, and the impact is great. From the 1950s, with the social movements and the influences of the leftists, the Chinese-educated were seen as being closely related to the communists.... Those who promoted Chinese education, Chinese language, became regarded as a pro-China power group. Even today, though the ideological shadow is gone, but in the multicultural, multilingual social environment, Chinese language remains a very usable political tool. The latest example is the Deng Lianghong [Tang Liang Hong] affair in the recent election. It shows yet again that this tool is very powerful.

The reference to the Tang Liang Hong affair deserves some contextualization (Lim, 1997; Kwok 1998a; Huang, 2009: 339–40). In brief, Mr Tang, a Singapore University-trained lawyer who had been active in Chinese-speaking cultural circles, stood as an opposition candidate (with Mr J.B. Jeyaratnam of the Workers' Party) during the January 1997 elections. During the campaign in December 1996, PAP leaders portrayed Tang as a Chinese chauvinist on the basis of certain actions and remarks made by him earlier. After a hotly contested election in the ward that Tang and Jeyaratnam stood for, with the PAP winning by an uncomfortably small margin, Tang was charged with libel against a group of PAP leaders, who were later awarded S$8 million in damages. Tang left the country following the election and settled in Australia. To be sure, many Chinese-educated intellectuals did not necessarily support Tang's causes or his characteristic ways of promoting them, but many felt that the wholesale charge of chauvinism against Tang amounted to a politicization of issues related to Chinese language and culture, and a potential vilification against those who have genuine concerns about cultural loss and language maintenance. The difficulty of coming to terms with the politicization of language and cultural issues and of responding to marginalization weighs heavily on those who, like Ms B, take up an intellectual vocation as writers and social commentators:

> The Chinese-educated are a group full of internal contradictions. This is a society where English is the dominant language. On one hand, you are happy that your children are English-educated and that they are able to do well in society. On the other hand you are sad that your mother-tongue culture [culture as transmitted by the Chinese language] is disappearing. So there is a certain internal imbalance. There is this group of people who reconcile: they see it as a sacrifice made in exchange for stability. Another group feels that Singapore is a small country, and if you, the younger ones, ignore the Chinese language, and fail to see the rise of China, you will lose out in the end, and you have to face the consequences yourself. So they just let them ['the younger ones'] be. There is yet another group that simply gives up; they just keep silent, they felt that it is useless to talk. But silence is another kind of crisis. Some people say that silence is way of making a stand. But silence also means that the group that has a loud voice will be at an advantage.

Thus, a significant historical reversal can be said to have taken place for the Chinese-educated. During the pre-Independence era, the Chinese-educated played a pre-eminent role in the political avant-garde and in a wide range of social and cultural movements. By the early 1980s, the voices of Chinese-educated intellectuals in the sphere of wider public discourse became either significantly withdrawn or simply mute, many reduced to attempting to stem the decline of Chinese-language standards, or wrestling with general demoralization.

The Social Memory of Nantah

If the zenith of the history of Chinese education was represented by the founding of Nanyang University, the historical reversal was marked by its demise. The event did not elicit any overt opposition, but this did not imply total or willing acquiescence. The memory of Nantah as a unique institution, as a special historical moment, persisted in many minds, as much as it was not publicly articulated. Another interviewee, Mr. C, has this to say:

> The period from the establishment of Nantah to the merger or closure has had great impact on Chinese society [in Singapore]. In 1950s, Tan Lark Sye, the then Chairman of Hokkien Huay Kuan, called for the establishment of a Malayan University, so that students in Singapore and Malaya had another choice, other than going to Taiwan and China. They overcame many obstacles and set up the university, but in the end, *it still could not escape the fate of being closed down.* Of course, we have to accept the decision, but for many of us activists in the Chinese society, when we speak about Nantah, *we felt very helpless. Many even dared not speak about their anger. Many felt resigned.* They had busied themselves for nothing. Their enthusiasm was misunderstood and distorted [i.e. misrepresented]. I also feel that the whole Nantah incident also indirectly caused many in Singapore to be oblivious to currents affairs and social development in Singapore. You know you busied yourself so much and poured in all the enthusiasm, and in the end it all comes to nothing, and you get into all the trouble and you still have to step down from the stage. The negative impact is so much more than anything positive [that Nantah represented]. This is not an issue that many will want to talk about even up till today. One typical Chinese characteristic is that you swallow everything into your own stomach, and just pretend that nothing happened. I can feel

> that *many have given up hope and lost interest in most things* [emphasis added].

This sense of demoralization — a mixture of fatalism, resignation, bitterness and ennui — contrasts sharply with the youthful idealism of earlier times, for example, among those who participated in the Nantah Student Association (Khe, 2006). The sentiment is echoed by Mr. A, who suggests that the glorious life of Nantah and its inglorious demise have been carried as a burden in the minds of older graduates:

> .... The so-called burden [of Nantah] is linked to the history, the so-called intellectual history of China. Every educated person [the educated] — maybe they took themselves too seriously — they like to think ... [in terms of] commitment to society, *youhuan yishi* ["a worrying mentality"], act for society, for nation. And they would certainly like to think about Nantah being that crystallization — being the highest institution of the Chinese-speaking world, a symbolic venue in the context of Southeast Asia.... It was a regional university.... If they were given a fair chance, perhaps they could make [could have made] better of it. But historical circumstances, social-political history, did not seem to enable them to realize their dream, and made them feel a little under-utilised — if not a bit useless. Some of them, those in their 50s, if not their early 60s, have been *living with that kind of complex*. They can't bend back; I've had ties with them [emphasis added].

But history could not be artificially brought back to life. When Nantah was closed down through merger with Singapore University to form the National University of Singapore (NUS), the Nantah graduate rolls were absorbed as part of the new entity because of its status as a predecessor institution. In May 1995, Mr Chia Ban Seng, President of the Association of Nanyang University Graduates, appealed to Prime Minister Goh Chok Tong for the transfer of the Nantah register from NUS to Nanyang Technological University (NTU). Earlier in the year, the Prime Minister had supported NTU's change of its abbreviated Chinese name, Litah (Technological University), to Nantah, identifying itself as the latter-day incarnation of Nantah and indicating continuity with an institution that was remembered but no longer in existence. The Prime Minister now supported the new request, and spoke favourably of the "Nantah spirit", which meant "unremitting efforts to improve oneself and become stronger". Moreover, he said: "In the past, some Nantah graduates felt left out of the mainstream of Singapore life. This unnecessary psychological baggage should now be thrown into the incinerator" (Goh, 1995: 26–7). In other words, the "Nantah spirit" should live on and thrive, but the Nantah "baggage" should not be needlessly carried by the graduates. Evidently, some Nantah graduates responded to the transfer of the register to NTU with great scepticism. Mr. C sums up their sentiments in the following way:

> You know, such blood relations have to be natural. You cannot do an operation and a transplant; it is very unnatural and uncomfortable. This is my feeling: it's very simple, your mother dies, and they find another woman, and ask you to call her 'mother'. This is blood relation you know, you cannot just call NTU Nantah and then you just accept. I don't know why the problem dragged on till now. Some of those involved were not bold enough to take certain actions. In the middle, there was a big break. After Nantah closed down, the campus was used for NTI [Nanyang Technological Institute], and then NTU. In fact if you change everything but keep the name, I think there will not be a problem. Now you change everything, except that Yunnan Yuan [Yunnan Garden, the focal point of the old Nantah campus] is still there, the word 'Nanyang' is there, but the institution is different. Many people I'm in touch with still find it hard to accept.

On the one hand, the burden of memory could be superficially considered as dispensable and debilitating "baggage" by those who did not have to carry it and had no apparent stakes in doing so. On the other hand, for many Nantah graduates, the burden involved a profound and painful sense of loss that admitted of no proper closure, engendering an emotional limbo. Indeed Mr. A's notion of their living with a "complex" suggests that the experience of marginalization has exacted psychological costs, which could not be mitigated by simply getting rid of baggage; the feeling of being trapped under the "burden" is still palpable among many of the older generation. Indeed, the near-Freudian themes of parental loss and incomplete mourning are neither accidental nor melodramatic. Yet there are those, like Mr. A, who could put some distance between themselves and the historical chain of events, and they did so, as it were, by moving beyond the legacy of Nantah and Chinese education, but not rejecting it as such:

> .... I and others may consider ourselves more fortunate in the sense of being able to go out of that little niche, to see a little bit more of the world because I have [had] the fortune of spending quite a few years overseas ... so that exposure in part liberated me, so to speak. *So I would not like go back to the old times, thinking in any chauvinistic manner, and I don't think I feel comfortable about that. Looking back at my roots, I certainly am proud, in a harmless way, of my upbringing, [of my] Chinese education.* But that gave me a certain appetite to reach out to the English-speaking world. This is a point I would like perhaps to elaborate a little. I often find it easier as I observe my peers and others, that it is often easier for those of us who began with Chinese education and later on [were] given the opportunity to become hopefully proficient in any other languages. The other way round is quite rare — not impossible but relatively more difficult. So I would like to consider myself a cosmopolitan man although that may be a little far-fetched, wishful thinking. Because I do travel a lot, and I take my Singaporean identity seriously.

Notice the carefully drawn contrast between a potentially harmful chauvinism and a liberating enlightened cosmopolitanism. This positioning, however, may be read as one that takes cognizance of the official warnings against the alleged chauvinism of those who question the decline of Chinese education. In Mr. A's "more fortunate" case, though, what is suggested is that his Chinese-educated upbringing had been a channel for him to be open to other cultures and is also not incompatible with being Singaporean. In a sense, such a perspective is akin to the "Malayan" and cosmopolitan thrust of the Wang Gungwu Report of 1965 and constitutes a departure from the perspective of its beleaguered detractors who feared the "anglicization" of the university and the loss of its distinctively "Chinese" character — which they defended vociferously.

With the ghosts of leftism safely exorcised by the 1990s, the state could appropriate Nantah as a positive symbol of Chinese values such as perseverance in the face of hardships and obstacles. Following the Prime Minister, PAP leaders began to extol the "Nantah spirit". In essence, this was a depoliticized and romanticized notion, which took no account of the role that Nantah students and the Chinese-educated played in the mass politics of the decolonization era and the official suppression against those who were accused of being communists and chauvinists.

Against this background, the case of the noted Chinese calligrapher and poet, Pan Shou, may be highlighted as an illustration of the persistence of memory and the difficulty of redressing official amnesia. Pan Shou had played a critical role in the founding of Nantah and served as its secretary-general, resigning from the position in early 1960. Among other things, he articulated the 'expansive and inclusive' vision of interracial bonds and a university committed to multiracialism evoked in Tan Lark Sye's speech at the opening of the Nantah campus in March 1958 (and, earlier, in the design of the university crest, which featured three interlocking rings representing the Chinese, Malay and Indian communities). Soon after the opening, however, he was denied Singapore citizenship from 1958 to 1983, after which he was recognized both nationally and internationally as a cultural icon, having won the Cultural Medallion in 1986. In late August 1998, at the age of 87, Pan Shou was conferred an honorary doctorate by Nanyang Technological University. On this occasion, he took the opportunity in his acceptance speech to suggest that the word 'technological' should be dropped from the university's name, in effect calling for the resuscitation of the name of Nanyang University. The suggestion was immediately rejected by the university and the Ministry of Education, with the Minister suggesting that "the Nantah spirit of self-help and hard work amidst adversity" should still be retained (Hong and Huang, 2008: 175–6).

Following Pan's death in 1999, a *Lianhe Zaobao* article (Li Huiling, 1999) revealed that in an interview Pan had expressed the paradox of his having once been regarded as a brigand (*qiangdao*) and later as a national treasure (*guobao*). This paradox, writ large, could just as well apply to Nantah, whose spirit in its earlier days was regarded as anti-national but later came close to the good old-fashioned 'Asian' values of diligence and determination. How did Nantah graduates respond to the official reinvention of the "Nantah spirit"? Evidently, some graduates welcomed it because the "spirit" did ring true to their life experiences as people who were discriminated against and yet managed to survive or thrive in a hostile environment; to them, some form of recognition was now being given, and it sat well with their self-perception, if not self-mythologization, as underdogs who have weathered the vicissitudes of the post-Independence era. Thus, following Pan Shou's call for the reinstatement of Nantah's name, some letters published in *Lianhe Zaobao* supported the idea as a revival of the "Nantah spirit". Others, however, suggested that "restoring the name would be like decorating brocade with flowers (*jin shang tian hua*) — a cosmetic change that would bring little more than psychological comfort to the old Nantah alumni". Indeed, one alumnus put it straightforwardly: "We must accept this painful fact: Nantah is history" (Kao, 1998). Indeed, these words epitomize the interplay between history and memory, although in this case, it would seem that memory struggles in vain against the 'fact' of history. This sentiment, accompanied by a sense of bitterness and irony, also emerged in the interviews, as summed up by Ms. B:

> Nantah graduates have a very sarcastic response — that we should thank them [the state] for closing down Nantah. If not for that, we [i.e. Singapore] would not have been able to achieve what we have achieved today in our society. We should thank them for killing Chinese education and closing Nantah.... This is one extreme response. It is very laughable but very helpless as well. It is like you've been played out by history.

The intensity of such feelings among the Nantah alumni also meant that there was no clear consensus on the issue of NTU restoring the name of Nanyang University in the years following Pan Shou's call in 1998. Dr Su Guaning, who became the University's president in 2003, proposed that the renaming could be timed with the fiftieth anniversary of Nantah's founding in 2005 and with the establishment of new faculties, including a school of humanities and social sciences, on the campus. Dr Su's own earlier schooling in Chinese-medium schools also led him to extol the "Nantah spirit" and to seek "closure of the period of hurt" experienced by the Chinese-educated. However, a year before the anniversary, the plan was suddenly and indefinitely postponed by Dr Su — a move which was endorsed by the Deputy Prime Minister Tony Tan as a "very sensible and responsible approach" (Huang, 2009: 344–5). In November 2010, with the announcement of the completion of his tenure as NTU president in the following year, Dr Su spoke about his role in straddling the worlds of the Chinese-educated and English-educated, and he concluded that the hardest part was over the issue of the renaming of the university: "Some in the Chinese-educated group [said], 'You're stealing the name of my dead mother.' I discovered how strong (those feelings) were, such that even if the Government and our other alumni accepted the renaming wholeheartedly, the renaming would have created controversy.... We don't need that. It's better to focus on building the university" (Cheong, 2010). From this perspective, it could be said that the fragmented social memory of Nantah was tenuously maintained by some alumni in the refusal of any symbolic 'closure' — a closure that was also not wholeheartedly offered by the state other than by superficial invocation of the "Nantah spirit". Both forms of social memory — in one case, the persistence of memory and, in the other, the reinvention of memory — are premised on the presence of an absence, the awareness that Nantah no longer existed other than as an abstraction: "Nantah" is either painfully recalled or sensibly consigned to the past, with its "spirit" appropriated for present day purposes.

Intergenerational Memory

At any rate, the appropriation of 'culture' and 'tradition' on the part of the state has been a longstanding practice in light of official concerns about 'deculturalization' in the face of 'Westernization'. The promotion of 'traditional values' and Confucianism during the 1980s found resonance among some segments of the Chinese-educated, especially among the leadership of clan associations, which played a role in such state-sponsored discourses. In this case, the importance of 'roots' was stressed alongside a narrow, superficial and essentialist idea of culture. It was a conception of Chinese values and Chinese identity (or Chineseness) that held up the Great Tradition formed over millennia, without any notion of twentieth-century Chinese modernism and devoid of critical political content. For the most part, the existing Chinese organizations avoided any role that would appear politically confrontational, as Ms. B observes:

> Many activities organised by these alumni and clan associations are in line with what the government wants, to preserve Chinese culture and all that. But they do not dare to touch any so-called controversial issues. But these issues are actually issues that the Chinese community is concerned with.... [In the early 1990s] Chinese school alumni began some activities, but they were not very active. Some of the NUS alumni were organizing political talks and things like that. But as for the Nantah graduate alumni, their activities were Happy Hours, *karaoke*.... You don't see their stand when we talk about issues. They are just there to keep the network. Even the Nantah alumni — they are very careful even when we talk about Nantah issues. They are so weighed down by their burden.

Along with the burden, however, were fears that discussions on issues concerning Chinese language and culture could still be regarded as chauvinistic activities. The 1997 elections, as pointed out earlier, saw the PAP campaigning against 'Chinese chauvinism', which by many accounts evoked negative sentiments among the Chinese-educated, who felt that they were being singled out as being potentially anti-national. In August that year, however, Prime Minister Goh Chok Tong put forward the idea of reproducing a "Chinese-educated elite" or "Chinese-proficient elite" (*huawen jingying*), a newer-generation "core group of Chinese Singaporeans who are steeped in and knowledgeable about Chinese culture, history, literature and the arts" so as to address the challenges of the Chinese community "in maintaining its roots" — challenges that paradoxically stemmed from the decline of Chinese education (Kwok, 1998a: 215). The idea did not translate itself into wide-ranging policies other than expanding the enrollment of students in Chinese Studies programmes at universities and the recruitment and training of Chinese-language teachers. But the official thinking behind these moves was met with a fair amount of skepticism on the part of some older Chinese-educated intellectuals like Mr. A:

> First of all, some of us seriously doubt whether a "culture" could actually be preserved by creating a tiny company or community of Chinese elites.... It's very questionable. And then the fact is those who have been promoting or have been trying quite desperately to preserve the so-called Chinese roots, values, are people who belong to the clan associations and some of the old guilds.... Well it's appealing in a way.... But in terms of preserving Chinese culture in the long run, I think that idea is really questionable.

In other words, the work of cultural transmission cannot be the sole responsibility of an elite. Ms. B also offered a fundamental critique of the idea of a Chinese-proficient elite:

> I think the starting point is problematic. The motive and the starting point are problematic. The government brought this up because they wanted to groom a batch of people who can handle the language and the culture, a younger generation who are basically bilingual. Their starting point is that our technocrats have not been successful in their business dealings because of the different cultural background [in China]. Their language proficiency was not sufficient. And you know, the government's view of Chinese elite is one who scored A1 [the top

> grade for the major examinations] in Chinese.... Do you think that scoring A1 in both Chinese and English means that you are a Chinese intellectual? The younger generation buys that view, because that was what the government suggests. Scoring good results in Chinese language does not mean that you also have good knowledge of issues related to Chinese culture and Chinese community. It does not mean becoming an intellectual either. We judge if a person is part of the elite on the basis of school results. This is very sad.... When the starting point is wrong, you can't see the issues.... What the government wants are those [younger people] groomed under the bilingual education system. When you have such an exclusive definition, how do you discuss the problem? So the older Chinese-educated feel that they have been excluded, marginalized. But intellectuals are intellectuals; you should not talk about "elites".

The crucial distinction here is that between 'elites' and 'intellectuals'. In this instance, elites are identified by conventional criteria and are groomed by the state for instrumental purposes, especially with the implied view that the erosion of Chinese cultural literacy hampers the country's ability to do business with a rising China. In contrast, as Ms B suggests, academic performance does not equate with cultural knowledge, and intellectuals should not be beholden to or co-opted by the state. By the same token, intellectuals could have been marginalized and excluded from the elite. Indeed, it might well be said that many intellectuals, especially among the Chinese-educated, have not been part of the Singapore elite, which is seen as overwhelmingly English-educated and technocratic in background.

Independent of the state's idea of a Chinese elite, however, some younger members of the Chinese-educated have taken the initiative to define their roles as intellectuals. From the late 1990s onwards, there have been renewed and concerted efforts by the Chinese-educated themselves in making their presence felt in public discourse. These efforts have been spearheaded by a group of intellectuals who in 2000 formed a group called The Tangent (*Yuanqiexian*). The make-up of the founding committee of The Tangent is telling. Most of their founding members were in their late twenties or early thirties and many had attended SAP schools and are alumni of one of the most prominent Chinese high schools, Hwa Chong. Led by Quah Sy Ren (Ke Siren), a former Chinese-language teacher at Hwa Chong, the group also comprised journalists from the Chinese press. Over the decade, they have organized a series of conferences on contemporary issues conducted mainly, although not exclusively, in Chinese. Most of these discussions were documented in their journal *Tangent*, whose inaugural issue (October 2000) carried the proceedings of their first conference as a registered society, with the theme "Walking on the Tangent: Alternative Reflections on Modern Singapore". The metaphor of a tangent is, of course, not accidental; it invokes an ironic sense of marginality and a yearning to break out of a circle of people or a circle of circumstances. Moreover, the emphasis of the group is on offering "alternative reflections" (*linglei sikao*), that is, alternative to the dominant views in Singapore, including those that have been offered by the older generation of Chinese-educated intellectuals and the broader Chinese-speaking segment of the population. Lee Huay Leng (Li Huiling), a founding member of the group who also served as its first president, explained the reasons that prompted them to register themselves officially as a civil society group (Li, 2000: 4):

> By starting first amongst ourselves, we hope to see members of the Chinese-speaking community cast aside their historical baggage [*paokai lishi de baofu*], and participate actively in dialogue during this time when Singapore is continuously progressing. Some of our preceding generation [*qianbei*] may have had very unhappy personal experiences, and we do not dare to forget them. However, instead of allowing ourselves to be constrained by the past, we should try to see things through a more proactive lens in this different era.

The reference to "historical baggage" here should not be interpreted as echoing Prime Minister Goh's earlier call to Nantah graduates to get rid of their "unnecessary psychological baggage". The Tangent could not have been founded without the example and support of older intellectuals in the media and educational circles, including Nantah graduates of the late 1960s and 1970s, who have served as their teachers and mentors. The self-identity of these younger intellectuals was in part shaped by the transmission of the memories of an earlier generation of the Chinese-educated. Nonetheless they saw themselves as belonging to a different generation (Chia, 2009). They wanted to widen the scope of Chinese-language public discourse in spite of the decline in Chinese-language standards in the country, which has been a longstanding preoccupation among the older Chinese-educated. In particular, Quah Sy Ren was critical of the new official appeal to the utilitarian value of the language in light of the rise of China (Huang, 2009: 346). In addition, Lee Huay Ling argued that poor language standards hamper "deep cultural engagement" (*shenceng wenhua de jiechu*) and that "the Chinese-speaking community need not respond to the new emphasis on the language, engendered by China's rise, in a manner that results in fear among other communities.... In the cultural realm, what is needed is a sincere effort to develop a sense among various communities that 'multiculturalism' has real substance" (Li, 2001: 114, 116).

When asked in a press interview about the shift away from Chinese culture of the group's focus, Quah Sy Ren replied: "I feel that it is already so deep within us members that we want to discuss broader things" (Oon, 2000). Their stance signalled a refusal to disengage from public dialogue and a distancing from the debilitating sense of hopelessness and helplessness that has plagued many among their elders. From this account, it could be argued that The Tangent continued to carry a sense of the role of the intellectual as, in Quah's words, the "voice of conscience" (*liangzhi de shengyin*) and as one who maintains "an inner sense of independence" (*xinlishang de duli*). In the second issue of *Tangent*, Quah Sy Ren wrote of the mission "to engage, to understand, [and] to communicate" (Ke, 2001). Absent, however, was any clear injunction "to remember" or to address the issues of marginalization that have preoccupied older Chinese-educated intellectuals; instead the call is to turn their attention to contemporary issues of social, cultural and political change.

Indeed, it may be said that these younger Chinese-educated intellectuals were sincerely and deftly grappling with what Charles Maier (1993: 150) has called a "surfeit of memory", which was "a sign not of historical confidence but of a retreat from transformative politics" in the case of Western societies in the last decade of the twentieth century. Jeffrey Blustein (2008: 16–7) extends Maier's concept in the following way:

> In one sense, we may speak of *too much* memory when a community, say, is obsessively preoccupied with wrongs perceived against itself in the past and constructs its collective identity predominantly around the notion of victimization. It may also as a result fail to properly acknowledge the seriousness of wrongs committed against others: these are either downplayed or disregarded.... In another sense, there's too much memory when preoccupation with the past hinders the collective action that is required for desirable social and political transformations.

The members of The Tangent were clearly imbued with a progressive sense of social change and oriented towards modern ideals such as inclusiveness and pluralism. Their attempt to break out of the preoccupation with marginalization on the part of the older Chinese-educated, however, did not entail a repudiation of the past. Instead, they also sought to rediscover the idealism of an earlier era as exemplified by some of their mentors. One example of such an effort may suffice here, and it is documented in the fifth issue of *Tangent*, a special bilingual issue on "Multiculturalism in Singapore" published in October 2002. It was dedicated to Kuo Pao Kun (1939–2002), the dramatist and public intellectual who had passed away a month earlier and was regarded by The Tangent as "a practising idealist of multiculturalism" (Kwok, 2003). In particular, it documented two fascinating discussions that showed the complex work of social memory among the younger Chinese-educated intellectuals. The first is a "cross-cultural dialogue" among members of The Tangent and the Association of Muslim Professionals in which issues that were normally deemed 'sensitive' in Singapore were openly discussed. For example, the former asked about Malay perceptions of the SAP schools and the Speak Mandarin Campaign, and the latter wanted to know how the Chinese community viewed the controversy over some Muslim parents insisting that their daughters wear the *tudung* or headscarf in schools. On the one hand, Quah Sy Ren recalled that the Chinese-educated of the 1950s and 1960s, infused with the spirit of Malayan nationalism, strove to learn and use the Malay language so as to communicate with non-Chinese. On the other hand, his counterpart, Yang Razali Kassim, emphasized the greater urgency of intercultural understanding in the aftermath of September 11. Indeed, the dialogue gave substance to the idea of multiculturalism in Singapore, which has been criticized as being based on a "minimalist understanding of tolerance" that is bereft of "any substantive cultural exchange, deep understanding and even less cultural crossing of boundaries" (Chua, 2003: 75).

The second discussion documented in the special issue of *Tangent* is an extensive online forum among a dozen members following the cross-cultural dialogue. One major thread of the discussion illustrates a critical response to The Tangent's shift of attention from the "unhappy experiences" of the older Chinese-educated to the challenges faced by other minorities. This was manifested in an intervention by Wang Changwei [Ong Chang Woei] to the effect that the group owed a responsibility to "the Chinese community" and it might have created the impression that it was "indifferent" to their elders in its newfound eagerness to empathize with other minorities. The suggestion, in turn, prompted a series of criticisms against an exclusivist discourse of victimhood and an essentialist sense of identity. In other words, the thrust of The Tangent was weighted against an inward-turning collective identity based on the idea of victimization and in favour of a more expansive solidarity with other minorities. This thrust led the group to take up other wider themes in subsequent issues of *Tangent*, including censorship, civil society, the economy, national elections, and alternatives to the state-centric historiography of the nation (compare Barr and Trocki, 2008; Loh and Liew, 2010; Tan, Tan and Hong, 2011).

Social Memory and Public Discourse

Throughout the post-Independence decades, the status of the Chinese language has declined steadily. In the early twenty-first century, fundamental shifts in patterns of language use in Singapore were evident. According to the 2000 Census, English was the language most frequently spoken at home for 23 per cent of the Chinese population (Leow, 2000: 27); by 2009, as many as 60 per cent of the Chinese children entering primary school spoke English at home (Ho, 2010). This linguistic shift set the stage for two rounds of public debate on the teaching of the Chinese language and on the place of the mother tongue in the education system. On 15 November 2009, Minister Mentor Lee Kuan Yew criticized the pedagogy of Chinese-language teaching for children from English-speaking families in a speech given at the official opening of the Singapore Centre for Chinese Language (Hoe, 2009):

> We started the wrong way. We insisted on *tingxie* (listening), *moxie* (dictation) — *madness*! We had teachers who were teaching in completely Chinese schools [teachers who had taught in Chinese-medium schools]. And they did not want to use any English to teach English-speaking children Chinese and that turned them off completely [emphasis added].

In April 2010, *The Straits Times* carried an interview with Ng Eng Hen, the Education Minister for Singapore, who commented that "the high weighting given to mother tongue languages in the Primary School Leaving Examination (PSLE) is now under review and could be reduced" (Davie, 2010). Under the existing policy, the scores obtained in

English, Mathematics, Science and the mother tongue language count equally towards the aggregate score for the PSLE — the yardstick for admission into secondary schools. Ng remarked this "high" weighting "could exclude someone from progressing in his educational pathway even if he did well in other subjects". He added that since the current system "requires him to do well in his mother tongue language to get into a good [secondary] school, it limits his space".

The two instances in which high-ranking government leaders signalled possible changes in language policies elicited many responses from members of the public, especially in letters to both the Chinese and English press. In the first instance, Wang Changwei [Ong Chang Woei], a Tangent member who wrote in his personal capacity, cited his own experiences in learning English as someone from a Chinese-speaking family (Wang, 2010):

> I remember that when I was schooling, English lessons were a chore, and they nearly killed my interest in schooling. MM Lee said that one of the mistakes of the bilingual policy was that it did not consider the feelings of those students who spoke English. Yet, since its beginning, the teaching of the English language also did not consider the feelings of those who spoke Chinese. Nevertheless, looking back now, I am grateful in hindsight that the system did not indulge me. By raising its standards [of the English language] continuously, I had no choice but to try to reach those standards for my own survival.

Wang's response highlighted an asymmetry in the bilingual education policy. On the one hand, those who came from Chinese-speaking families were expected to perform well in English as a school subject regardless of the difficulties they experienced. These pupils were not given any special pedagogical consideration in the education system; they were channelled into various streams on the basis of "academic ability" as measured by their performance in national examinations (Kwok, 1999: 61). On the other hand, pupils from English-speaking families were offered concessions when requirements in the Chinese-language were judged too demanding for them. In 2001, for example, a less rigorous Chinese Language 'Basic' syllabus was introduced as an alternative to the standard Chinese-language curriculum in secondary schools to cater to those who had "exceptional difficulties" in coping with the Chinese language (Hussain and Leow, 2010).

In the second instance, public responses to Ng's comments proved even more vociferous. There was, firstly, an immediate response from leaders and members of the Singapore Federation of Chinese Clan Associations (SFCCA), who quickly convened a meeting to discuss the issue. Following what has been described as "an emotionally charged two-hour session", the group planned to petition the government to reconsider the possible reduction in weighting of mother tongue language at the PSLE (Leong, 2010). In addition, in a span of two weeks, *Lianhe Zaobao* received 64 letters, almost all of which were against any reduction in weighting. Over the same period, *The Straits Times* received about 102 letters, of which 81 were opposed to weighting reduction while the rest were in favour (Oon, 2010a). Apart the petition from SFCCA and letters to the press, the issue of language policy was also taken up through other channels of public discourse by a segment of the population that has been described as "younger mother tongue advocates" who "speak good English and do not carry the historical baggage of their predecessors, many of whom would have been from Chinese-medium schools and the now-defunct Nanyang University" (Leow, 2010). For example, a petition-signing session was held at the Speakers' Corner at Hong Lim Park to "save mother tongue on Mothers' Day", which fell on 9 May. Organized by Danny Yeo, Lim Sau Hoong and Kok Heng Luen, the petition gathered over 2,500 signatures in a few hours. When interviewed by *The Straits Times*, Yeo offered his thoughts on the value of the Chinese language in "opening doors":

> I am English-educated. I studied at Anglo-Chinese School from primary school to junior college, and I furthered my studies in the United States. But I still see the value of mother tongue. Doors have opened for me because I can speak two languages at a certain level (Leow, 2010).

Although Yeo did not elaborate on the "doors" that were opened, the economic value of Chinese was highlighted by signatories in an online petition,"Mother Tongue Weighting in PSLE Should Not Be Cut". The petition, started by Timothy Low, an undergraduate majoring in Chinese at NTU, gathered over 1,000 signatures. Members of the public and signatories of the two petitions had various reasons for opposing any change in the policy. Nevertheless, it is possible to identify two broad categories of responses. First, many responses highlighted the instrumental value of the Chinese language in the context of China's rise as an economic power. For example, one signatory to the online petition appealed to "the ever practical parents" by stating that "salaries for certain professional positions are now higher in China than in Singapore. Bilingual Singaporeans are highly prized in China to bridge the communication gap between the locals and the head offices of MNCs". Second, a significant number also emphasized the function of the Chinese language in transmitting an essentialized "Chinese culture", as reflected in a signatory's concern with "instilling in our younger generation a strong sense of cultural identity and moral values through mother tongue education".

To be sure, these responses resonated strongly with the state's repeated dual emphasis on the cultural function of the mother tongue and the increasingly practical value of the Chinese language in the wake of China's rise. Moreover, the highly 'ethnicized' and 'instrumentalized' thrust of the public discourse hardly touched on issues related to social equity for those who were not from English-speaking backgrounds — issues which had been highlighted, for example, by members of The Tangent in their efforts to give substance to multiculturalism. Nevertheless, the weight of these responses proved strong enough to result in what may be seen as a recantation of possible changes to the bilingual policy. On 11 May 2010, Singapore's Prime Minister Lee Hsien Loong convened a press conference to "explain the Government's thinking on the question of mother tongue language". During the press conference, PM Lee clarified that there would be no reduction in the weighting of mother tongue language at the PSLE. He also attributed the strong resistance that has emerged through various channels to the "success" of Singapore's bilingual education policy, which has produced "a whole new generation of Singaporeans who are competent in and proud of their mother tongues" (Oon, 2010b). These "successful" products of the system, ironically, were now also able to reproduce the official rhetoric in advancing apparently contrary views vis-à-vis the state.

Among the older generation of Chinese-educated intellectuals, the intervention of the "young mother tongue advocates" drew varied responses. Some were exceedingly relieved and grateful that the tide was stemmed by efforts of a younger generation. Such were the sentiments expressed by Liu Peifang (2010) in her *Lianhe Zaobao* article, which was entitled *Bixie Danxin* [or "loyalty unto death"]:

> It is comforting that the plea [to maintain the weighting of mother tongue] came from our younger generation, and I wept with joy as my emotions welled up. When I met an old friend and told her about my thoughts, I could see that she was also moved as tears welled up in her eyes.... If more young people have such a level of concern for their mother tongue and are courageous in voicing their opinions publicly, then the future of mother tongue education will radiate with hope.

Others, however, found it difficult to share the same exuberance. In responding to Liu's article, Phoon Yew Tien [Pan Yaotian], a Chinese-educated composer, offered the following remarks in a blog entry (Phoon, 2010):

> The title "*Bixie Danxin*" [loyalty unto death] is especially striking. Personally, I just feel that it seems a little exaggerated to use such a 'heavy' title in reference to a modest petition drive that attracted only about 2,000 people. I believe that Madam Liu knows that those occasions which could be described as *Bixie Danxin* did occur in Singapore during its earlier years. However, for many, these occasions are already distant memories and as transient as a passing cloud [*guoyan yunyian*] .... [Liu Peifang wrote that one's] "mother tongue is as dear as one's mother, one should not give it up, and neither should one escape from it, because escapism will eventually lead one to give it up" — surely, these words make sense, and I am not trying to bicker here, but it is often the case that the one who speaks is sincere, but the one who listens is contemptuous [*yanzhe zhunzhun tingzhe miaomiao*]. Those who already appreciate the importance of the mother tongue need not be told again. As for those who don't, there's no use in saying anything more to them!

Underlying these divergent responses is the sense of embattlement among the older generation of Chinese-educated intellectuals as they have tried, time and again, to stand up loyally against the decline of Chinese language standards — albeit, ultimately, in vain. This sentiment could be gleaned from the account offered by Yan Mengda (2010), Senior Executive Editor of *Lianhe Zaobao*, on the possible change to the language policy:

> Many people have said that this is the last frontier (*zuihou yi dao fangxian*) for the Chinese language, and it is indeed so. The older generation have already been so drained, both mentally and physically,

> in guarding earlier frontiers that they no longer have the will to fight. Even if they insist on standing guard at this frontier, their capacities would fall short of their will.

The "young mother tongue advocates", who did not carry the burden of memory, succeeded only in legitimizing the official discourse. The older Chinese-educated, enervated by past battles and mired in memories of victimization, could do little to defend the "last frontier". If social memory was conspicuously absent in the one case, it was indelibly inscribed in the other; in both cases, the possibility for critical questioning was precluded. Blustein (2008: 22) has argued that "whether or not attention to past wrongdoing constitutes objectionable preoccupation with the past, as opposed to a "decent quotient" of collective memory, partly depends on its consequences for other social goods and obligations". The stakes in retaining and reclaiming a "decent quotient" of social memory are significant because "an excessive preoccupation with the past ... clouds judgment, prevents constructive engagement with contemporary injustices and social needs, and impedes the realization of other important social goods" (Blustein, 2008: 168). In the case of the Chinese-educated in Singapore, such stakes have tended to be compromised by both the surfeit of memory on the part of the older generation and the collective amnesia in the larger society. This makes the efforts of intellectuals in maintaining a "decent quotient" of memory at the margins all the more significant.

Note

Portions of this study are based on a project on Southeast Asian Pluralisms, led by Prof. Robert Hefner of the Institute for the Study of Economic Culture at Boston University. Chua Beng Huat and Kwok Kian-Woon directed the research on Singapore in 1999 and early 2000 (see Chua and Kwok, 2001). Thanks are due to Prof. Hefner for leading the project, Prof. Chua for his collaboration, Mr Lee Chee Keng for help in conducting, transcribing and translating some of the interviews, and the interviewees for sharing their experiences and views, only a portion of which could be reflected in this paper.

References

Barr, Michael and Carl Trocki (2008). *Paths Not Taken: Political Pluralism in Post-War Singapore*. Singapore: NUS Press.

Benjamin, Geoffrey (1976). "The Cultural Logic of 'Multiracialism'", in Riaz Hassan (ed.), *Singapore: Society in Transition*. Kuala Lumpur: Oxford University Press, pp. 115–33.

Berger, Peter L. (1986). *The Capitalist Revolution: Fifty Propositions About Prosperity, Equality, & Liberty*. New York: Basic Books.

Berger, Peter L. and Michael Hsiao Hsin-huang (eds) (1988). *In Search of an East Asian Development Model*. New Brunswick, NJ: Transaction Books.

Bloodworth, Dennis (1986). *The Tiger and the Trojan Horse*. Singapore: Times Books International.

Blustein, Jeffrey (2008). *The Moral Demands of Memory*. Cambridge: Cambridge University Press.

Borthwick, Sally (1988). "Chinese Education and Identity in Singapore", in Jennifer Cushman and Wang Gungwu (eds), *Changing Identities of the Southeast Asian Chinese since World War II*. Hong Kong: Hong Kong University Press, pp. 35–59.

______ (1990). "Chinese Education and Employment in Singapore", in Guo Liang (ed.), *Zhanhou Haiwai Huaren Bianhua: Guoji Xueshu Yantaohui Lunwenji* [The Postwar Transformation of Overseas Chinese]. Beijing: Zhongguo Huaqiao Chubanshe.

Chelliah, D.D. (1947). *A History of the Straits Settlements with Recommendations for A New System Based on Vernaculars*. Kuala Lumpur: The Government Press, Kuala Lumpur, Federation of Malaya.

Cheng Lim Keak (1985). *Social Change and the Chinese in Singapore: A Socio-Economic Geography, with Special Reference to Bang Structure*. Singapore: Singapore University Press.

______ (1990). "Reflections on the Changing Roles of Chinese Clan Associations in Singapore". *Asian Culture* 14: 57–71.

Cheong Suk-Wai (2010). "Changing Mindsets to Build Top Varsity", *The Straits Times*, 14 October.

Chew, Melanie (1996). *Leaders of Singapore*. Singapore: Resource Press.

Chia Kwok Wai, Kelvin (2009). "Chinese-Educated Intellectuals in Singapore: A Case Study of The Tangent". B.A. (Honours) Final Year Project, Division of Sociology, Nanyang Technological University.

Chua Beng Huat (2003). "Multiculturalism in Singapore: An Instrument of Social Control". *Race & Class* 44: 58–77.

Chua Beng Huat and Kwok Kian-Woon (2001). "Social Pluralism in Singapore", in Robert Hefner (ed.), *The Politics of Multiculturalism: Pluralism and Citizenship in Malaysia, Singapore, and Indonesia*. Honolulu: University of Hawai'i Press, pp. 86–118.

Chua Mui Hoong (1999). "Who is the Chinese Intellectual?", *The Straits Times*, 2 March.

Clammer, John (1993). "Deconstructing Values: The Establishment of a National Ideology and Its Implications for Singapore's Political Future", in Garry Rodan (ed.), *Singapore Changes Guard: Social, Political and Economic Directions in the 1990s*. Melbourne: Longman Cheshire, pp. 3–51.

Davie, Sandra (2010). "Mother Tongue Weighting in PSLE Could be Cut", *The Straits Times*, 21 April.

Davis, Gloria (1993). "'Star Wars' and the Confucian Ethic", in Mabel Lee and A.D. Syrokomla-Stefanowka (eds), *Modernization of the Chinese Past*. Sydney: The University of Sydney, School of Asian Studies Series Number 1.

Drysdale, John (1994). *Singapore: Struggle for Success*. Singapore: Times Books International.

Fang Xiu (1977). *Notes on the History of Malayan Chinese New Literature, 1920–1942*. Translated by Angus W. McDonald, Jr. Tokyo: The Centre for East Asian Cultural Studies.

Foong Choon Hon (ed.) (1997). *The Price of Peace: True Accounts of the Japanese Occupation*. Translated by Clara Show, original Chinese edition 1995. Singapore: Asiapac.

Goh Chok Tong (1995). "The Nantah Spirit". *Speeches* 19 (3): 24–5.

Goh Keng Swee *et al.* (1979). *The Report on the Ministry of Education 1978*. Singapore: Ministry of Education.

Gopinathan, Saravanan (1991). "Education", in Ernest Chew and Edwin Lee (eds), *A History of Singapore*. Singapore: Oxford University Press.

——— (1998). "Language Policy Changes 1979–1997: Politics and Pedagogy", in S. Gopinathan, Anne Pakir, Ho Wah Kam and Vanithamani Saravanan (eds), *Language, Society and Education in Singapore: Issues and Trends* (2nd ed.). Singapore: Times Academic Press.

Harper, T.N. (2001). "Lim Chin Siong and the 'Singapore Story'", in Tan Jing Quee and Jomo K.S. (eds), *Comet in Our Sky: Lim Chin Siong in History*. Kuala Lumpur: INSAN, pp. 3–55.

Ho Cheeng Cheeng (2010). "Heated Debate in Chinese Daily", *The Straits Times*, 1 May.

Hoe Yeen Nie (2009). "Insistence on Bilingualism in Early Years of Education Policy was Wrong: MM Lee". <http://www.channelnewsasia.com/stories/singaporelocalnews/view/1018826/1/.html> [accessed 17 November 2009].

Hofheinz Jr., Roy and Kent Calder (1982). *The Eastasia Edge*. New York: Basic Books.

Hong Lysa and Huang Jianli (2003). "The Scripting of Singapore's Heroes: Toying with Pandora's Box", in Tan Liok Ee and Abu Talib Ahmad (eds), *New Terrains in Southeast Asian Historiography*. Athens: Ohio University Press, pp. 219–46.

——— (2008). *The Scripting of a National History: Singapore and its Pasts*. Singapore: NUS Press.

Huang Jianli (2008). "Dilemma and Anguish of the Chinese-educated", in Bridget Welsh *et al.* (eds), *Impressions of the Goh Chok Tong Years in Singapore*. Singapore: NUS Press, Lee Kuan Yew School of Public Policy and Institute of Policy Studies, pp. 336–49.

Hussain, Zakir and Leow Si Wan (2010). "Community Groups Welcome Clarifications", *The Straits Times*, 12 May.

Kahn, Herman (1979). *World Economic Development: 1979 and Beyond*. London: Croom Helm.

Kao Chen (1998). "Reviving Nantah's Name", *The Straits Times*, 14 October.

Ke Siren [Quah Sy Ren] (1999). "Shehui de Bianchui yu Xiandaixin de Zhongxin: Xinjiapo Huawen Zhishifenzi de Jingyu" [The Periphery of Society and the Centre of Modernity: Singapore Chinese Intellectuals in Context]. Paper presented at conference on "The Role and Responsibility of Singapore's Chinese Intellectuals in the 21st Century", organized by the Hwa Chong Alumni, 28 February 1999.

______ (2001). "Jiechu, Liaojie, Jiaoliu: Wenhua Sikao de Yiyi" [To Engage, To Understand, To Communicate: The Significance of Cultural Relations]. *Tangent* 2: 1–4.

Kee Pookong and Choi Kwai Keong (eds) 2000. *A Pictorial History of Nantah*. Singapore: Chinese Heritage Centre.

Khe Su Lin (2006). *Lixiang yu xianshi: Nanyang Daxue Xueshenghui Yanjiu*, 1956–1964 [Idealism and Reality: The Student Association of Nanyang University 1956–1964]. Singapore: Global Publishing & NYU Centre for Chinese Language and Culture.

Kotkin, Joel (1992). *Tribes: How Race, Religion, and Identity Determine Success in the New Global Economy*. New York: Random House.

Kuo, Eddie, C.Y. (1996). "Confucianism as Political Discourse in Singapore: The Case of an Incomplete Revitalization Movement", in *Confucian Traditions in East Asian Modernity: Moral Education and Economic Culture in Japan and the Four Mini-Dragons*. Cambridge, Mass.: Harvard University Press, pp. 294 –309.

Kwok Kian-Woon (1995). "Social Transformation and the Problem of Social Coherence: Chinese Singaporeans at Century's End". *Asiatische Studien/ Etudes Asiatiques*, XLLX (1): 217–41.

______ (1998a). "Singapore", in Lynn Pan (ed.), *Encyclopedia of the Chinese Overseas*. Singapore: Archipelago Press/Landmark Books; Cambridge, Mass.: Harvard University Press, pp. 200–17.

______ (1998b). "Being Chinese in the Modern World", in Lynn Pan (ed.), *Encyclopedia of the Chinese Overseas*. Singapore: Archipelago Press/Landmark Books; Cambridge, Mass.: Harvard University Press, pp. 121–6.

______ (1999). "The Social Architect: Goh Keng Swee", in Lam Peng Er and Kevin Y.L. Tan, (eds), *Lee's Lieutenants: Singapore's Old Guard*. St Leonards, NSW: Allen & Unwin.

——— (2003). "Remembering Kuo Pao Kun (1939–2002)". *Inter-Asia Cultural Studies* 4: 193–201.

Lai Ah Eng (1995). *Meanings of Multiethnicity: A Case-study of Ethnicity and Ethnic Relations in Singapore*. Kuala Lumpur: Oxford University Press.

Lee Ting Hui (1977). *The Open United Front: The Communist Struggle in Singapore, 1954–1966*. Singapore: The South Seas Society.

——— (1987). "Chinese Education in Malaya 1894–1911: Nationalism in the First Chinese Schools", in Lee Tai To (ed.), *The 1911 Revolution: The Chinese in British and Dutch Southeast Asia*. Singapore: Heinemann Asia, pp. 48–65.

Leong Weng Kam (2010). "Chinese Clans to Petition Government on Language Weighting", *The Straits Times*, 4 May.

Leow Bee Geok (2000). *Census of Population 2000: Advance Data Release*. Singapore: Singapore Department of Statistics.

Leow Si Wan (2010). "New Breed of Bilingual Advocates Stepping Up", *The Straits Times*, 13 May.

Li Huiling (1999). "Pan Shou de Nanda Leihen" [Pan Shou"s Sorrow Concerning Nanyang University], *Lianhe Zaobao*, 6 March.

——— (2000). "Yuan Qie Xian Chuang She Yan Tao Hui Zhu Xi Bao Gao" [Chairperson's Report for The Tangent's Inauguration Conference]. *Tangent* 1: 3–5.

——— (2001). "Wei Huawen Huayu de Cunbu Nanxing Fuchu Daijia" [Paying the Price for the Predicament of Chinese Language in Singapore]. *Tangent* 2: 108–16.

Li Yuanjin (1994). "Xinjiapo Huawenjiao yu Bianqian (1959–1987) xia, Zhishifenzhi de Baogen Xintai" [Changes in Chinese Education in Singapore and the Attitude of Intellectuals towards the Preservation of Roots], in *Traditional Culture and Social Change*. Singapore: Tung Ann District Guild, pp. 47–97.

——— (1999). "Zuo Chu Lishi, Kua Yue Shiji: Xinjiapo Huawen Zhishifenzhi Jueshe de Yanbian" [Transcending History, Crossing the Century: The Changing Roles of Chinese Intellectuals in Singapore]. Paper presented at conference on "The Role and Responsibility of Singapore's Chinese Intellectuals in the 21st Century", organized by the Hwa Chong Alumni, 28 February.

Lim Jim Koon (1997). "Forget the Sedan Chair, Let's Get on a Jetliner — Together: A Chinese-Educated's View on the Tang Liang Hong Affair." Speech delivered at the Third National Education Seminar on 23 January 1997, Ngee Ann Polytechnic, Mimeo.

Liu Peifang (1994). "Lishi Changhezhong de Yiduan Jiyi" [A Section of Memory in the Long River of History], *Lianhe Zaobao*, 25 September.

——— (2010). "*Bixie Danxin*" [Loyalty Unto Death], *Lianhe Zaobao*, 13 May.

Loh Kah Seng and Liew Kai Khiun (eds) (2010). *The Makers & Keepers of Singapore History*. Singapore: Ethos Books; Singapore Heritage Society.

MacFarquhar, Roderick (1980). "The Post-Confucian Challenge", *The Economist*, 9 February.

Maier, Charles (1993). "A Surfeit of Memory? Reflections on History, Melancholy and Denial", *History and Memory* 5 (2): 136–51.

Mother Tongue Weighting in PSLE Should Not Be Cut (2010). <http://www.petitionspot.com/petitions/pslemothertongue> [accessed 25 June 2010].

Oon, Clarissa (2000). "Not Flying Off at a Tangent: A SAP School Product, With No Nantah Baggage", *The Straits Times*, 14 September.

______ (2010a). "Much Ado about Mother Tongue", *The Straits Times*, 8 May.

______ (2010b). "No Change to PSLE Mother Tongue Weightage", *The Straits Times*, 12 May.

Oon, Clarissa and Kor Kian Beng (2009). "Was Chinese Wrongly Taught for 30 Years?", *The Straits Times*, 27 November.

Pendley, Charles (1983). "Language Policy and Social Transformation in Contemporary Singapore", *Southeast Asian Journal of Social Science* 11 (2): 46–58.

Phoon Yew Tien (2010). "Bi Xie Dan Xin [Loyalty Unto Death]", *Pan Yaotian Boke* [Phoon Yew Tien's Blog]. <http://phoonyewtien.blogspot.com/2010/05/blog-post_13.html> [acessed 20 June 2010].

PuruShotam, Nirmala (1998). *Negotiating Language, Constructing Race: Disciplining Difference in Singapore*. Berlin and New York: Mouton de Gruyter.

Redding, S. Gordon (1990). *The Spirit of Chinese Capitalism*. Berlin: Walter de Gruyter.

Sai Siew Min and Huang Jianli (1999). "The "Chinese-educated" Political Vanguard: Ong Pang Boon, Lee Khoon Choy and Jek Yeun Thong", in Lam Peng Er and Kevin Y.L. Tan (eds), *Lee's Lieutenants: Singapore's Old Guards*. St Leonards, NSW: Allen & Unwin, pp. 132–68.

Sai Siew Yee (1997). "Post-Independence Educational Change, Identity and Huaxiao-sheng Intellectuals in Singapore: A Case Study of Chinese Language", *Southeast Asian Journal of Social Science* 25 (2): 79–101.

Tan Jing Quee, Tan Kok Chiang and Hong Lysa (2011). *The May 13 Generation: The Chinese Middle School Students Movement and Singapore Politics in the 1950s*. Petaling Jaya: Strategic Information and Research Development Centre.

Tang Eng Teik (1988). "Uniqueness of Malayan Chinese Literature: Literary Polemic in the Forties", *Asian Culture* 12: 102–15.

Tu Wei-Ming (1984). *Confucian Ethics Today: The Singapore Challenge*. Singapore: Curriculum Development Institute of Singapore, Federal Publications.

Tu Wei-Ming (ed.) (1991). *The Triadic Chord: Confucian Ethics, Industrial East Asia and Max Weber*. Singapore: Institute of East Asian Philosophies.

——— (1994). *The Living Tree: The Changing Meaning of Being Chinese Today*. Stanford: Stanford University Press.

——— (1996). *Confucian Traditions in East Asian Modernity: Moral Education and Economic Culture in Japan and the Four Mini-Dragons*. Cambridge, Mass.: Harvard University Press.

Wang Changwei [Ong Chang Woei] (2010). "Wo Guo Hua Wen Jiao Yu Shi Bai De Zheng Jie" [The Crux of the Failure of Our Country's Chinese Language Education], *Lianhe Zaobao*, 20 November.

Wang Gungwu (1964). "A Short Introduction to Chinese Writing in Malaya", in T. Wignesan (ed.), *Bunga Emas: An Anthology of Contemporary Malaysian Literature (1930–1963)*. Kuala Lumpur: Rayirath (Raybooks) Publications.

Wee, C.J. W-L (1999). "The Vanquished: Lim Chin Siong and a Progressivist National Narrative", in Lam Peng Er and Kevin Y.L. Tan (eds), *Lee's Lieutenants: Singapore's Old Guards*. St Leonards, NSW: Allen & Unwin, pp. 169–90.

Wee-Davies, Gloria [Gloria Davies] (1994). "East Asia's Link with Confucianism", *Trends, Business Times*, 31 December.

Willmott, W.E. (1989). "The Emergence of Nationalism", in Kernial Singh Sandhu and Paul Wheatley (eds), *Management of Success: The Moulding of Modern Singapore*. Singapore: Institute of Southeast Asian Studies, pp. 578–98.

Yan Mengda (2010). "Gai ting nianqingren de le!" [Time to Listen to the Young People!], *Lianhe Zaobao*, 1 May.

Yao Souchou (2008). "All Quiet on Jurong Road: Nanyang University and Radical Vision in Singapore", in Michael Barr and Carl Trocki (eds), *Paths Not Taken: Political Pluralism in Post-War Singapore*. Singapore: NUS Press, pp. 170–87.

Yeo Song Nian (1993). "Chinese Language Literature in Malaya and Singapore (1919–1942)", in Leo Suryadinata (ed.), *Chinese Adaptation and Diversity: Essays on Society and Literature in Indonesia, Malaysia, and Singapore*. Singapore: Singapore University Press, pp. 169–80.

Yeo Song Nian and Leung Yuen Sang (1985). "In Search of Identity: Chinese Literature in Malaysia and Singapore, 1919–1983", *Asian Culture* 5: 18–23.

Yong Chin Fatt (1992). *Chinese Leadership and Power in Colonial Singapore*. Singapore: Times Academic Press.

Zahari, Said (2001). *Dark Clouds at Dawn: A Political Memoir*. Kuala Lumpur: Insan.

CHAPTER 10

Living with the Spectre of the Past: Traumatic Experiences among Wives of Former Political Prisoners of the '1965 Event' in Indonesia

Budiawan

Introduction

As with the end of authoritarian rule elsewhere, the fall of Suharto in Indonesia created an opportunity for survivors of past political violence to break their silence publicly. Among those who have taken the chance to express themselves are former political prisoners of the '1965 event' (or *eks-tapol,* as the popular Indonesian term goes).[1] These former prisoners have claimed the right to be regarded as victims, instead of perpetrators, of the past tragedy. Their claims have appeared in memoirs, autobiographies or other forms of self-narrative — publication of which began only a few months after Suharto stepped down in May 1998, and has been booming ever since. Twenty-five memoirs or autobiographies of former political prisoners of the 1965 event have been published since early 1999, in addition to dozens of books — both translations of foreign scholars' works and those written by Indonesian academics — presenting various alternative versions of the 1965 event and its aftermath.[2] A number of organizations have also been formed to campaign for rehabilitation. The primary objective of these self-articulations is to seek public recognition of their claims about what happened, in order to find release from their own burden of the past.

At least four organizations of *eks-tapol* have been established since early 1999, such as YPKP 1965–66 (Yayasan Penelitian Korban Pembunuhan 1965–66, Foundation for Research into the Victims of the 1965–66 Massacres), LPKP 1965–66 (Lembaga Penelitian Korban Pembunuhan 1965–66, Institute for Research into the Victims of the 1965–66 Massacres), LPKrop (Lembaga Perjuangan Rehabilitasi Korban Rezim Orde Baru, Institute for the Struggle to Rehabilitate Victims of the New Order Regime), and Pakorba (Pagayuban Korban Order Baru, Community of the Victims of the New Order Regime). In principle, these four organizations struggle for public acknowledgement of victims of the past violence and for the rehabilitation of their civic rights. What makes them different is, among other things, the methods they employ to achieve their aspirations. LPKP 1965–66, for instance, not only builds its networks within Indonesia but also lobbies international agencies such as the International Court. Pakorba, for its part, has formed an alliance with victims of other gross human rights violations of the New Order regime. The other two, YPKP 1965–66 and LPKrop, cooperate with legal aid organizations and human rights advocates within Indonesia only.

However, not every survivor of the 1965 event welcomes this opportunity. Rather than taking part in these memorial movements, some prefer to remain silent about what they have experienced. Among these are wives of *eks-tapol*, particularly those who 'committed adultery' (*berselingkuh*) or started another relationship while their husbands were imprisoned. These survivors were never jailed, tortured, raped or even detained for interrogation; they were not political prisoners. Yet their 'adultery' has made them feel imprisoned in the past. It is easy to see how their situation might have led them to enter into other relationships. The imprisonment of their husbands placed them in a position of great insecurity — nobody knew how long their husbands would be in jail, leaving them to struggle for survival in the meantime. Yet, since many other wives of political prisoners did remain faithful to their absent spouses, they have had to suffer the harsh judgment of those around them for having chosen this path. They are left with the feeling that they lost the struggle to master their situation. It is partly this feeling that has left them unable to express their memories. In other words, although they suffered 'only' the indirect effects of the past political violence, they are still living with the spectre of the past.

This chapter is concerned with several such cases. There are at least two reasons why they are worth discussing. Firstly, when mass political violence leads to some sections of society being either imprisoned or killed by the party that seizes power, not a few children are orphaned and wives widowed, whether permanently or temporarily while the father/husband is imprisoned. Children grow up without their fathers and wives are stuck in an ambiguous, liminal state so long as their husbands remain in prison. However, these victims are absent from or under-represented in public discourse. Practitioners of mainstream social sciences and history are partly responsible for this lack of concern. Any attempt at discussing the experiences of such 'hidden' survivors will bring a better understanding of the (continuing) effects of mass political violence. Secondly, in spite of having endured 'only' the indirect effects of the political violence, the experience of these children and wives is still very traumatic, partly because these experiences are completely beyond their expectation. Making sense of the past may be an even heavier burden for them compared to those who were imprisoned, who might perceive of their own bitter experiences as a consequence of their engagement in political activism. This means that studying such survivors carries serious implications for the notion of victim and the category of victimhood. This chapter, however, focuses its concern on wives of *eks-tapol*, particularly those who entered into a relationship with another man while their husbands were in prison. Of those experiencing the *indirect* effects of the 1965 event, the latter have suffered from the most traumatic experiences. This is observable in their continuing silence and anxious or apathetic expressions about the current 'wind of change', instead of enthusiastic celebration. To show the degree of their trauma, it is necessary to make some comparison with wives who struggled for survival without the assistance of illegitimate spouses.[3]

This chapter is organized as follows. Firstly, it will present a brief account of the 1965 event and its aftermath. This will provide the historical setting for the cases in question. Secondly, the case histories will be described in detail. Thirdly, I will analyze the cases, setting them within the theoretical framework of recent writings on trauma, memory and identity. The data on which I rely are drawn from my personal observation during fieldwork conducted from October 1999 to January 2000. They are also partly derived from the field notes of a research project currently conducted by Syarikat, a non-governmental organization initiated by a number of young activists of the Muslim organization Nahdlatul Ulama (NU), which is concerned with the issue of reconciliation between NU and the families of former political prisoners at the grassroots level. This organization has drawn together young people from both sides to work together in researching and collecting stories of their parents' past involvements in the 1965 event and its aftermath.[4]

What Syarikat has achieved is a real breakthrough in enhancing the discourse of (communal) reconciliation. The young activists who joined it have initiated a break with the standard official account of communism in Indonesia's past. This is because NU, like other Muslim organizations and nationalist organizations as well, actively took part in the killings of the so-called communists in 1965–66. In line with the national memory of Suharto's New Order regime, they claim that they acted as such in order to save the state, nation and religion (viz., Islam) from the communist threat. However, in the past few years, a number of young activists of NU have redefined their sense of self. Instead of claiming to be the children of heroes, they call themselves children of slaughterers. In their perception, what happened in 1965–66, when hundreds of thousands of alleged communists were either imprisoned without trial or killed, was a crime against humanity.[5]

The '1965 Event' and Its Aftermath

The term '1965 event' refers to what happened on 30 September 1965. The official version of Suharto's regime narrates the events as an abortive Communist coup. The Indonesian Communist Party (PKI) is said to have masterminded a putsch by the Presidential Guards' Regiment (*Cakrabirawa*) to kidnap and kill six top Army officers on the eve of 1 October 1965 "as a way of controlling the military before eventually controlling the state."[6] This narration relies on "evidence from the trials of the top PKI leaders and those who were involved in the September 30, 1965 Movement".[7]

According to Suharto's regime, the 1965 event was the climax of the PKI's efforts to transform the state ideology *Pancasila* (Five Principles)[8] and the National Constitution to Communism. However, according to the official narrative, due to the close co-operation of the military under the leadership of Major-General Suharto, by then the strategic commander of the Army (*Pangkostrad*) — who was not himself a target of the '30 September 1965 Movement' — and the people, the PKI's last attempt could be crushed. *Pancasila* and the Constitution were saved, and so was the existence of the state and the nation.[9]

What remains unspoken in this account concerning the military campaigns against the PKI and its subsidiary organizations is the fact that from the end of 1965 to mid-1966, an estimated 500,000 people accused of being communists were killed, either by armed civilians who had the support of the military, or by the military itself.[10] Meanwhile, over one million more people were imprisoned without trial for periods varying from just a few years to over 20 years. One source notes that 1,375,320 people categorized under Group C (those who had "indications of having links with the PKI") were detained for less than ten years, while 34,587 people (including more than 10,000 people interned on the Island of Buru) categorized as Group B (those who had "indications of having links with the 30 September Movement") were detained for more than ten years, and 426 people categorized as Group A (those who were "involved in the Movement") were tried, some being sentenced to death and the rest to life imprisonment.[11]

The extermination of the PKI following the event of 30 September 1965 was in turn a way of bringing Sukarno's rule to an end since the PKI was his largest supporter. It paved the way for Suharto (and his generals) to seize power. From its inception, Suharto's regime produced and reproduced the story of the communist threat. Former political prisoners of the 1965 event were almost always blamed whenever there was a riot. Being labelled as 'ideologically and historically unclean' (*tidak bersih diri*) made them vulnerable scapegoats; they also lost their civic rights. Their offspring, labelled as 'genealogically unclean' (*tidak bersih lingkungan*), found their access to public service jobs (for instance, the military services, the civil service, or state-owned companies, etc.) cut off. In short, anyone associated with what the regime branded as communism was repressed or silenced. By doing so, a continued fear of communists and communism was maintained, and partly, if not mainly, explains how Suharto's regime sustained itself in power for 32 years.

After the fall of Suharto, the anti-communist discourse has been reproduced less frequently by state apparatuses. However, it still persists since parts of society still find an interest in sustaining it due to their own memories of conflicts with the PKI. This means that attempts to re-examine the past violence are still challenged by certain sectors of society. This fact is partly responsible for the continuing silence of some of the survivors of the 1965–66 massacres. In the cases examined below, silence is symptomatic of disbelief that the country has reached a 'point of no return' (or, in the Indonesian phrase, '*tiada titik balik*'). Exploring the manifestations of such disbelief will help us to understand to what degree their traumatic experiences still haunt these victims and constrain them from imagining another possible future. Time is not always conceived as linear; in fact, the traditional Javanese view of time is cyclical, expressed in the Javanese phrase '*wolak waliking zaman*', meaning that there is a possibility of the past returning in the future, even if not in precisely the same form. It is my observation that many victims of the 1965 event have recourse to this conception of time in being cautious, perhaps too cautious, in their interpretations of recent history and current events. Victims of political violence are in general deeply troubled by the sense that the world has become unpredictable, and are unlikely to relinquish such fears so long as the perpetrators go unpunished in a "culture of impunity" (Zur, 1994). As such, the adherence to a cyclical notion of time in Java is hardly surprising, but it is also a serious obstacle for individuals trying to cope with a traumatic past. The following section explores the cases in question.

Three Wives of Former Political Prisoners

As mentioned earlier, mass political violence has always had the effect of leaving a significant number of children without fathers and wives without husbands, either temporarily or permanently, since the primary targets of violent actions are mostly men. For women whose husbands are killed or imprisoned, their primary concern is survival and seeking some social protection. This problem is critical in a class of society where the man is positioned as the sole breadwinner of the family while the woman is regarded as only the manager of household affairs. Although this is not necessarily the case in Indonesian cultures generally, it tended to be so for many of the victims, who were part of an urban middle-class culture. The political violence left wives almost totally alone to struggle for their own survival and that of their children. In many cases the extended family served as a social safety net, with grandparents, uncles or aunts providing some economic assistance or even taking over as the source of economic support. But in other cases, these victims were shunned by their extended family members and treated like social lepers. No single factor can explain why the former happens in some cases and what conditions lead to the latter instead. In the context of the 1965 event and its aftermath, where the anti-communist campaigns were run on a massive scale and very effectively, people tended to put a distance between themselves and those being stigmatized as communist or the relative of a communist. To be seen to have a close relationship with such persons could drag one into trouble with the security apparatuses. Consequently, even if one sympathized with them, one dared not express it openly, unless one was a member of the security forces oneself. In many cases the wives of political prisoners had to struggle for survival alone. Some received economic support from their parents. Many married again legally, after asking for a divorce from their imprisoned husbands. But not a few committed adultery or entered into an illegitimate second marriage in order to survive.

Below are the stories of three wives of *eks-tapol*. They came from the same social stratum, that is, the relatively well-educated, urban middle class where men tend to be the sole breadwinners of the family. Each had a different experience during the imprisonment of their husbands, which played out differently in their everyday lives. The first wife, Mdm Surti (not her real name), struggled for survival completely alone, without any assistance from her parents and relatives. The second wife, Mdm Siti (not her real name), at first had to manage alone but later found a married man, a police officer, who showed sympathy and finally cohabited with her. The third wife, Mdm Sri, completely relied on her parents' assistance for rearing her children.

Mdm Surti

Mdm Surti has two children, a son and a daughter. They were seven and four years old respectively when the 1965 event happened. She was a full-time housewife while her husband was a military officer of lower-middle rank.

Since Mdm Surti's husband belonged to the military unit under the line of command of the commander of the 30 September 1965 Movement, he was arrested and imprisoned without trial for 13 years, although he was not involved in and had never known about the Movement. This changed Mdm Surti's course of life. To rear her two children she had to earn a living alone. She could not expect any assistance from her poor and aged parents or parents-in-law. Neither could she expect a helping hand from her own relatives or the relatives of her husband, since they were having a hard time as well.

At first Mdm Surti worked for a small home industry producing rice flour. She worked from 4.00 am–5.00 pm every day, except on Sundays. Her two children were left at home, where her son took care of his sister for the whole day.

With the money she earned, she could feed herself and her two children, as well as buy some food for her imprisoned husband. She was also able to save a little. But in the early 1970s, when her son had to enter secondary school, where the school fee was of course higher, she turned to running her own business. With her savings of the past six years and a loan from her former boss, she ran her own rice flourmill as a home industry. Her business went well enough for her to be able to send her two children to universities where they obtained their degrees.

In 1978 her husband was released. It was a happy moment since the whole family was reunified and could live together. However, the good times did not last long. Her husband was unhappy that his wife had become a successful businesswoman. What made him unhappy was not her success as such, but its social and psychological consequences as he saw it. To him, the fact that she was now the breadwinner of the family was unacceptable. In his eyes his wife seemed to have changed — she was not as subservient as she had been before he was imprisoned. They did not live in harmony. Eventually they decided to live separately. She built a new house and lived with her daughter, while her son took care of her husband in the other house. They did not get divorced but they have become like strangers to each other.

For Mdm Surti, her most bitter memory of the past is not of the time when she had to work hard to rear her two children, but of the unwillingness of her husband to acknowledge her role as a successful breadwinner of the family. What she could not understand, and even felt hurt by, was her husband's attitude towards her years of hard struggle to ensure the family's survival. Instead of being thankful to find that the family had been able to endure those difficult years without depending on other people, he resented her success as he felt it eroded his authority as the head of the family.

Every time she remembers the disharmony, she wonders whether every man is like her husband. Sometimes she wants to forget but is unable to as long as her husband does not take any initiative to apologize. However, expecting her husband to apologize is like expecting a leopard to change its spots. She would like to forget him but knows that she will never be able to. All she can do is to keep her tale just for her two children,[12] in the hope that her son will not turn out to be like his father. Ironically, despite her deep disappointment about her husband, she still conforms to the so-called Javanese cultural wisdom that 'a woman should protect her husband's dignity'.

Obviously the central problem for Mdm Surti is the embodiment of a patriarchal value system in her husband's perception of gender relations. Below is another story which reveals the ways in which such a value system has shaped how an *eks-tapol*'s wife has dealt with her bitter past.

Mdm Siti

Mdm Siti already had two children — a boy of three-and-a-half and a girl of one-and-a-half years old — when her husband was arrested and imprisoned in early November 1965. Her husband was previously a secondary school teacher while she was a full-time housewife.

She had to depend on herself to earn a living as both her parents and parents-in-law had only a small plot of land each. Neither could she expect any economic assistance from her relatives or the relatives of her husband since many of them were also imprisoned. She ran a small shop selling basic goods while minding her two children. The profit she earned was actually enough to support her family. Unlike most children of political prisoners, her two children were not underfed; she could even afford to buy them toys, which was at that time a luxury for most families of political prisoners.

However, she was not sure for how long she could continue to do all the work by herself; she also did not know the length of time her husband would remain in prison. With the future so uncertain, she could not refuse the sympathy of a man, a police officer.[13] Initially she simply accepted his helping hand but later started to think of him as a substitute father for her two children, although she knew that he was already married and had children of his own. However, she was not sure if she was making the right decision since her husband was still alive. In this state of indecision, she started a relationship with him and became pregnant. After she gave birth, the man came to her house more often and they even cohabited. Relatives and neighbours started to talk about her behind her back. Mdm Siti did not know (and will never know) exactly what other people said and thought about her but it was their 'silence', ironically, that made her feel condemned. Her problem, she felt, was how to defend herself against such 'silent' social condemnation.

In mid-1969 the government announced a plan for releasing thousands of political prisoners by the turn of the decade.[14] Mdm Siti wondered if her husband would be among them. She was torn about her situation: it was likely that her husband would come home, but someone else had entered her life, giving her some economic and psychological protection and acting like a father to her three children. Upon learning that her husband was to be released immediately, she asked her lover to leave, begging for his understanding.

By the end of 1969, Mdm Siti's husband was released. He had heard that his wife had had a child with another man during his imprisonment.[15] He could not deny the fact that there was a stepchild in the family and tried to live with the new reality. His wife, however, instead of apologizing to him for her adultery, blamed him for the scandal. She insisted that she would not have committed adultery had he not been imprisoned; and that he would not have been imprisoned had he not followed his brother's example to become engaged in political activism. This conviction of hers has shaped the communication between the couple, as manifested in their everyday life, and also the way they have 'managed' their memories. To Mdm Siti, the cause of her bitter past is politics. Since her husband's release, she has steered him away from anything associated with politics: she controls the newspaper stories he should read, the TV programmes he should watch, and the conversations he should have with other people, especially with his brother who lives next door.

Mdm Sri

Unlike the stories of the two wives above, Mdm Sri's is less dramatic. Hers is probably the most common among wives of former political prisoners.

When her husband was arrested toward the end of October 1965, Mdm Sri's four children — two daughters and two sons — were aged seven, five, and three respectively, while her youngest child was only six months old. She was a full-time housewife, while her husband taught in a secondary school. He is the elder brother of Mdm Siti's husband.

Their house was built not on their own land but on land rented from her husband's uncle. After her husband was arrested, she and her four children were driven out, with only a small sum of money as 'compensation' given by her husband's uncle. Since they were now homeless, her parents took care of her and the two sons, while her parents-in-law took care of her two daughters. In the first months after her husband was imprisoned, she made some money by selling the remaining household goods, including many books from her husband's collection, but after only a couple of months, there was nothing left to sell.

Mdm Sri did not think at all of running a business to earn a living. She relied completely on her father's pension in order to survive. Her father was a retired schoolteacher while her mother ran a small business selling traditional clothes from door to door. In addition to taking care of her two boys, she periodically visited her two daughters who lived outside of town with her parents-in-law. She and her mother took turns every other month to visit her husband, bringing him food[16] and other personal equipment. They visited him routinely until his release toward the end of 1969.

Despite living in dire straits, which meant that she had to manage the money received from her parents very carefully, Mdm Sri does not harbour any bitter memories. She does not blame her husband for the difficult times she had to go through because she realizes that thousands, even hundred of thousands, of other families shared similar hardships. She perceives of her husband (and other former political prisoners) as victims of the party in its bid to seize power. It is such a perception that she and her husband have passed on to their children. After Mdm Sri's husband was released, the whole family was reunited and went to live with her parents-in-law outside the town. To make a living, her husband began to learn to cultivate some plots of land owned by his own parents. He did this for around five years before migrating to Jakarta to apply for a teaching job. In the case of Mdm Sri, the memory of the years after the 1965 event is not burdensome since there was nothing to hide or repress. The 'current wind of historical change' has given her husband an opportunity to recover his sense of self by actively joining some non-governmental organizations initiated by *eks-tapol*s.

Trauma, Memory and Identity: Social and Cultural Perspectives

In order to achieve a better understanding of these case histories in the context of current debates about trauma, memory and identity in social and cultural perspectives, I outline below a theoretical framework.

In its most basic definition, trauma refers to a special category of experience connected to loss. People perceive trauma as fundamentally involving loss. All traumas involve loss, but not all losses are traumas (Harvey, 2002). In the context of loss, people often experience a sense of missing something very important, a sense of incompletion and a feeling of disappointment.

Trauma resulting from collective violence is the result of victimization. Trauma and victimization thus play a central role in the politics of memory. Memories, however, are never simply records of the past, but are "interpretive reconstructions that bear the imprint of local narrative conventions, cultural assumptions, discursive formations and practices, and social contexts of recall and commemoration" (Antze and Lambek, 1996: vii). In other words, trauma is best understood in its relation to the complexities of memory, while memory is linked to identity. To put the three concepts together within the social, cultural and political settings will bring a better understanding of why some survivors of past political violence continue to live with the spectre of the past, and why they do not see the fall of an authoritarian regime as an opportunity to negotiate a fresh interpretation of the past.

If trauma is connected to loss, the first two of the three cases above show different experiences of loss in 'dealing with men'. In the case of Mdm Surti, it was a loss of respect for her husband that she experienced. His lack of appreciation for her efforts to survive was a major disappointment, just as his feeling threatened by her success in running a business made her wonder if every man was self-centred. However, having bowed to the social convention that a wife should protect her husband's 'social dignity', she faces a cultural constraint that prevents her from expressing her deep disappointment openly. In this case, memory is then "a culturally specific field", in the sense that remembering is indeed personal, but how it is communicated (or not) is shaped by the cultural context. Here memory is, in Teski's words, "neither a cultural given nor an individual creation, but something between the two" (Teski, 1995: 50).

It is such 'in-between-ness' that prevents the accommodation of some memories, as Mdm Siti has discovered. In her case, it was the loss of her dignity as a woman. She knows that committing adultery is a violation of the moral conventions of societies that regard the institution of marriage as sacred. But she also knows that society reserves a harsher condemnation for the woman who has committed adultery than the man — it is as if there is no excuse for an adulterous woman while an adulterous man is, to some degree, tolerated. It is this unfair treatment that prompted Mdm Siti's protestations, of which her husband, as the closest man in her life, has been her immediate target. In this context, she represses some of her memories and wipes them out of history. I use the term 'repression' here not to refer to "the sort of psychological mechanism of repression of painful memories" in which it is postulated that a person actually "loses all recall of a painful past event or events", but rather the "conscious suppression of memories that challenge present identities and actions of individuals and groups" (Teski and Climo, 1995: 5). Since they cannot be accommodated within one's current life circumstances, these memories are given no place in one's life narrative.

From such a perspective, Mdm Siti's new domination over her husband is a manifestation of her challenging the phallocentrism of society. However, since the result of such a covertly expressed challenge is the victimization of her own husband, instead of receiving sympathy, she receives double the social condemnation — for her adultery and for the transfer of her guilt to her husband. This condemnation is observable in how the people around her (relatives and neighbours) communicate with her. They tend to boycott any communication she initiates, or pretend to listen to what she is saying.

In the case of Mdm Siti, it is obvious that a failure to negotiate with the social and cultural context will only result in a sort of social isolation. She is isolated not primarily for what people see as her past wrongdoing, but for how she has dealt with it. Her social isolation has in turn caused her to distrust other people. She realizes that other people only pretend to talk to her, so she in turn pretends to talk to them. A pseudo-communication has thus arisen from one person's failure to negotiate with the patriarchal social and cultural order.

On the other hand, the case of Mdm Sri shows how a conformist attitude to the existing social and cultural order has resulted in a continued smoothness of social communication. In her case, there was no traumatic experience of the past, as she lost nothing in her relationship with her husband as a result of the 1965 event. After her husband was released, each returned to his/her accustomed place within the family. He has gone back to being the head of the family while she takes care of the household affairs. Having no experience of being a breadwinner has enabled Mdm Sri to uphold her belief that women should be subservient to men, so as to ensure what she believes to be harmonious relations between them. Unlike the other two cases, Mdm Sri's experience does not contain any unspeakable parts. She can relate her memories of the hard living conditions of the past without any sort of constraint. To a great extent, it is even a source of pride for her that she did not fall into the same sort of situation as Mdm Siti. In other words, her pride does not lie in her past experiences as such, but in her successfully avoiding any of the 'temptations' that could have trapped her into incurring the condemnation of others. This bears out exactly what John Shotter argues, namely, that "our ways of talking about our experiences work, not primarily to represent the nature of those experiences in themselves, but to represent them in such a way as to constitute and sustain one or another kind of social order" (Shotter, 1990: 121–2).

The three cases above show how the existing patriarchal cultural values work in a particular class of society experiencing the effects of mass political violence. Such values are formulated around an unequal relation of power between genders whereby women are subordinated to men. The man is typically the only breadwinner while the woman is expected to manage the household. Being accustomed to such a division of labour, most wives were shocked to have to earn their own living and struggle for survival alone when their husbands were either killed or imprisoned after the 1965 event. However, as is seen in the case of Mdm Surti, it is, ironically, also an expression of this patriarchal value system that the husband fails to show any appreciation of his wife's struggle to keep the family together. So long as the husband is still alive, a woman's role in earning a living is perceived as merely substitutive or complementary. It is also this same patriarchal value system that inhibits a woman from openly expressing her disappointment with her husband. In such a case, past experiences turn out to be traumatic, not because of the nature of the experiences as such, but because of the way that they have been rationalized within the dominant system of cultural values.

In Mdm Siti's case, the workings of the patriarchal system of cultural values are observable in the way her neighbours and relatives gossip about her adultery. Such social condemnation reflects the unequal status between men and women since in such a scandal, it is the woman who takes the blame. The reasons for this apportioning of blame are connected not only to the ethical principles bound up in the institution of marriage, but also to the cultural value which holds that a woman should maintain her loyalty and obedience to her husband regardless of the circumstances. Unable to protest, Mdm Siti has developed her own self-defence mechanism. More than merely a political condition, it is politics itself that she blames as the very source of her bitter experiences. Her husband was imprisoned because of politics, which in turn thrust upon her such unexpected experiences. As such, she shares the depoliticization agenda of Suharto's regime, which exploited the public's fear of politics in order to establish control over citizens.

Mdm Siti also believes that her husband's experience could be repeated in the future if he were to become politically engaged again. That is why she strictly forbids him from participating in the memorial movements initiated by groups of *eks-tapol* since the fall of Suharto. She does not believe that this current 'wind of change' has brought Indonesia to a 'point of no return'. She has retained the Javanese cultural conception of the cyclical nature of time. She does not welcome the opportunity for the survivors of the 1965 event to articulate their sense of self publicly because she believes that the past can return in the future. For her, the future seems to be non-existent since it risks being merely a repetition of the past. These discourses, both political and cultural, prevent a resolution of her distress. Minow (1998: 61 ff.), discussing the effects of trauma in societies recovering from mass violence, and the problematic potential for victims to find ways of healing their pain, reviews some of the evidence that telling one's story and having it acknowledged by serious listeners can indeed bring cathartic relief. The individual (and by implication, the nation) must be able to reintegrate the narrative of the traumatic event into their life story as a whole. Until they are able to do so, they may suffer conflicting feelings both of a loss of autonomy, and the loss of connections with others. Minow cites Eric Santner (1992) who, in writing of Holocaust testimonies, defines trauma as "the overstimulation of a person's psychic structures so that the individual needs to reinvent or repair the basic ways of making meaning and bounding the self and others". He warns that this takes time, and that it is important to avoid "prematurely invoking normalcy before the trauma has been worked through" (Minow, 1998: 64). When Santner speaks of "bounding the self and others", he refers to the sense of a breaching of the self's own boundaries, since the experience of traumatic violence forces the individual to relinquish his/her own autonomy. For healing to take place, that autonomy must somehow be reclaimed. But another problem is the rupturing of social *bonds* with others. Where trauma causes a loss of trust in human nature, mending those bonds can be equally difficult to achieve.

The remarkable number of autobiographies of former political prisoners published in the few years since the fall of Suharto would seem to testify to the impulse to surmount the past by telling one's story. These authors, however, are almost all men, who have received public acknowledgement of their narratives. The problem for Mdm Siti, by contrast, would seem to lie in the lack of an audience willing to validate her experience. She is faced with the reverse situation — a lack of social sympathy, if not outright condemnation. As a result, she has not only broken the social bond with others but also experiences a foreclosing of any possible futures. What I refer to by 'breaking the social bond with others' is not complete self-isolation (except from her family), but the suspicion she conveys in her every communication with others. To her everybody looks like a stranger.

The cases of Mdm Surti and Mdm Siti show that traumatic experiences may also be dealt with by repression, in the sense referred to earlier of a conscious exclusion from one's life story. To them, especially to Mdm Siti, the past has produced a "humiliated memory", which makes recollection painful (Kirmayer, 1996: 183). This has shaped the ways they construct their identities, which are themselves indelibly shaped by the predominant system of cultural values. They both identify themselves as victims — not only of the past violence but also of the patriarchal system. Both perceive that men always want to be right. Mdm Surti's silence about the earliest moments of disharmony in her relationship with her husband is a way of escaping from the contradictions created by this system of cultural values. By contrast, Mdm Siti's hatred of anything associated with politics is a way of protesting against the unequal judgment of women who have committed adultery, when the same act is tolerated for men. Her tight control over what her husband should do in his everyday life is the very manifestation of such a protest. As a victim of male domination, she has found the means of dominating the closest man in her life. Mdm Sri's case shows how one woman has escaped being re-victimized by a society that still adheres to a patriarchal system of values — by offering no resistance to it, she has kept herself within the system and, in this way, has managed to avoid any traumatic experience.

If trauma is inseparable from the system of cultural values, then the process of healing should begin with a radical criticism of it. Unless this agenda for cultural change is working, then such traumatized survivors of mass political violence will be forced to continue living with the spectre of the past, regardless of how the 'winds of change' may blow. Cultural changes, however, must begin not at the centres of power but within the family — the site where political violence has its most painful effects.

Closing Remarks

This chapter has demonstrated that it is not the nature of past experiences per se, but how a system of cultural values (in addition to social and political discourses) makes sense of the experiences, which may result in trauma. Trauma, like memory and identity, is thus always mediated through social, cultural and political complexes. This implies that any effort to help traumatized survivors of collective political violence will always involve a negotiation with social, cultural and political discursive practices. To work through the trauma fully will undoubtedly take a long time. A law was passed in 2004 mandating the establishment of a Truth and Reconciliation Commission to investigate the events of 1965–66, but after opposition from a group of NGOs that objected to the idea of amnesty for perpetrators, this law was then annulled as unconstitutional in a shock verdict by the Constitutional Court in December 2006. It now seems very unlikely that there will ever be a TRC. Even if such a commission had been established, this would not in itself have guaranteed any automatic healing of the nation's wounds. At best it might have opened up a path toward such a goal, but it seems clear that reconciliation will now have to proceed through other initiatives and activities at grassroots level. Although Syarikat has not had the time to publish the results of its research, its activists are also working to this end. Their hope is that ultimately, previously unheard narratives, such as those presented here, will have a chance to become part of a new national narrative of the 1965 event.

My chapter has been concerned to suggest that women who suffered 'only' the indirect effects of the past political violence may, nevertheless, in some ways, experience more lasting trauma than men, even those who were imprisoned without trial for years. If the fall of Suharto has opened up an opportunity for these former political prisoners (almost all men) to break out of their social imprisonment and to reconstrue the meaning of their experiences, it has not been the same for women such as Mdm Surti and Mdm Siti. They remain imprisoned by the patriarchal system of cultural values, not past political violence. Because of this past violence, they have in effect experienced a double imprisonment. Consequently, any advocacy on behalf of such survivors should be undertaken in close co-operation with those who are deeply engaged with movements for the emancipation of women and the establishment of more equal power relations between genders.

Notes

1. *Tapol* is an acronym derived from the Indonesian term *tahanan politik* (political prisoner).
2. In the former category, see, for instance, Setiawan (2003, 2004), Sukanta (1999), Sudjinah (2003), Raid (2001), Moestahal (2002), Sulami (1999), Soepardjan (2004), etc.; in the latter, see, for instance, Wierenga (1999), Cribb (2003), Anderson and McVey (2002) and Sulistyo (2000).
3. By 'illegitimate spouse', I mean men with whom wives of political prisoners had an intimate relationship without marriage. These women had not asked their husbands for a divorce, although there were some other wives of political prisoners who did do so in the years after 1965. But this is beyond the concern of this chapter.
4. As an advisory board member of Syarikat, I was asked to participate as a facilitator at a training workshop organized in December 2003, which gathered activists from 22 cities in different regions of Java and Bali to present their findings.
5. On the discourse of anti-communism and the politics of reconciliation in post-Suharto Indonesia, see Budiawan (2004).
6. According to the so-called Council of Revolution (Dewan Revolusi), which claimed to be behind the Movement, the killings were a response to the persistent rumour that these officers, as members of the so-called Council of Generals (Dewan Jenderal), had planned to remove President Sukarno, whose health was reportedly in decline, from office. Regardless of the truth of this claim, this indicates how crucial the political contestation between

the PKI and the military, especially the Army, had been, while President Sukarno stood above both parties.

7. *Gerakan 30 September Pemberontakan Partai Komunis Indonesia: Latar Belakang, Aksi dan Penumpasannya* (Jakarta: Sekretariat Negara Republik Indonesia, 1994). This is called the *Buku Putih* [White Book], or the revised official version of Suharto's New Order about what happened in the 1965 event. However, finding that the editorial of the PKI's daily *Harian Rakjat* on October 2, 1965 declared its support for the formation of the Dewan Revolusi (Council of Revolution) announced by the commander of the putsch, Lt. Colonel Untung, Suharto and the Army began their campaign to crush the PKI and its subsidiary organizations a few days afterwards, while the 'trials' alone were carried out later. This means there had been executions before the 'trials', and the fairness of the 'trials' was suspect.
8. The five principles are (a) Belief in One God, (b) Humanitarianism, (c) Nationalism, (d) Democracy and (e) Social Justice.
9. Since the fall of Suharto, this version has been seriously challenged by at least four different scenarios that were formerly circulated within limited circles of academics only. These four alternative scenarios are: first, the 'attempted coup' was the result of an internal struggle in the armed forces; second, Suharto was the coup's actual instigator, or at least he influenced, manipulated and distorted the killing of the generals for his own ends; third, President Sukarno allowed or encouraged disaffected officers to act against others said to be part of a secret Council of Generals; fourth, foreign intelligence operations, that is, the CIA and MI-6, were involved in an attempt to oust the left-leaning Sukarno from his influential position in Indonesia and among Third World nations. Which version(s) is (are) true is debatable and beyond the concern of this chapter. They are mentioned here only to underline the fact that since Suharto stepped down, the official version put forward by his regime is no longer the only version of the event appearing in public discussions.
10. On the various estimations of the number of victims of the 1965–66 massacres in Indonesia, see Cribb (1990: 12).
11. *Tapol Bulletin*, No. 80, April 1987.
12. This is how I came to know the story of Mdm Surti — her son used to be a colleague of mine in a private university in Central Java.
13. In a situation where wives were widowed or left alone, either temporarily or permanently, because their husbands were either imprisoned or killed as a result of mass political violence, it was common for policemen or military officers to take the chance to act as the protectors of such 'widows'. Stories abound of women with similar experiences as Mdm Siti's in the years after the 1965 event.

14. The main reason for this policy was that the government did not have the budget to provide food for those prisoners. Toward the end of 1969, the government held a screening operation. Group B prisoners remained under detention, more than 10,000 of whom were exiled to the island of Buru, where they were left to live or die under the harsh living conditions and hard labour to which they were subjected. Searing accounts of their misery can be found in the works listed in note 1. One account that is available in English is the memoir of novelist Pramoedya Ananta Toer, *The Mute's Soliloquy* (1999). Group C prisoners, on the other hand, were released in stages in the early 1970s.
15. According to one of his cellmates — his own brother (and also one of the interviewees for this paper) — the news, when he was still in prison, that his wife had given birth came as a great shock to him. He was unable to accept the reality. But with the psychological support of his brother, he slowly came round to it as he realized that he could not control what was happening at home.
16. Food sent from home supplemented in a small way the food provided in the prisons, which was poor in terms of both quantity and quality. In the first months of their imprisonment, political prisoners only received around 200 kernels of maize and 2 cups of drinking water a day. Not a few died of starvation while many others suffered from beriberi.

References

Anderson, Benedict R.O.G and Ruth T. McVey (2002). *Kudeta 1 Oktober 1965: Sebuah Analisis Awal.* Translated from *A Preliminary Analysis of the October 1, 1965, Coup in Indonesia.* Yogyakarta: Syarikat.

Anonymous (1994). *Gerakan 30 September Pemberontakan Partai Komunis Indonesia: Latar Belakang, Aksi, dan Penumpasannya.* Jakarta: Sekretariat Negara Republik Indonesia.

Antze, Paul and Michael Lambek (eds) (1996). *Tense Past: Cultural Essays in Trauma and Memory.* London & New York: Routledge.

Budiawan (2004). *Mematahkan Pewarisan Ingatan: Wacana Anti-Komunis dan Politik Rekonsiliasi Pasca-Suharto.* Jakarta: Elsam. Translated from "Breaking the Immortalized Past: Anti-Communist Discourse and Reconciliatory Politics in Post-Suharto Indonesia", PhD thesis, Southeast Asian Studies Programme, National University of Singapore, 2003.

Cribb, Robert (2003). *Pembantaian PKI di Jawa dan Bali 1965–1966.* Translated from *The Indonesian Killings 1965–1966: Studies from Java and Bali.* Yogyakarta: Mata Bangsa & Syarikat.

——— (ed.) (1990). *The Indonesian Killings 1965–1966: Studies from Java and Bali.* Melbourne: Center of Southeast Asian Studies, Monash University.

Harvey, John H. (2002). *Perspectives on Loss and Trauma: Assaults on the Self.* London: Sage Publications.

Kirmayer, Laurence J. (1996). "Landscape of Memory: Trauma, Narrative, and Dissociation", in Paul Antze and Michael Lambek (eds), *Tense Past: Cultural Essays in Trauma and Memory*. London & New York: Routledge.

Minow, Martha (1998). *Between Vengeance and Forgiveness: Facing History after Genocide and Mass Violence*. Boston: Beacon Press.

Moestahal, Achmadi (2002). *Dari Gontor ke Pulau Buru: Memoar H. Achmadi Moestahal.* Translated from *The Islamic Boarding School of Gontor to the Prison-Island of Buru: A Memoir*. Yogyakarta: Syarikat.

Pramoedya Ananta Toer (1999). *The Mute's Soliloquy: A Memoir*. Harmondsworth: Penguin.

Raid, Hasan (2001). *Pergulatan Muslim Komunis: Otobiografi Hasan Raid* [The Struggle of a Communist Moslem: An Autobiography]. Yogyakarta: LKPSM-Syarikat.

Santner, Eric (1992). "History Beyond the Pleasure Principle: Some Thoughts on the Representation of Trauma", in S. Friedlander (ed.), *Probing the Limits of Representation: Nazism and the "Final Solution"*. Cambridge, Mass.: Harvard University Press.

Setiawan, Hersri (2003). *Aku Eks-Tapol* [I Am a Former Political Prisoner]. Yogyakarta: Galang Press.

——— (2004). *Memoar Pulau Buru* [The Island of Buru: A Memoir]. Magelang: IndonesiaTera.

Shotter, John (1990). "The Social Construction of Remembering and Forgetting", in David Middleton and Derek Edwards (eds), *Collective Remembering*. London: Sage Publications.

Soepardjan, Adam (2004). *Mendobrak Penjara Rezim Soeharto* [Breaking the Prison House of Soeharto's Regime]. Yogyakarta: Ombak.

Sudjinah (2003). *Terhempas Gelombang Pasang: Riwayat Wartawati dalam Penjara Orde Baru* [In a Jakarta Prison: Life Stories of Women Inmates]. Jakarta: Pustaka Utan Kayu.

Sukanta, Putu Oka (1999). *Merajut Harkat* [Knitting the Human Dignity]. Yogyakarta: Pustaka Pelajar.

Sulami (1999). *Perempuan-Kebenaran-Penjara* [Woman-Truth-Prison]. Jakarta: Cipta Lestari.

Sulistyo, Hermawan (2000). *Palu Arit di Ladang Tebu: Sejarah Pembantaian Massal yang Terlupakan, 1965–1966.* Translated from *The Forgotten Years: The Missing History of Indonesia's Mass Slaughter (Jombang — Kediri 1965–1966)*. Jakarta: Kepustakaan Gramedia Populer.

Tapol Bulletin, No. 10, October 1987. London.

Teski, Marea C. (1995). "The Remembering Consciousness of a Polish Exile Government", in Marea C. Teski and J. Climo Jacob (eds), *The Labyrinth of Memory: Ethnographic Journeys*. Westport, Conn. & London: Bergin & Garvey.

Teski, Marea C. and Jacob J. Climo (1995). "Introduction", in Marea C. Teski and Jacob J. Climo (eds), *The Labyrinth of Memory: Ethnographic Journeys*. Westport, Conn. & London: Bergin & Garvey.

Wierenga, Saskia E. (1999). *Penghancuran Gerakan Perempuan di Indonesia*. Translated from *The Politization of Gender Relations in Indonesia: Women's Movement and Gerwani until the New Order State*. Jakarta: Garba Budaya & Kalyana Mitra.

Zur, Judith (1994). "The Psychological Impact of Impunity", *Anthropology Today* 10/3: 12–7.

CONTRIBUTORS

Budiawan obtained his Ph.D. in Southeast Asian Studies from the National University of Singapore in 2003. He is a Lecturer in the Graduate School of Media and Cultural Studies, Gadjah Mada University, Yogyakarta, Indonesia. His publications include: *Mematahkan Pewarisan Ingatan: Wacana Anti-Komunis dan Politik Rekonsiliasi Pasca-Suharto* (2004) (a translation of his Ph.D. thesis, "Breaking the Immortalized Past: Anti-Communist Discourse and Reconciliatory Politics in Post-Suharto Indonesia"), and "Seeing Indonesia's Past from my Village: A Narrative Report", in Priscilla Chua (ed.), *The Past in the Present: Histories in the Making* (Singapore: National Heritage Board, 2009).

Kelvin Chia obtained a B.A. (First Class Honours) in Sociology from the Nanyang Technological University in 2009, and a M.Sc. in Sociology from the London School of Economics and Political Science in 2010. His areas of interest include critical social theory, higher education, social memory and urban studies.

Dayang Istiaisyah bte Hussin graduated with Honours from the Department of Sociology, National University of Singapore, in 1999. Her chapter is drawn from research conducted for her Honours thesis. She obtained her Master's Degree in Sociology from the same university in 2004, with research on *madrasah* (Islamic educational institutions) in the context of nation-building in Singapore. After working as a Principal Executive of the Children, Youth & Family Services Department of the National Council of Social Services, Singapore, she is currently an Assistant Manager with the MUIS Academy (Islamic Religious Council of Singapore).

Heddy Shri Ahimsa-Putra is Professor of Anthropology in the Department of Cultural Anthropology, Universitas Gadjah Mada, Yogyakarta, Indonesia. He studied at Universitas Gadjah Mada, Universitas Indonesia, the University of Leiden and Columbia University. He has been a visiting professor at a number of other universities in both Indonesia and Myanmar. From 2000–2008 he was a member of the team of specialists for the study and conservation of Borobudur. His publications include: *Minawang: Hubungan Patron-Klien di Sulawesi Selatan pada Akhir Abad 19* [*Minawang: Patron-Client Relationships in South Sulawesi at the end of the 19th Century*] (Yogyakarta: Gadjah Mada University Press, 1989); *Strukturalisme Lévi-Strauss, Mitos dan Karyasastra* [*Lévi-Strauss's Structuralism, Myth and Literature*] (Yogyakarta: Galang Press, 2001), and *Jejak Masa Lalu, Sejuta Warisan Budaya* [*History and Cultural Heritage*] (with Arwan Tuti Artha) (Kunci Ilmu, 2004). He has also published widely in Indonesian academic journals. His research interests include South Sulawesi and Java, social-cultural change, ecological anthropology, political anthropology and theory in anthropology.

Ricardo T. José is a Professor in the Department of History, University of the Philippines. He obtained his Master's Degree in History from the University of the Philippines, and his Ph.D. in History/Area Studies from the Tokyo University of Foreign Studies. He specializes in the Second World War in the Philippines, as well as in Philippine military history, and has also worked on Philippine diplomatic history and the Philippines' relations with Japan.

Kwok Kian-Woon received his Ph.D. in Sociology from the University of California at Berkeley. He is Head of the Sociology Division and Associate Provost (Student Life) at Nanyang Technological University, Singapore. His teaching and research interests concern the historical and comparative understanding of modern social transformation and contemporary social change. His focus has been on the study of Chinese societies, American society and Southeast Asian societies, especially Singapore. His publications include numerous co-edited books, journal articles and book chapters on Singapore society, the Chinese Overseas, cultural policy and the arts, social memory, and mental health.

Adeline Low Hwee Cheng graduated with Honours from the Department of Sociology, National University of Singapore, in 1998. Her chapter is drawn from research conducted for her Honours thesis. Adeline earned a Diploma in Education at the National Institute of Education in 2000 and thereafter taught at Yishun Town Secondary School where she was the Head of Department for English Language and Literature from 2005 to 2010. She is currently pursuing a Master of Education degree in Curriculum and Teaching at the National Institute of Education, Singapore.

Maitrii Aung-Thwin is Assistant Professor of Southeast Asian/Burmese history in the Department of History, National University of Singapore. His fields of interest include comparative colonialisms, socio-legal studies and public history. He is the author of *The Return of the Galon King: History, Law, and Rebellion in Colonial Burma* (Singapore: NUS Press 2011) and co-author of *A New History of Southeast Asia* (Palgrave, Macmillan, 2010).

Vatthana Pholsena is a research fellow at the French National Centre for Scientific Research (CNRS). Currently based in Singapore, she is also the representative for the Institute of Research on Contemporary Southeast Asia (IRASEC). From 2004–2006 she was Assistant Professor in the Southeast Asian Studies Programme, National University of Singapore. Her research in Laos focuses on issues of ethnicity and nationalism, particularly as they have affected 'peripheral' upland populations, and the connections between history, historiography and memory in Laos. She is the author of *Post-War Laos: The Politics of History, Culture and Identity* (Singapore: ISEAS, 2006); "Highlanders on the Ho Chi Minh Trail: Representations and Narratives", *Critical Asian Studies*, vol. 40, no. 3, 2008; "Life under Bombing in Southeastern Laos (1964–1973): Through the Accounts of Survivors in Sepon", *European Journal of East Asian Studies*, vol. 9 (2), 2010.

Sharon Seah Li-Lian graduated with Honours from the Department of Sociology, National University of Singapore, in 1999. Her chapter is drawn from research conducted for her Honours thesis, which won the 1999 Chng Heng Lay Memorial Prize. Her main interests are issues of history, memory, truth, narratives, and feminist works. She has contributed to a collection of essays based on "Ways of Seeing", a workshop on Southeast Asian history and art, jointly conducted by the University of New South Wales and the National University of Singapore in February 2000. Currently she is working with the Ministry of Foreign Affairs, Singapore.

Roxana Waterson is a social anthropologist (Ph.D. Cambridge, 1981) and Associate Professor in the Department of Sociology, NUS. She has done fieldwork with the Sa'dan Toraja people of Sulawesi (Indonesia) since 1978. Her publications include *The Living House: An Anthropology of Architecture in Southeast Asia* (4th edition, Tuttle, 2009); *Southeast Asian Lives: Personal Narratives and Historical Experience* (Singapore/Athens: NUS Press/Ohio University Press, 2007); and *Paths and Rivers: Sa'dan Toraja Society in Transformation* (Leiden: KITLV, 2009). She has a special interest in social memory and life narrative research, and has published articles on social memory, trauma, testimony and reconciliation.

INDEX

Abdurrahman Wahid 6
Acting out 36, 40
Alexander, Jeffrey 26
Amnesia 4, 28, 100
  collective 263
  official 250
  politics of 31
  technology of 94
  see also forgetting
Anderson, Benedict 3, 101, 127–8, 287
Australia 37–8, 144, 159, 190, 196, 245

Baddeley, Alan 20
Benjamin, Geoffrey 3, 230
Benjamin, Walter 226
Bloch, Maurice 18
Bosnia 36–7
Browning, Christopher 40
Burma 3, 53–77
Buruma, Ian 31–2, 44

Cambodia 34, 96, 100, 122
Carruthers, Mary 24
China 28, 38–9, 86, 130, 151, 231–4, 238, 240–7, 253–4, 256, 261
  Cultural Revolution (1966–1976) 27–8, 34, 41, 45, 243
Climo, Jacob 19, 282
'Comfort Women' 37–8, 40, 185–6, 194, 197
Commemoration 5–8, 32, 281
  in Burma 53, 55, 57, 61
  in Indonesia 156–7, 159–61, 164–7, 174–6
  in Laos 100
  in Philippines 188–93
  in Singapore 202
  in Vietnam 110, 116
Connerton, Paul 11, 202
Contestation 4, 11, 27, 30, 42–3, 57, 73, 75, 157, 243, 287
Conway, Martin 20–1
Counter-memory 25
Cultural trauma, *see* trauma

Debouzy, Marianne 205

Elias, Norbert 23
Estonia 29–30

Fang Lizhi 41
Fentress, James 25, 157–8, 205, 220
Forgetting 2, 4, 11, 25, 28, 83, 121, 156–7, 172, 189, 195
  enforced 31, 42
  prevention of 33, 159
  see also amnesia
Foucault, Michel 25, 60, 108, 129, 203

Freud, Sigmund 34–6, 248
Friedländer, Saul 33–4

Gellner, Ernest 3, 128, 130
Goldhagen, Daniel 40

Halbwachs, Maurice 22–4, 157, 202, 218, 226
Hamengkubuwono IX, Sultan of Yogyakarta 6, 156–78
Hiroshima 39, 44, 188
History 2, 4, 6, 8–9, 17, 22–7, 30–1, 42, 85, 106–8, 118–9, 125, 218–9, 247, 251, 272
  and identity 26, 42–3, 53–4, 61, 100–1, 119, 125, 202, 207, 226, 233
  and morality 2, 37, 39, 41, 112, 138, 157, 177, 208
  Burmese 54–77
  democratization of 11
  Indonesian 156–77
  Laotian 83–102
  Singapore 125–7, 132–6, 148–51, 205–8, 224
  'straightening history' (*meluruskan sejarah*) (Indonesia) 176
  textbooks 9, 12, 39, 41, 90, 97, 176, 195
  'Technique of Forgetting History' (China) 41
  Vietnamese 109–122
'Historians' Debate' (Germany) 36
Holocaust 25, 31, 33–4, 36, 38, 40, 43, 284

Indonesia 6, 9–10, 42, 43, 53, 130, 142, 145, 148–9, 151, 242
  'Confrontation' with Malaysia (1962–66) 212
  fall of Suharto (1998) 9, 30, 176, 270, 274, 284–5, 287–8
  Japanese Occupation 153, 188, 198
  massacres (1965–6) 270–88
  'New Order' 6, 156, 166, 174–5, 271, 273, 288
  War for Independence (1945–49) 6, 156–78

Japan 7, 34, 37–41, 43–5, 233, 238, 242
  relations with Philippines 185, 187–91, 194–8
Japanese Occupation of Southeast Asia 197–8

Kansteiner, Wulf 24–6
Keyes, Charles 25–6
Kleinman, Arthur 27–8
Koizumi, Junichiro 39–40
Kuo Pao Kun 41, 257

LaCapra, Dominique 25, 33–6, 40
Levi, Primo 31, 33, 40
Lieux de mémoire, *see* memory, sites of
Lukacs, John 11

Malaysia 43, 53, 227, 233–5, 242
  Independence 5
  Japanese Occupation 198
  Merger with Singapore (1963) and Separation (1965) 5, 127–52, 206, 208, 212, 215, 217, 233–4
  Racial riots (1969) 221–2
Memorials 53, 74, 109, 118, 189–93, 195, 271, 284

Memory
accuracy of 19, 25, 157–8
and censorship 30, 258
and delay 3, 27, 31, 34, 36
and emotion 6, 19, 22, 28, 36, 40–1, 91, 131, 136, 185, 187, 248
and identity 3, 6, 8, 17, 20, 25–6, 31, 35, 43, 126, 205, 256, 281, 286
and 'working through' 27, 36, 40, 42
autobiographical 20–1, 202, 224
burden of 10, 248–9, 263
collective 1, 8, 34, 75, 121, 126, 201–3, 205, 219, 223–4, 263
colonial 61, 76–7
dominant 5, 205, 218
embodied 9, 27, 74
episodic 18–21
frameworks of 202, 205, 211
humiliated 285
key 20
national 42, 207–8, 215, 218–20, 223, 273
oral 22, 84, 92, 204
perceptual 20
politics of 36–7, 281
popular 7–8, 121, 195, 199, 201, 217–8, 220, 225
psychological approaches 1, 17–8, 20, 22, 27
revisions of 7, 157
selectivity of 1, 20, 28, 119, 121
semantic 18, 21
silencing of 5, 10, 30, 38, 44, 65, 116, 204, 235, 245, 270, 272, 274–5, 279, 285
sites of 24, 39, 61
surfeit of 256, 263
tensions in 2, 7–8, 37, 190, 225
traumatic 2–3, 9, 26–7, 34, 42–4, 270, 272, 275, 281, 283–6
vicarious 19
work of 2–3, 7, 23, 29, 38, 257
see also social memory
Monuments 5–7, 29, 74, 107, 109–10, 117, 122, 156–7, 160–7, 175–6, 192
'war of' 29
Mourning 33, 35–6, 248
Museums 5, 56, 74, 76, 93, 109–15, 119–22, 156, 163, 177, 204, 207, 225

Nanjing, Rape of 38
Nanyang University (*Nanyang Daxue*, Singapore) 231–3, 237, 239, 246–51, 260
'Nantah burden' 252
'Nantah spirit' 247, 252
social memory of 246–52
Narrative 107–8
and historical writing 43, 131, 219
conventions 281
dominant and suppressed 2, 26, 41–2, 53, 116, 119, 131
fetishism 35
national or official 3–6, 25, 30, 42–3, 85, 116, 175, 205, 207–8, 210, 213–4, 219, 227, 273, 286
occlusion 29
of illness 28
of trauma 284
personal or autobiographical 29, 201, 204, 219, 270, 282, 284–5
Nationalism 3, 6, 27, 53, 100–1, 121, 126–30, 205, 207, 233–4, 236, 257

Neisser, Ulric 17–8
Neurology 17
Nora, Pierre 24, 39, 58, 61

Olick, Jeffrey 22, 25–6, 42
Ong Keo 4, 84, 86–102

Philippines 5, 7, 38, 53, 185–99
PKI (*Partai Komunis Indonesia*, Indonesian Communist Party) 9, 12, 273–4, 288
Portelli, Alessandro 24, 224, 226

Raphaël, Frédéric 23
'Return of the repressed' 28, 34
Ricoeur, Paul 43, 134
Ritual 7, 9, 26, 32, 35, 59, 65, 84, 87, 95, 156, 163–6, 176, 190, 202
Robbins, Joyce 22, 25–6
Rose, Stephen 17
Ross, Bruce 17

Santner, Eric 33–6, 284–5
Saya San Rebellion 3, 57, 59, 64, 66, 75, 77
Schacter, Daniel 3, 17
Serangan Oemoem 1 Maret 1949 (General Attack of 1 March 1949, Yogyakarta) 6, 156–77
Singapore 11, 43
  Chinese-educated in 10–11, 230–63
  Japanese Occupation 41
  Maria Hertogh Riots (1950) 136, 213, 221–2, 227
  Memories of 1950s 31
  Merger with Malaysia (1963) and Separation (1965) 5, 125–52, 206–8, 212, 217, 227, 233–4
  National Education Programme 8, 125, 131, 153, 226
  national identity 8, 130, 148, 226
  'Racial Riots' (1964) 8, 126, 129, 132, 136, 138, 142–3, 148, 201–28
Spain, Franco era 44
Suharto (Soeharto) 6, 9, 12, 30, 156, 158–77, 270, 273–4, 284–5, 287–8
Sukarno (Soekarno) 145, 159, 161, 167, 174–5, 177, 274, 287–8
Social memory 1, 9, 11, 18, 20, 53, 75, 77, 157, 160, 246, 252
  and history 22, 25–6, 85, 106, 117–9, 157–8, 174–6, 224, 251
  and media 6, 175
  and morality 2–3, 25, 27–8, 32–4, 37–9, 41, 112, 138, 146, 157, 177, 208
  and public discourse 258, 263
  and resistance 2, 4, 10, 28, 30, 43, 53–8, 68, 71, 73, 75, 90, 118, 121, 187–8, 190, 195, 286
  and totalitarian regimes 6, 29, 30, 32, 41–2, 97, 174–7, 271–4, 281, 284, 288
  and trauma 26–7, 34–5, 43, 272, 281, 286
  and truth 8, 11–2, 22, 25, 31, 106, 119–22, 171, 176, 185, 222
  new literature on 1, 22, 42
  processes of 2, 22, 27–8, 34, 36, 41–2, 43, 58, 201, 257

transmission 19, 22, 25
see also memory
Soedirman, General 161, 163, 168–70
South Africa 9–10
Southeast Asia 1, 2, 7, 30, 33, 34, 37, 41–3, 53, 55, 65, 196–8, 233, 247, 263

Taiwan 38, 41, 231, 238, 240, 242, 246
Uprising of 28 February 1947 42
Tanabe, Shigeharu 25–6
Tangent, The (*Yuanqiexian*) (Singapore) 254–61
Thailand
October 1976 massacre, Bangkok 42
Tonkin, Elizabeth 85, 205, 220
Trauma 2, 6, 9–10, 43
and Cultural Revolution in China 27–8
and Holocaust 33–6, 43–4, 284
and Indonesian massacres (1965–66) 270–87
and Japanese Occupation 34, 194
cultural or social 26–8, 36, 42
Truth and Reconciliation Commission 286
Tulving, Endel 18, 20

Vietnam 4–5, 86, 88–9, 94–6, 98–102, 188
American War in 106–23

Wachtel, Nathan 202, 204
Watson, Rubie 84, 94
Wickham, Chris 25, 157–8, 205, 220
Winichakul, Thongchai 42, 53
World War II 7, 32–3, 37–45, 54
Philippine experience of 185–99
Working through 27, 36, 40, 42
see also Acting out

Yasukuni Shrine 39–40
Yogyakarta 6, 156–77
Yugoslav War Crimes Tribunal 37

Zerubavel, Eviatar 25
Zurburchen, Mary 11, 12, 30, 53